The
OXFORD
Children's Encyclopedia of
Science &
Technology

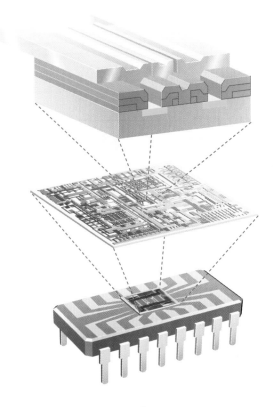

OXFORD
UNIVERSITY PRESS

OXFORD
UNIVERSITY PRESS

Great Clarendon Street, Oxford OX2 6DP

Oxford University Press is a department of the University of Oxford.
It furthers the University's objective of excellence in research, scholarship,
and education by publishing worldwide in

Oxford New York

Athens Auckland Bangkok Bogotá Buenos Aires Calcutta
Cape Town Chennai Dar es Salaam Delhi Florence Hong Kong Istanbul
Karachi Kuala Lumpur Madrid Melbourne Mexico City Mumbai
Nairobi Paris São Paulo Singapore Taipei Tokyo Toronto Warsaw

with associated companies in Berlin Ibadan

Oxford is a registered trade mark of Oxford University Press
in the UK and in certain other countries

British Library Cataloguing in Publication Data

Data available

ISBN 0-19-910778-5

1 3 5 7 9 10 8 6 4 2

Typeset by Oxford Designers and Illustrators
Typeset in Photina and Rotis
Printed in Britain by Butler and Tanner

Contents

Contributors

Editor
Ben Dupré

Coordinating editors
Ian Crofton
Joanna Harris

Proofreaders
Helen Maxey
Susan Mushin

Indexer
Ann Barrett

Design
Jo Cameron
Oxford Designers and Illustrators

Art editor
Hilary Wright

Assistant art editor
Jo Samways

Cover design
Jo Cameron

Photographic research
Charlotte Lippmann

Consultants
Bridget Ardley
Neil Ardley
John R. Brown
Frank Eckardt
Esmond Harris
Dr Stuart Milligan
Colin Mills
Dr Jacqueline Mitton
Iain Nicolson
Joyce Pope
Stephen Pople
Elspeth Scott
Michael Scott
Professor Charles Taylor
Eric Tupper
Bob Unwin
Elizabeth Williamson
Dr Robert Youngson

Authors
Bridget Ardley
Neil Ardley
Jill Bailey
John Becklake
Susan Becklake
Ian Crofton
Frank Eckardt
David Glover
Susan Goodman
Sonia Hinton
Dr Terry Jennings
Dr Jacqueline Mitton
Iain Nicolson
Dr Stuart Owen-Jones
Chris Oxlade
Joyce Pope
Stephen Pople
R. J. Ritchie
Dr Alisdair Rogers
Michael Scott
Andrew Solway
John N. Stringer
Professor Charles Taylor
Dr Philip Whitfield
Elizabeth Williamson

Acknowledgments

Key t top; b bottom; c centre; r right; l left
NHPA = Natural History Photo Agency; SPL = Science Photo Library; OSF = Oxford Scientific Films

Photos are reproduced by kind permission of:
Front cover Corbis/Getty Images. 7b SPL, Dr George Gornacz. 8t Image Bank, Erik Simonsen. 9b Getty Images, Tony Hutchings. 12t Getty Images. 12b SPL. Space Telescope Science Institute/NASA. 14t SPL, Patrice Loiez. 15b SPL, Los Alamos National Laboratory. 16t Getty Images. 17t Images of Africa, David Keith Jones. 17b SPL. 18b SPL. 20tr Robert Harding, Nigel Frances. 20tl Robert Harding, M. Leslie Evans. 20b Image Bank, Walter Bibikow. 21t Topham. 21b SPL, Jean-Loup Charmet. 22b NHPA, Stephen Dalton. 23t NGIC, Dean Conger. 25t SPL, Maximilian Stock Ltd. 25b SPL, Alexander Tsiaras. 26br Image Bank, T. Chinami. 27t SPL, Tony and Daphne Hallas. 28t SPL, David Parker. 29b SPL, Los Alamos National Laboratory. 30t Bridgeman Art Library, Bibliotheque Nationale, Paris. 30cr SPL, Jeremy Burgess. 30b SPL, Eye of Science. 31t Mary Evans. 31b Bridgeman Art Library, Downe House, Kent. 32tr Oxford Scientific Films, Hjalmar R. Bardarson. 34t NHPA, Daniel Heuclin. 35t SPL. 35b SPL, J. L. Charmet. 36t SPL, Adam Hart Davis. 38b SPL, Nelson Morris. 39t SPL, Vaughan Fleming. 41t SPL, Department of Energy. 41b SPL, Peter Menzell. 42t Science and Society Picture Library. 43t SPL. 44b Image Bank, Roland Dusik. 45t SPL. 47t SPL, US Naval Observatory. 47b SPL. 48t Sally and Richard Greenhill. 49b SPL, Philippe Plailly/Eurelios. 50b NGIC, James L. Stanfield. 51t SPL. 52t SPL. 53b SPL, Martin Bond. 54t SPL, James King-Holmes. 54b The Guardian, Don McPhee. 55b Getty Images. 56t SPL. 57b SPL, Will & Deni McIntyre. 58b SPL, Richard Nowitz. 59b Mary Evans. 62t SPL, Alex Bartel. 62b Image Bank, Wendy Chan. 63t NHPA, Stephen Krasemann. 63b SPL. 64t SPL, Richard Folwell. 65t Getty Images, Seth Resnick. 65b SPL, Jean-Loup Charmet. 66t SPL, Ed Young. 66b SPL, Malcolm Fielding. 67t Michael Holford. 68t Robert Harding, Michael Short. 68b SPL, John Mead. 69t NGIC, Walter Meayers Edwards. 69b SPL, Dr Jeremy Burgess. 71t Robert Harding, Kodak. 71cr SPL. 73t Suzuki. 74b SPL, David Parker. 75t Governor and Company of the Bank of England. 75b SPL, Geoff Tompkinson. 76t Getty Images, James Wells. 77t Image Bank, Steve Allen. 77b SPL, Rosenfeld Images Ltd. 79b SPL, David Parker & Julian Baum. 80bl NHPA, Anthony Bannister. 81t NHPA, G. I. Bernard. 82t Image Bank, Marc Romanelli. 83tr SPL, NOAA. 83br Image Bank, Yiu Chun Ma. 83bl Topham, Kurt Adams. 85t SPL, Martin Bond. 85b SPL, Sandia National Laboratries. 86t SPL, Pascal Nieto. 87t Robert Harding, T. Waltham. 88t SPL. 89t Getty Images, Paul Chesley. 90t Milepost 92½. 90b Robert Harding, John Miller. 92t Redferns, Suzi Gibbons. 93t Robert Harding, Gavin Hellier. 93b Image Bank, Steve Allen. 94t SPL, David Parker. 95cl, c, cr. 96t, b Geo Science Features/Dr B. Booth. 97t Image Bank, P. & G. Bogwater. 97b SPL, European Space Agency. 98t SPL, Will & Deni McIntyre. 98b SPL, David Vaughan. 99t Getty Images, Arnulf Husmo. 100t NGIC, Wilbur E. Garrett. 101t NGIC, David A. Harvey. 102t Mike Dudley. 104t SPL, US Geological Survey. 104c SPL. 105bl Image Bank, Jaime Villaseca. 106tr, bl SPL. 107t Novosti. 109t SPL. 109b SPL, Tony and Daphne Hallas. 110t NGIC, Jonathan Blair. 111tr SPL. 112t SPL. 112b SPL, J. L. Charmet. 113b SPL, David Parker. 115t SPL. 115b Rex Features. 116bl South American Pictures. 117t Robert Harding, Bildagentur Schuster. 117b SPL. 118tr Image Bank, Ted Kawalerski. 120cl SPL, Space Telescope Science Institute/NASA. 121b SPL, Hank Morgan. 123t Robert Harding, Financial Times. 124t SPL, David Parker. 124b SPL, Abeles Bsip.

Illustrations are by:
Baker, Julian: 38tr, 39b, 50t, 59t, 76b, 78, 87b, 91, 94b, 99b, 102b, 110, 113t, 116br
Beckett, Brian/Gecko: 11tr
Bull. Peter: 100b, 101b
Doherty, Paul: 103
Gecko Ltd: 19, 22, 24, 52bl, 72, 73, 84, 86b
Gecko Ltd/Sneddon, James: 82b
Hardy, David: 71b, 74, 108, 111tl, 120t
Hawken, Nick: 51b
Hinks, Gary: 32bl, 95, 122
Kennard, Frank: 53t
Milne, Sean: 33b, 34b
Milne, Sean/Richardson, Paul/Roberts, Steve: 10 foreground, 60 foreground
Oxford Illustrators: 8, 9, 13, 14, 26ct, br, 36, 37, 42b, 43b, 56, 57t, 92, 107, 118, 119
Oxford Illustrators/Sneddon, James: 61
Polley, Robbie: 119t
Seymore, Steve: 49tl
Sneddon, James: 6t, b, 7, 10 background, 15t, 16b, 18b, 23b, 26tr, 27b, 28b, 29b, 33t, 40, 45b, 46t, 48b, 49tr, 52r, 55tr, 58t, 60 background, 62tl, 64b, 70, 79t, 81 background, 88b, 89b, 105, 111br, 114, 121t, 123b
Sneddon, James/Woods, Michael: 80br
Spenceley, Annabel: 46b
Visscher, Peter: 81 foreground
Wiley, Terry: 44t
Woods, Michael: 11b

Finding your way around

The *Oxford Children's Encyclopedia of Science and Technology* has many useful features that will help you find the information you need quickly and easily.

The articles in the encyclopedia are arranged in alphabetical order from Acids to X-rays. When you want to find out about a particular topic, the first step is to see whether there is an **article** on it in the A–Z sequence. If there is no article, there are two things you can do.

First of all you can look at the **footers** at the bottom of the page.

These may include the topic you want, and give you the name of the article where you can find out about it. If there is no footer, the next thing to do is to look the topic up in the alphabetical **index** at the back of the book. This will tell you which page or pages you can look at to find out what you want to know.

The **header** tells you what articles are on the page, for quick reference.

Articles are arranged alphabetically, so that they are easy to find.

Captions not only describe the photographs and illustrations but give additional information on the topic.

The **opening paragraph** gives a friendly introduction to the topic.

The **main text** gives an account of the topic in a continuous and readable way. Key terms are picked out in *italic text*.

Colourful illustrations and photographs bring the topic to life.

The **find out more panel** points you to other articles related to the topic.

Boxes highlight records, statistics and amazing facts, or cover a particular aspect of the topic.

The **footer** provides a short cut to topics that do not have their own articles.

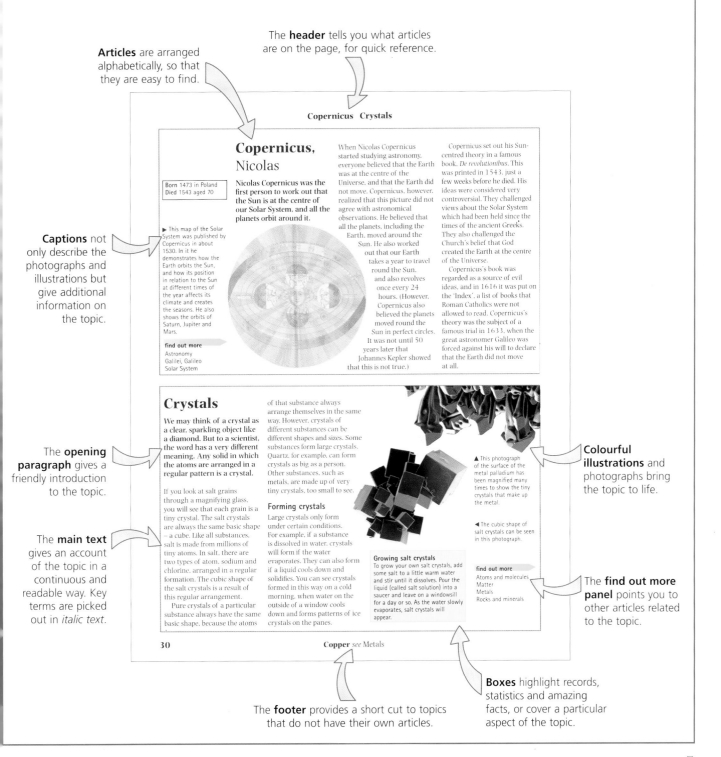

Copernicus Crystals

Copernicus, Nicolas

Born 1473 in Poland
Died 1543 aged 70

Nicolas Copernicus was the first person to work out that the Sun is at the centre of our Solar System, and all the planets orbit around it.

▶ This map of the Solar System was published by Copernicus in about 1530. In it he demonstrates how the Earth orbits the Sun, and how its position in relation to the Sun at different times of the year affects its climate and creates the seasons. He also shows the orbits of Saturn, Jupiter and Mars.

find out more
Astronomy
Galilei, Galileo
Solar System

When Nicolas Copernicus started studying astronomy, everyone believed that the Earth was at the centre of the Universe, and that the Earth did not move. Copernicus, however, realized that this picture did not agree with astronomical observations. He believed that all the planets, including the Earth, moved around the Sun. He also worked out that our Earth takes a year to travel round the Sun, and also revolves once every 24 hours. (However, Copernicus also believed the planets moved round the Sun in perfect circles. It was not until 50 years later that Johannes Kepler showed that this is not true.)

Copernicus set out his Sun-centred theory in a famous book, *De revolutionibus*. This was printed in 1543, just a few weeks before he died. His ideas were considered very controversial. They challenged views about the Solar System which had been held since the times of the ancient Greeks. They also challenged the Church's belief that God created the Earth at the centre of the Universe.

Copernicus's book was regarded as a source of evil ideas, and in 1616 it was put on the 'Index', a list of books that Roman Catholics were not allowed to read. Copernicus's theory was the subject of a famous trial in 1633, when the great astronomer Galileo was forced against his will to declare that the Earth did not move at all.

Crystals

We may think of a crystal as a clear, sparkling object like a diamond. But to a scientist, the word has a very different meaning. Any solid in which the atoms are arranged in a regular pattern is a crystal.

If you look at salt grains through a magnifying glass, you will see that each grain is a tiny crystal. The salt crystals are always the same basic shape – a cube. Like all substances, salt is made from millions of tiny atoms. In salt, there are two types of atom, sodium and chlorine, arranged in a regular formation. The cubic shape of the salt crystals is a result of this regular arrangement.

Pure crystals of a particular substance always have the same basic shape, because the atoms of that substance always arrange themselves in the same way. However, crystals of different substances can be different shapes and sizes. Some substances form large crystals. Quartz, for example, can form crystals as big as a person. Other substances, such as metals, are made up of very tiny crystals, too small to see.

Forming crystals

Large crystals only form under certain conditions. For example, if a substance is dissolved in water, crystals will form if the water evaporates. They can also form if a liquid cools down and solidifies. You can see crystals formed in this way on a cold morning, when water on the outside of a window cools down and forms patterns of ice crystals on the panes.

▲ This photograph of the surface of the metal palladium has been magnified many times to show the tiny crystals that make up the metal.

◀ The cubic shape of salt crystals can be seen in this photograph.

Growing salt crystals
To grow your own salt crystals, add some salt to a little warm water and stir until it dissolves. Pour the liquid (called salt solution) into a saucer and leave on a windowsill for a day or so. As the water slowly evaporates, salt crystals will appear.

find out more
Atoms and molecules
Matter
Metals
Rocks and minerals

Acids and alkalis

Acids and alkalis are chemical opposites. An acid is a sour-tasting substance, such as lemon juice or vinegar. Alkalis are rather soapy substances. Both acids and alkalis are widely used to make products ranging from soap and paper to explosives and fertilizers.

Lemons taste sour because they contain citric acid. The sour taste of vinegar is due to acetic acid, while sour milk contains lactic acid. All these are weak acids. Strong acids are far too dangerous to taste or touch. They are corrosive, which means that they can eat into skin, wood, cloth and other materials.

Alkalis can be strong enough to burn your skin, just like strong acids. If you mix an alkali and an acid together in the right quantities, you will make a neutral substance. This is neither an acid nor an alkali, and it will not burn. Scientists measure the strength of acids and alkalis on a scale of numbers called the pH scale. The scale ranges from 14 (the strongest alkalis) to 0 (the strongest acids).

One of the best-known strong acids is sulphuric acid. It is used to make fertilizers, explosives, plastics, paints, dyes, detergents and many other chemicals.

The modern chemical industry, which began 200 years ago, was based on the manufacture of alkalis. Alkali mixtures containing the metals sodium and potassium are widely used in the manufacture of glass, paper, soap and textiles, and in the refining of crude oil.

• Hydrochloric acid is produced in your stomach. It kills most of the germs that you swallow with your food, and helps your stomach to digest the food.

find out more
Chemistry
Soaps and detergents

▼ The pH scale. Neutral substances, such as pure water, have a pH of 7.

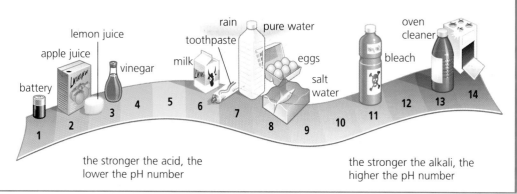

the stronger the acid, the lower the pH number

the stronger the alkali, the higher the pH number

Aerosols

Paints, polishes, deodorants, air-fresheners, fly-killers, shaving creams and oven cleaners are just some of the substances that can be sprayed by aerosol cans.

An aerosol can consists of a metal container with a concave (curving inwards) base. The base is shaped this way to withstand the high pressure of the substances inside the can. In the top of the can is a plastic nozzle, connected to a valve and a plunger. A narrow tube passes from these almost to the bottom of the can.

The can contains the substance to be sprayed, together with a liquid called a *propellant*. The propellant is unusual because it turns into a gas when it is released. When

the nozzle is pressed, the pressure of this gas forces the paint, polish or whatever else the can contains, through the hole in the nozzle. It is this that creates the fine spray.

Aerosols and the ozone layer

In recent years scientists have discovered that some of the propellants used in aerosol cans have polluted our world. They have found that some of the most commonly used propellants, substances known as chlorofluorocarbons (CFCs), have damaged the ozone layer in the upper atmosphere. The ozone layer protects us from the harmful ultraviolet rays in sunlight. If it is badly damaged, humans are likely to suffer more from skin cancer. CFCs also help to cause the greenhouse effect and global warming.

Scientists have developed safer propellants, and most countries have banned the use of CFCs in aerosol cans. Aerosol cans that contain safe propellants often have 'Ozone Friendly' written on them.

• Before the word 'aerosol' came to be used to mean 'spray', scientists were already using it. When tiny solid or liquid particles are held in gas, that is an aerosol. So smoke, fog and clouds are all really examples of aerosols.

◀ Many hair sprays come from an aerosol can like this.

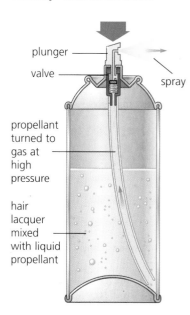

plunger

valve

spray

propellant turned to gas at high pressure

hair lacquer mixed with liquid propellant

find out more
Atmosphere
Greenhouse effect
Pollution

Air

Although air is all around us, we cannot see, smell or taste it. We can feel it moving when the wind blows. Without air, our planet would be a waterless, empty desert with no living creatures. Air is a mixture of gases, mainly nitrogen and oxygen. We breathe air to obtain the oxygen we need to stay alive.

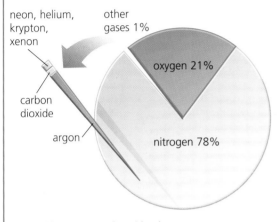

neon, helium, krypton, xenon

other gases 1%

oxygen 21%

carbon dioxide

argon

nitrogen 78%

▲ The different gases found in air.

Air contains tiny amounts of carbon dioxide gas. This is very important as green plants use it, together with water, to make their food. As they do so, they produce oxygen, which is used by humans and other animals. Air also contains many other things: rare gases (such as neon and argon), dust, water vapour, pollen, seeds, tiny microscopic animals, bacteria and pollution from cars and factories.

Atmospheric pressure

A bucketful of air weighs about the same as two pages of this book. The weight of the air above is always pressing down on us. This force pressing on a given area is called atmospheric pressure. At sea level, atmospheric pressure is equivalent to the weight of about 1 kilogram pressing on every square centimetre. This pressure does not squash our bodies because we have air inside us as well as outside.

Atmospheric pressure is measured with a *barometer*. In an aneroid barometer, the most common kind, there is a flat metal box from which most of the air has been removed. The atmospheric pressure tries to squash the box flat but, because the metal is springy, it is not squashed completely. If the atmospheric pressure varies, the lid of the box rises and falls, moving a pointer around a dial to give a reading. A barometer reading is often given in millibars

(mb) or in kilopascals (kPa). One kind of barometer, called a barograph, is used in weather forecasting.

Atmospheric pressure is one example of air pressure (the force of air pressing down on a given area of a surface). We can increase the air pressure of a bicycle tyre, for example, by pumping more and more air into the space available.

Vacuums

A vacuum is a completely empty space from which even the air has been removed. Because it is impossible to remove all the air, by 'vacuum' we really mean a partial vacuum from which most of the air has been removed. Space is a vacuum, although it contains some dust and gas particles. Vacuums are used in Thermos flasks and inside some electrical equipment such as televisions and vacuum cleaners. The vacuum inside a Thermos flask is between the inner and outer walls of the container. The flask keeps drinks hot or cold because heat cannot travel very well through the vacuum, so the heat is kept in a hot drink and away from a cold drink.

Air-conditioning

An air-conditioning system keeps the temperature and moisture of the air in a room at comfortable levels (usually between 20 °C and 25 °C and a relative humidity of 35–70 per cent). In an average room, fresh air and air from the room are mixed in an air-conditioning unit about the size of a large box. Some of the air is warmed by passing it over hot pipes, and the rest is cooled over cold water pipes. A mixture of the warm and cold air produces the required temperature.

• In a space as big as a school hall, there is probably over one tonne of air. That is more than the weight of a small car!

• Neon and argon are two of the rare gases found in air. They produce a coloured glow when an electric current is passed through them. The shaped lighting tubes used in colourful advertising signs are filled with neon and argon.

find out more
Atmosphere
Greenhouse effect
Matter
Oxygen
Plants
Pollution
Water

▼ Scuba divers carry their own air supply in metal tanks filled with compressed air, which are strapped onto their backs. A special device controls the flow of air into the diver's lungs.

Aircraft

Aircraft is the name we use for flying machines. There are many types of aircraft in use today, for commercial, military, private and recreational purposes. Planes, gliders and helicopters are heavier-than-air aircraft, which need wings or blades to keep them in the air. Hot-air balloons and airships are also aircraft. They stay in the air because they are filled with a lighter-than-air gas.

Most planes and gliders have a central body called a fuselage, with wings near the middle and a smaller tailplane and fin at the back. Straight wings work best for carrying heavy loads at low speed, but swept-back wings give a better airflow for fast flying. Some military jets, such as the Panavia Tornado, have 'swing wings', which swing further back for high-speed flight. Some aircraft, such as Concorde, do not have a tailplane. Instead, the wings form a triangular shape, called a delta, which goes all the way to the back. Delta wings are good for high-speed flight but do not perform well at low speed.

Aircraft normally have a frame made from a light alloy (metal mixture) such as duralumin. This frame is covered with a skin of light metal, which acts as a shell and makes the fuselage very strong, like a tube. The wings are built in a similar way. Building aircraft with a rigid shell is called monocoque construction. Before it was developed in the 1920s, aircraft had wood or metal frames covered in fabric and strengthened by wires.

▲ A Boeing 777 passenger jet, one of the new generation of air liners.

How an aircraft flies

Most aircraft have wings with an arched cross-section like those of birds. The shape is called an *aerofoil*. Air moving over this aerofoil creates lift, but unlike bird's wings, aircraft wings cannot be flapped. Therefore air must be kept flowing over them.

The aircraft in the picture (below) is moved forwards using a propeller that turns very quickly. As the aircraft builds up speed, the air rushing over the wings creates the lift needed to raise it into the sky. Aircraft designers have to ensure that the shape of the plane is streamlined. This reduces drag, which is caused by the resistance of the air as a plane moves through it.

Aircraft power

Powered aircraft come in many shapes and sizes, ranging from simple lightweight microlights to the latest wide-bodied jets that can carry more than 600 passengers over very long distances. Most modern aircraft use jet engines in one form

• It is now possible to build human-powered aircraft (HPAs) by using new, very strong and light materials such as carbon fibre. These aircraft have an overall weight of just 60 kg. The pilot turns the propeller by pedalling.

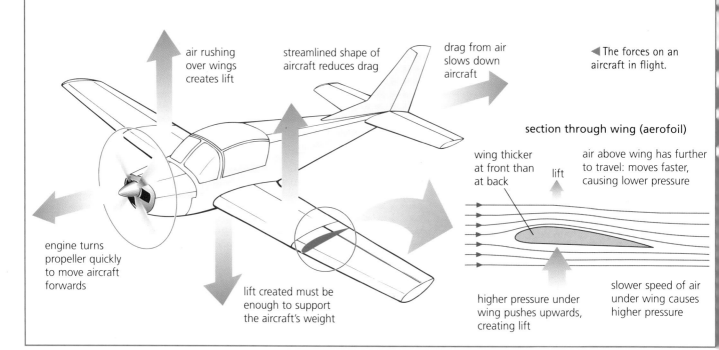

air rushing over wings creates lift

streamlined shape of aircraft reduces drag

drag from air slows down aircraft

◄ The forces on an aircraft in flight.

engine turns propeller quickly to move aircraft forwards

lift created must be enough to support the aircraft's weight

section through wing (aerofoil)

wing thicker at front than at back

lift

air above wing has further to travel: moves faster, causing lower pressure

higher pressure under wing pushes upwards, creating lift

slower speed of air under wing causes higher pressure

 Airships *see* Balloons and airships

Aircraft

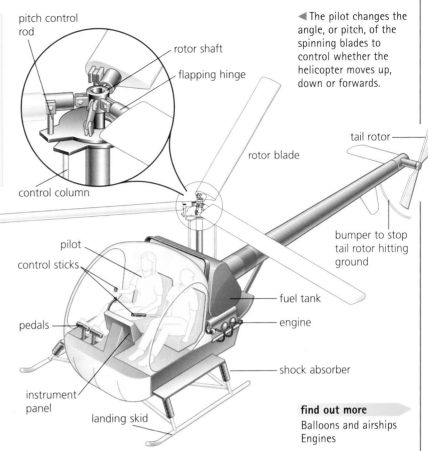

pitch control rod

rotor shaft

flapping hinge

control column

rotor blade

◀ The pilot changes the angle, or pitch, of the spinning blades to control whether the helicopter moves up, down or forwards.

tail rotor

bumper to stop tail rotor hitting ground

pilot

control sticks

pedals

instrument panel

landing skid

fuel tank

engine

shock absorber

or another. Even where a propeller is fitted, the power may come from a turboprop engine, which is based on the jet engine. Some small aircraft have propellers turned by piston engines, which work in a similar way to a motor-car engine. Microlight aircraft are powered by an engine barely bigger than that of a motorcycle.

Using computers

Computers are an important part of a modern airliner. The autopilot is a computer which can navigate and fly the aircraft for most of its journey. On some aircraft, the pilot does not directly control the plane. Instead, the pilot's controls send instructions to a computer and the computer works out the best way to fly the plane. This system is known as fly-by-wire.

Helicopters

Helicopters can take off and land vertically from any flat area, even a roof. They are used to carry people and equipment on short-distance journeys to and from inaccessible places such as ships and offshore oil rigs, and between airports and across towns.

Instead of wings, helicopters have long thin blades (the rotor) on top. The engine makes the blades turn. As they spin round, they push air downwards and this lifts the helicopter upwards. By tilting the blades the pilot can make the helicopter take off, hover or land. Helicopters usually have a smaller tail rotor to stop the helicopter spinning round in the opposite direction from the main rotor. Helicopters are noisier, slower and smaller than most other types of aircraft.

Gliders and hang-gliders

Gliders and hang-gliders do not have engines to keep them moving. Instead, they use the force of the wind to stay up in the air. They are flown for pleasure and in competitions.

A glider's fuselage is lightweight and streamlined to cut down air resistance. The wings are long to create as much lift as possible at the glider's low cruising speed. Most gliders have one seat, although those used for training have two.

Gliders are either towed up into the air behind a powered aircraft or launched from the ground by a car or powered winch. Once in the air, the pilot releases the towline and is free to soar like a bird.

A glider can gain height if the pilot finds a *thermal*, a current of warm air that rises from the ground on a sunny day. If the glider circles in the thermal, it will gain height. Pilots can also use the air flow over a hill to gain height.

Hang-gliders are really fold-up gliders with portable wings. Most hang-gliders carry one person, the pilot, who hangs underneath in a special harness. The pilot becomes airborne by running into the wind off a hill or cliff.

find out more
Balloons and airships
Engines

▼ A view along the wing of a banking glider. Gliders have long flexible wings, a thin streamlined body and a distinctive tail.

Animals

Animals live almost everywhere in the world, from polar regions to hot, dry deserts and steamy forests. The biggest weigh over 100 tonnes, the smallest can only be seen through a microscope.

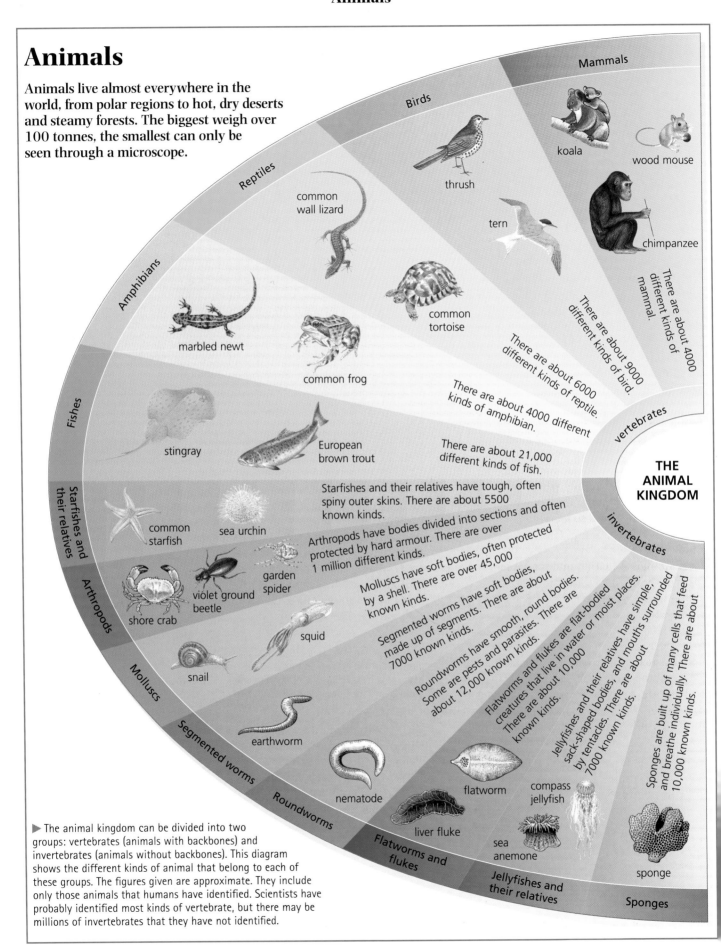

Mammals

koala

wood mouse

chimpanzee

Birds

thrush

tern

There are about 4000 different kinds of mammal.

There are about 9000 different kinds of bird.

Reptiles

common wall lizard

common tortoise

There are about 6000 different kinds of reptile.

Amphibians

marbled newt

common frog

There are about 4000 different kinds of amphibian.

Fishes

stingray

European brown trout

There are about 21,000 different kinds of fish.

vertebrates

THE ANIMAL KINGDOM

invertebrates

Starfishes and their relatives

common starfish

sea urchin

Starfishes and their relatives have tough, often spiny outer skins. There are about 5500 known kinds.

Arthropods

violet ground beetle

garden spider

shore crab

Arthropods have bodies divided into sections and often protected by hard armour. There are over 1 million different kinds.

Molluscs

snail

squid

Molluscs have soft bodies, often protected by a shell. There are over 45,000 known kinds.

Segmented worms

earthworm

Segmented worms have soft bodies, made up of segments. There are about 7000 known kinds.

Roundworms

nematode

Roundworms have smooth, round bodies. Some are pests and parasites. There are about 12,000 known kinds.

Flatworms and flukes

liver fluke

flatworm

Flatworms and flukes are flat-bodied creatures that live in water or moist places. There are about 10,000 known kinds.

Jellyfishes and their relatives

compass jellyfish

sea anemone

Jellyfishes and their relatives have simple, sack-shaped bodies, and mouths surrounded by tentacles. There are about 7000 known kinds.

Sponges

sponge

Sponges are built up of many cells that feed and breathe individually. There are about 10,000 known kinds.

▶ The animal kingdom can be divided into two groups: vertebrates (animals with backbones) and invertebrates (animals without backbones). This diagram shows the different kinds of animal that belong to each of these groups. The figures given are approximate. They include only those animals that humans have identified. Scientists have probably identified most kinds of vertebrate, but there may be millions of invertebrates that they have not identified.

Animals

Animals are one of the five main groups (called kingdoms) into which all living things are divided. It is not always easy to tell animals from plants, but generally animals are able to move about and must eat food to survive.

All animals eat things that have once been alive. Most, like horses and snails, are *herbivores*, and eat plants. Some, like tigers and sharks, are *carnivores*, and kill and eat other animals. Some, like human beings and worms, are *omnivores*, and eat almost anything. Others, like vultures and dung beetles, are *scavengers*, and feed on dead and rotting plants and animals.

Activity

Some animals – birds and mammals – are 'warm-blooded'. This means they are able to keep their body at a constant temperature, however hot or cold their environment. They are always able to be active, but they pay a high price as they have to find a great deal of food to fuel their activity. However, most animals, including reptiles, amphibians, fishes and all invertebrates, are 'cold-blooded'. This means that their body temperature rises and falls with the temperature of their surroundings. In sunshine or hot weather, they can be quite warm and active, but at night or in winter, they are often cold and inactive. The advantage to being so inactive is that they do not need so much food.

Reproduction

Most animals are either male or female, and after mating, the young are born sharing the characteristics of both parents. A small number of animals, such as greenfly and water fleas, are almost all females and, without mating, are able to produce many female young. A few kinds of animal, such as garden snails, are both male and female at the same time, and are able to produce both eggs and sperm. A few others, such as oysters and some fishes, change sex at a certain time in their lives or as a result of changes in their environment. Others still, like some sea anemones, are able to divide their own body, splitting off pieces that grow to make the next generation.

Some animals produce huge numbers of young, but most of these die early, eaten by other creatures. Animals that have long lives and care for their young tend to have smaller families. The female is usually most important in caring for the family, but in some cases the male helps equally, or even looks after the offspring himself.

How animals work

The bodies of nearly all animals work in similar ways. Most animals are made up of billions of cells. All animals take in food, break it down and absorb nutrients into their bodies. This is called *digestion*. These nutrients, together with oxygen from the air or water, are carried by the blood to every cell in the body. This is called *circulation*. Each cell uses oxygen to produce energy from food. This is called *respiration*. The blood also takes away waste matter from every part of the body. Filters (the kidneys in vertebrates and some invertebrates) clean the blood, and the waste matter passes out of the body. This is called *excretion*. Other waste matter passes out from the body through the gut.

All these activities are controlled by the *nervous system*. In simpler animals the nervous system is a network of nerves. In more complicated animals there is also a spinal cord and a brain. The nervous system also controls movement, and takes in messages from the senses. The simplest animals only have the senses of touch, taste and smell, but more complicated animals also have the senses of sight and hearing.

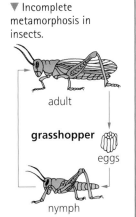

▼ Incomplete metamorphosis in insects.

adult

grasshopper

eggs

nymph

▼ Complete metamorphosis in insects.

adult

butterfly

pupa   eggs

larva

find out more
Biology
Carbon
Cells
Darwin, Charles
Ecology
Energy
Evolution
Genetics
Human body
Living things
Nitrogen
Oxygen
Plants
Water

▼ Animal life cycles. All animals change form at some point in their lives. For most animals these changes happen when they are still either inside an egg or in their mother's womb. However, some animals, such as insects and frogs, go through big changes after they are born. This process of change is called *metamorphosis*. The diagrams below illustrate metamorphosis in frogs. The diagrams to the right show two kinds of metamorphosis in insects: incomplete metamorphosis and complete metamorphosis.

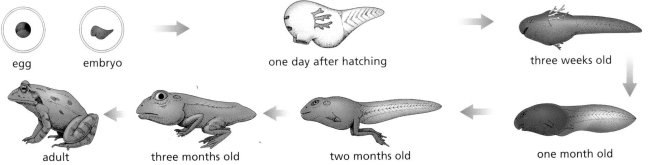

egg   embryo

one day after hatching

three weeks old

one month old

adult   three months old   two months old

Archimedes

Born about 287 BC in Sicily, Italy
Died 212 BC aged about 75

Archimedes was one of the greatest engineers and mathematicians in ancient Greece. He spent his life studying geometry, and using his ideas to develop new types of machine.

• One of the machines that Archimedes is best remembered for is the Archimedean screw, which is used to raise water. In fact, in spite of its name, the screw may have been invented by the Egyptians.

Archimedes was born in the town of Syracuse in Sicily, which at that time was a Greek city-state. He was a wealthy man and a friend of the king of Syracuse.

There is a story that the king wanted to know if his crown was pure gold. He suspected that his goldsmith had mixed some cheaper metal in it. Archimedes could not solve the problem until one day, stepping into his bath, he realized that the water level rose higher the more of his body he immersed.

He ran outside naked shouting 'Eureka! Eureka!' ('I've got it! I've got it!'). Archimedes then put the crown in a bath and worked out its volume by the rise in the water level. Next he immersed a piece of pure gold weighing the same as the crown. As the water level did not rise to the same height, the crown could not have been pure gold and the goldsmith was executed.

Other stories tell of the amazing war machines Archimedes invented to protect Syracuse from the invading Romans. These included large mirrors that focused the Sun's rays and set the Roman ships on fire.

When Syracuse was eventually captured, Archimedes was killed by a Roman soldier.

▼ The engineer, mathematician and philosopher Archimedes at work on one of his inventions.

ARCHIMEDES PHILOSOPHE
Grec. Chap. 23.

Astronomy

Astronomy is the study of the planets, stars and galaxies that make up the Universe. Astronomers try to explain all the things that you can see in the night sky. They also investigate, for example, the age of stars and their distance from the Earth.

• Most distances in space are so enormous that it is meaningless to measure them in kilometres. So astronomers use a measurement called a light year (the distance light travels in a year), which is equal to 9.5 million million kilometres.

• The word 'astronomy' comes from the Greek words *astron* meaning 'star' and *nomia* meaning 'arrangement'.

find out more

Copernicus, Nicolas
Galaxies
Galilei, Galileo
Newton, Isaac
Solar System
Stars
Telescopes
Universe

Early astronomers watched the movements of the Sun, Moon and stars in order to keep track of time and the seasons. Modern astronomers make observations with the help of telescopes, usually in large observatories. The telescopes gather the light from objects that are too faint to see with the naked eye. As well as sending out light, stars and galaxies give off other kinds of radiation,

such as X-rays and radio waves. Astronomers detect these rays with the help of sophisticated telescopes, space satellites and other equipment.

Computers are an important tool in astronomy, helping astronomers to work out what their observations mean. You need to know a lot about science and mathematics to do

astronomy as a job, but amateur astronomers can make useful observations as well as have fun with a pair of binoculars or a small telescope.

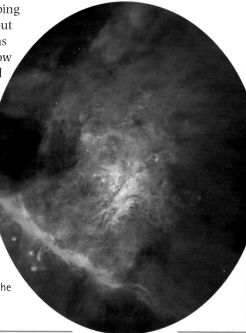

▶ The Orion Nebula, a huge cloud of glowing gas about 1300 light years away from the Earth. The photograph is made up of a series of pictures taken by the Hubble Space Telescope (HST) in orbit round the Earth. Astronomers use powerful telescopes like the HST to help them find out about the very distant parts of the Universe.

Atmosphere

The atmosphere makes it possible for us to live on the Earth. It consists of layers of air that surround our planet. They are wrapped around the Earth rather like orange peel is wrapped around the fruit inside. The air itself is a mixture of gases, mainly nitrogen and oxygen.

The weight of the atmosphere is quite considerable. Every cubic metre of the air around us contains more than 1 kilogram of air. The weight of all this air above pushing down on us is called atmospheric pressure. It is like having 1 kilogram pressing on every square centimetre of our bodies.

The different layers of the atmosphere merge into one another, so it is difficult to give their exact heights. They vary depending on the time of year, the latitude, and activities of the Sun, such as sunspots and solar flares. We live in the *troposphere*, the lowest layer. It contains 90 per cent of the air in the atmosphere. As you move up through the troposphere, the temperature drops, and on high mountains there is not enough oxygen to breathe easily. The air in the layer above the troposphere, the *stratosphere*, is much thinner, and the temperature rises. The stratosphere contains a gas called ozone, which is a type of oxygen. It absorbs much of the harmful ultraviolet radiation from the Sun.

Above the stratosphere, the temperature drops rapidly. Higher up, in the *ionosphere*, there are layers of particles called ions which carry electrical charges. These layers are very important in bouncing radio signals around our planet. The *exosphere* is where the Earth's atmosphere really becomes part of space. In this layer temperatures can be as high as 1000 °C.

Auroras

High up in the atmosphere, between 80 and 600 kilometres above the ground, huge patches of glowing coloured lights sometimes appear in the night sky. Scientists call this display the aurora. The pattern of lights can look like rays from a searchlight, twisting flames, shooting streamers or shimmering curtains. In the northern hemisphere, the popular name for this display is the 'northern lights'. We are more likely to see an aurora when there are big sunspots on the Sun. Atomic particles from the Sun collide with atoms in our atmosphere, giving off the different coloured lights.

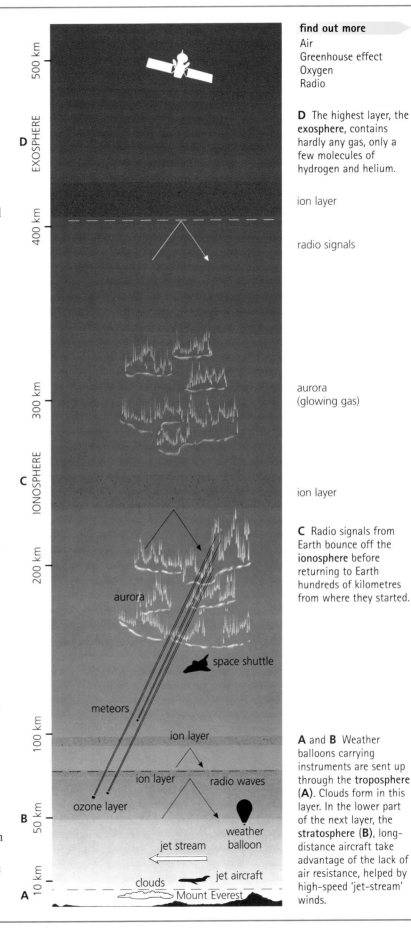

find out more
Air
Greenhouse effect
Oxygen
Radio

D The highest layer, the **exosphere**, contains hardly any gas, only a few molecules of hydrogen and helium.

C Radio signals from Earth bounce off the **ionosphere** before returning to Earth hundreds of kilometres from where they started.

A and **B** Weather balloons carrying instruments are sent up through the **troposphere** (**A**). Clouds form in this layer. In the lower part of the next layer, the **stratosphere** (**B**), long-distance aircraft take advantage of the lack of air resistance, helped by high-speed 'jet-stream' winds.

Atoms and molecules

Every material is made from tiny particles called atoms. Often, these are clumped together in groups known as molecules. Atoms are far too small to be seen with a normal microscope.

Everything is made from about 100 basic substances called *elements*. An atom is the smallest bit of an element you can have. It is so small that more than 4000 million of them would fit across the dot on this letter i! Around 200 years ago, the chemist John Dalton found that the atoms of different elements have different weights. We now know that each element has its own type of atom.

Although there are only about 100 elements, there are millions of different substances. This is because atoms of different elements can join together to make completely new substances called *compounds*. For example, water is a compound of two elements, hydrogen and oxygen.

Compounds and molecules

The smallest bit of water you can have is called a *molecule* of water. It is made up of two hydrogen atoms joined to one oxygen atom. The simplest molecules contain just two or three atoms, sometimes of the same element. But the largest molecules can contain millions of atoms. Many of the molecules in plants and animals are like this.

Inside atoms

Atoms are themselves made of smaller particles, called *electrons*, *protons* and *neutrons*. The protons and neutrons are clumped together in a central *nucleus*. The much lighter electrons speed around this. Each electron carries a negative (−) electric charge and each proton an equal positive (+) charge. Neutrons do not have any charge. Each atom has equal numbers of electrons and protons, so overall it is neutral.

J. J. Thomson discovered the electron in 1897, when he found that tiny electrical particles could come from atoms. In 1911 Ernest Rutherford studied how atomic particles were deflected by gold foil and concluded that an atom must be mainly empty space, with a concentrated blob of matter at its centre. He called this the nucleus. Rutherford suggested that electrons might orbit the nucleus rather like planets round the Sun. Nowadays, scientists find it more useful to think of the electrons as clouds of electric charge. To describe their behaviour, they use the mathematics of *quantum mechanics*. They also think that protons and neutrons are themselves made of even smaller particles, called *quarks*.

● Atoms are mostly empty space. If you imagine an atom the size of a concert hall, then its nucleus would be no larger than a grain of salt.

● Most of the molecules in your body are made from four elements – oxygen, carbon, hydrogen and nitrogen.

▼ A model of a carbon atom. The nucleus of protons and neutrons is surrounded by clouds of fast-moving electrons. The electrons are all the same, but different colours have been used to show different types of movement.

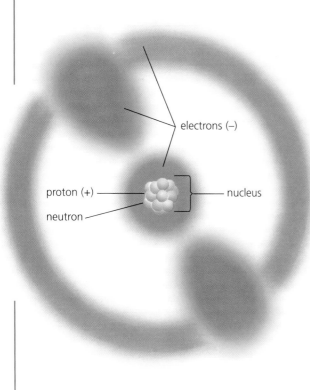

electrons (−)

proton (+)

neutron

nucleus

▶ Scientists have found many ways of detecting subatomic particles (electrons, protons, neutrons and quarks). One of the earliest was the bubble chamber. It is filled with a super-heated liquid, which reveals the tracks of electrically charged subatomic particles. In this artificially coloured picture of a bubble chamber you can see the particles' spiralling tracks.

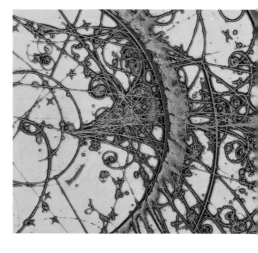

▼ The molecules of three common substances.

molecule of oxygen gas

molecule of water

molecule of methane gas

hydrogen atom

oxygen atom

carbon atom

Atoms and molecules

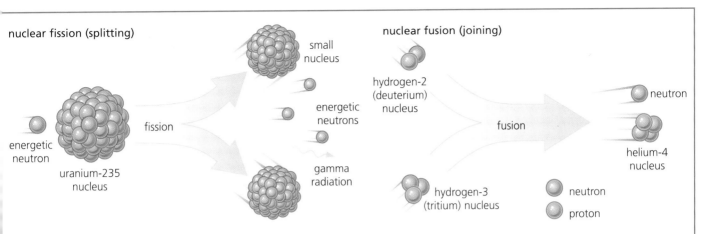

nuclear fission (splitting)

energetic neutron

uranium-235 nucleus

fission

small nucleus

energetic neutrons

gamma radiation

nuclear fusion (joining)

hydrogen-2 (deuterium) nucleus

hydrogen-3 (tritium) nucleus

fusion

neutron

helium-4 nucleus

neutron

proton

Atoms and elements

The atoms of different elements have different numbers of particles in them. Hydrogen, the lightest element, has just one proton in its nucleus. Uranium, one of the heaviest, has 92.

Atoms of any particular element all have the same number of protons (and electrons). But they may have different numbers of neutrons. These different versions of the same element are called *isotopes*. To name isotopes, scientists put a number after the name of the element. Uranium-235, for example, is an isotope of uranium with 235 neutrons and protons.

Fission and fusion

The nuclei of some atoms are unstable. In time, they break up by shooting out tiny particles and, sometimes, high-energy waves. Atoms like this are *radioactive*. The particles and waves carry energy once stored in the nucleus.

Uranium-235 is radioactive. Normally, its nuclei break up slowly. But the process can be speeded up using a *nuclear reactor*. In the reactor, atoms of uranium-235 are bombarded by neutrons. If a neutron strikes a uranium-235 nucleus, the nucleus splits, releasing energy and more neutrons. These may split other nuclei,

and so on, in a chain reaction. The splitting process is called *nuclear fission*. In a nuclear power station, a controlled chain reaction gives a steady supply of heat. In atomic weapons, an uncontrolled chain reaction gives an almost instant release of energy.

Nuclear energy can also be released in another way – by making hydrogen nuclei fuse (join together). This process is called *nuclear fusion*. It is the way the Sun gets its energy and is the power behind the hydrogen bomb. Fusion power stations have yet to be built, but in the 21st century they may become an important source of electricity.

▲ Nuclear fission and nuclear fusion.

find out more
Einstein, Albert
Elements
Matter
Radiation

▼ A test explosion of a nuclear weapon in 1953. The lines on the left of the picture are smoke trails, used to show the shock waves caused by the explosion. An exploding atom bomb releases as much energy as 16,000 tonnes of high explosive.

Balloons and airships

In 1783 the first people to fly freely through the air travelled 9 kilometres in a hot-air balloon designed by the Montgolfier brothers in France.

- Toy balloons are filled with helium, which is lighter than air. This explains why they shoot upwards when you let them go.

find out more
Air
Aircraft
Atmosphere

Nowadays balloon flights are usually for pleasure or sport. Balloons are also used to collect information about the weather, and to carry out scientific experiments high up in the atmosphere.

Balloons float in air in the same way as ships float in water. To make a balloon light enough to float, it has to be filled with a gas that is lighter than the surrounding air. So balloons are filled with helium or hot air.

Until the 1930s, passenger-carrying balloons and airships were filled with hydrogen, the lightest gas. Unfortunately, hydrogen catches fire easily, and was no longer used after a series of bad accidents.

◄ The hydrogen-filled airship *Graf Zeppelin*. In 1929 it took 10 days to travel all the way around the world.

A hot-air balloon is made of nylon and can be as large as a house when it is inflated. A basket hangs from wires or ropes under the balloon. The basket carries the crew and passengers. The gas burner is fixed to the basket's frame and is used in short bursts to heat the air to make the balloon rise and then keep it at the chosen height. When the air inside cools, the balloon loses height.

Airships are sausage-shaped balloons powered by engines. Modern airships are filled with helium gas, which does not burn. They are quiet, safe and comfortable, with an enclosed gondola below, which can carry as many as 20 passengers. The motors which turn the propellers to move the airship forwards are attached to the gondola. The pilot uses a large rudder to steer.

Batteries

Batteries produce electricity when the chemicals inside them react with each other. Small batteries provide the power for torches, radios, watches and pocket calculators. Large batteries can start car engines and can even provide all the power to drive vehicles such as milk-floats.

- The first battery was invented in 1800 by an Italian physicist, Alessandro Volta. During an experiment he placed card soaked in a salt solution between two piles of coins made of different metals. This produced an electric current, and Volta had made the world's first-ever battery.

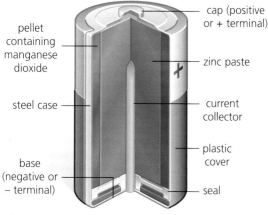

▲ A cutaway view of a long-life alkaline battery.

All materials have positive (+) and negative (−) charges in their atoms. In an electric cell, reactions between chemicals cause the negative charges to concentrate around one terminal, and the positive charges around the other. A battery is really two or more electric cells joined together. However, single cells like the ones used in torches are often called batteries. A car battery consists of six separate cells joined together in the same case.

Different kinds of battery have different chemicals in them. *Zinc chloride* batteries are cheapest, and are often used in torches. *Alkaline* batteries cost more, but last longer because they store more energy. *Lithium* batteries store the most energy, but are much more expensive. In hearing aids, watches and calculators, the batteries need to be thin and small. They are often called *button cells*. Silver oxide, mercury and zinc–air batteries are all button cells.

When batteries are 'flat' and can produce no more electricity, most have to be replaced. Some batteries, such as *nickel–cadmium* ones, are rechargeable. The large *lead–acid* batteries used in car engines are also rechargeable. As the chemicals in rechargeable batteries run out, they can be restored by recharging.

find out more
Atoms and molecules
Electricity

Biology

Biology is the study of living things and the ways in which they interact with the world around them. Biologists study everything about the living world, from the workings of minute bacteria, to the evolution (change) that occurs in animals and plants over millions of years.

Biology is a very broad subject, and it can be studied in many different ways. Some biologists look at large groups of living things. *Population biologists* study whole populations of animals or plants, while *taxonomists* try to classify the different kinds of living things into groups, depending on how closely they are related. *Ecologists* look at how different animals and plants in the same area interact with each other and with their environment.

Other areas of biology look at animals and plants on an individual level. *Anatomists*, for example, study the structure of individual plants or animals, while *physiologists* look at what the different parts do and how they work. Some biologists become experts on particular types of

living thing. *Zoologists* study animals; *botanists* study plants. *Ornithologists* study only birds, while *entomologists* specialize in insects.

The area of biology that has grown most in the last 100 years is the study of living things at the microscopic level. All living things are made up of tiny cells, and *cell biologists* look at the different kinds of cell and how they work. *Molecular biologists* work on an even smaller scale, studying the chemicals (molecules) that make up cells. These complex molecules, and the chemical reactions that occur between them, are basic to all life on Earth.

◀ Some students of biology go on to become veterinarians (vets). In the same way that doctors know all about human biology, vets are expert in animal biology. This vet is applying medicine to the eye of a white rhino, an endangered animal, in Kenya.

find out more
Animals
Cells
Ecology
Evolution
Genetics
Living things
Plants

Biotechnology

Biotechnology is the use of living things to make large amounts of useful products such as drugs, vaccines and medicines. It often involves the use of microbes – tiny single-celled creatures such as bacteria and yeasts.

Microbes have been used in the production of some foods for centuries. Bakers and brewers use microbes called yeasts to make bread and beer. Cheese-making involves the use of bacteria and fungi.

Most modern biotechnology relies on a process known as *genetic engineering*, in which scientists alter the cells of simple animals and plants to give them useful properties. An example of this is the production of human insulin.

• Genetic engineering can also be used to make 'improved' plants. Food plants such as wheat and rice can be given genetic material from other plants to improve their resistance to disease or to help them grow in difficult conditions.

Insulin is a chemical that controls the levels of sugar in the blood. People with the disease diabetes need insulin as part of their treatment. To make insulin, scientists take a few human cells and extract from them the genetic material (DNA) that has instructions for

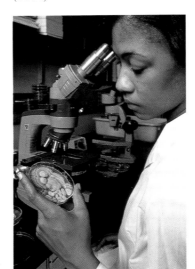

making insulin. They copy this material many times, and insert it into microbes, which then produce insulin.

Biotechnology has many other uses in medicine. Microbes can be genetically engineered to produce new drugs and vaccines. They are also used to make human antibodies, substances normally produced in the body, which fight disease.

Other products that can be made include enzymes. These are biological substances that speed up chemical reactions in the body. They have many uses in medicine and industry.

◀ Once a microbe has been modified to produce a substance, large numbers have to be grown. Colonies are first grown on flat dishes containing food, as with these fungi. Later, huge numbers are grown in large containers.

find out more
Cells
Genetics
Living things
Medicine

Black holes

When a massive star collapses it becomes a black hole. Nothing can escape from a black hole because the pull of its gravity is so strong. Only about one star in a thousand is massive enough to have any chance of becoming a black hole. Black holes are difficult to find because they cannot be seen!

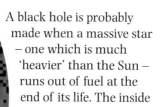

A black hole is probably made when a massive star – one which is much 'heavier' than the Sun – runs out of fuel at the end of its life. The inside

◄ Scientists believe that this falsely coloured image made by the Hubble Space Telescope is evidence of a black hole. It shows a spiral disc of hot gas at the centre of the M87 galaxy. The black hole's mass is about 3 billion times greater than the Sun's mass.

of the star falls in on itself and keeps on falling until all its material is crushed down to a tiny volume. While the star is collapsing, the force of gravity at its surface quickly grows stronger. As soon as its gravity becomes strong enough to stop light from escaping, the star becomes a *stellar black hole*. Anything that comes close enough to it will fall in and disappear.

A black hole has to have at least two or three times the mass of the Sun. A less massive star cannot collapse in this way because its gravity is not strong enough. A black hole with 10 times the Sun's mass would have a diameter (width) of 60 kilometres. If the Sun could be made into a black hole, it would have a diameter of 6 kilometres. A black hole with the mass of the Earth would be less than 2 centimetres across!

When material falls in towards a black hole, it becomes very hot and gives off X-rays. Astronomers believe that some of the X-ray 'stars' they have found may be black holes. There are probably 'supermassive' black holes at the centre of certain kinds of galaxy. The very bright centres of these galaxies are lit up by material falling into *galactic black holes* that 'weigh' up to several billion times more than the Sun.

find out more
Astronomy
Galaxies
Gravity
Stars
X-rays

Bridges

find out more
Railways
Roads

• The longest suspension bridge in the world is the bridge over the Akashi Strait in Japan.

Bridges carry roads, railways or footways over water, valleys and ravines or above other roads. Most are fixed, but some can be raised or swung round.

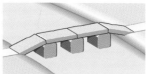
clapper bridge

arch bridge

truss-girder bridge

cantilever bridge

cable-stayed bridge

suspension bridge

◄ Some types of bridge.

With all bridges, the problem for engineers is to design and build structures which will not sag or crack under the weight they have to carry. There are several ways of doing this.

Beam bridges have rigid beams which are supported at each end. The earliest bridges used this idea. They were just tree trunks or slabs of stone resting between the banks of a stream. Modern beam bridges are often long, hollow boxes made of steel or concrete.

A *clapper bridge* is a beam bridge in which two or more stones or pieces of wood act as beams and are supported by piers of stone or wood. A *truss-girder bridge* is a type of beam bridge which uses a rigid steel framework as a beam.

Cantilever bridges have long, rigid sections like beam bridges. However, these sections are supported in the middle rather than at their ends. Each section extends out equally on either side of its supporting pier so that it balances.

Arch bridges take the strain of the main span with an arch that pushes on the ground at each end. Modern arch bridges often have a light structure.

Suspension bridges are best for very large spans. The road or rail deck is suspended from steel cables which hang between towers. The ends of these cables are anchored on either side of the span. Older suspension bridges have chains or even ropes rather than cables.

Cable-stayed bridges have cables attached to masts. The cables support the deck and transfer its load to the masts.

Building

Building work uses a wide range of materials. These range from simple ones such as clay and wood, to the steel, glass and concrete used to create the giant multi-storey structures found in modern cities.

There are two main methods of building. One involves constructing walls of a solid material like earth, brick or stone. These are called *load-bearing walls*, and they support the floors and the roof of the building. The other method involves constructing a framework of timber, steel or concrete. The frame bears the load of the floors and often the roof. The framework of timber buildings usually includes the roof structure. The frame can be covered or filled in with material (cladding or infilling), which can be lightweight as it does not carry loads.

Building a brick house

Before work can begin on building a brick house, a surveyor examines the soil and underlying rocks on the site to decide what foundations will be needed. The surveyor makes a plan of the plot of land to show its size and shape, and the nearest roads and water, gas and electricity supplies. Next, an architect draws a detailed plan showing every wall, door and window with exact measurements and information about the materials to be used. The builders use this to estimate the costs.

During building, an inspector from the local council checks regularly that building regulations are being observed. These regulations make sure the building is well built and safe.

Next, bulldozers level the ground ready for building work. The builders dig trenches where the house walls are to be built and pour concrete into them. The concrete sets hard to make a firm

• One of the most famous iron buildings of the 19th century was the Crystal Palace in London, which looked like a giant greenhouse. Glass was used to fill the spaces in the framework.

▼ How a typical single-storey brick house is built.

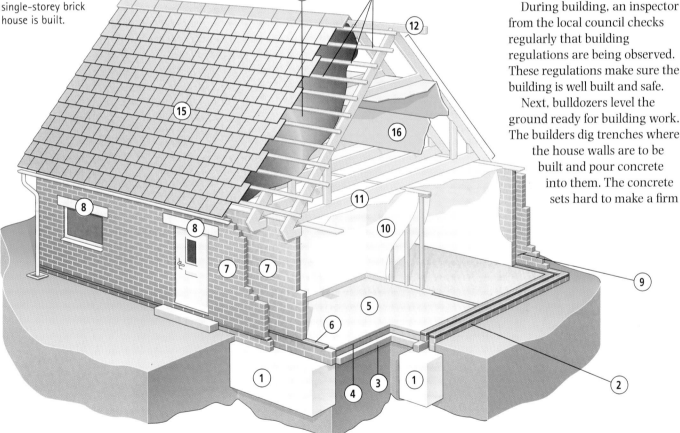

Strong, firm **foundations** (**1**) are needed for a house, to prevent it sinking into the ground or tilting over. **Footing walls** (**2**) finish level with the ground floor. They support the concrete slab of the ground floor and the structure above. To make the ground floor, **hardcore** (**3**) (broken bits of building material) is spread around the footing walls, and concrete is poured on. A **waterproof membrane** (**4**) (plastic sheet) goes on next, followed by a layer of **concrete flooring** (**5**).

The **damp-proof course** (**6**) prevents moisture from being sucked up the **walls** (**7**) from the earth (rising damp). Steel 'ties' in the mortar hold the inner and outer walls together. Concrete **lintels** (**8**) span the openings of doorways and windows. The **wall cavity** (**9**) keeps out rain and helps to keep the house warm in winter and cool in summer. Inner dividing walls are often made of **plasterboard** (**10**).

The main pieces of the roof framework are triangular **trusses** (**11**). A **ridge piece** (**12**) joins the trusses together at the top. **Waterproof felt** (**13**) covers the timber framework. **Battens** (**14**) (thin strips of timber) are laid on top of the felt, and **tiles** or **slates** (**15**) are nailed to the battens. **Insulating material** (**16**) is laid inside the roof space, to stop heat escaping through the roof.

Building materials

Bricks are moulded from clay and baked in a kiln. *Mortar*, a mixture of sand and cement, is used to stick the bricks together. It sets hard when it dries. The simplest framed buildings are made with a framework of timber (wood). Some Malaysian, Japanese, Chinese and medieval European timber-framed houses are decorated with ornate patterns and carving. Nowadays timber-framing is usually covered with bricks, wooden boards (weatherboarding) or panels. Iron and later steel have been used since the 18th century to make framed buildings. On modern steel-framed buildings, glass can be used as cladding as well as for windows. The concrete used for frames is reinforced with steel to make it stronger.

▲ In many hot countries, bricks are still made from clay in the traditional way. They have to be baked hard in the sun before they can be used for building work.

▲ The timber-framed guildhall at Thaxted in Essex, England, dates from the 15th century.

wide base as foundations for the walls. Once the 'footing' walls have been built on the concrete foundations, the concrete floor is laid, together with a layer of waterproof material, called the damp-proof course (DPC). It separates the foundations from the walls above. As the bricklayers build the walls upwards from the footings, they lay the bricks in horizontal patterns (bonds), overlapping them to prevent weak vertical joins up the face of the wall.

Most houses in wetter climates have a pitched (sloping) roof, so that rainwater runs off easily. As soon as the roof is in position, the carpenters fit the doors and windows and, if the house has more than one storey, the staircase. Plumbers fit the water system and electricians lay wiring for lights and electrical sockets. Plasterers finish the inside walls with a layer of plaster, which is decorated when dry. The new house is finally ready.

Multi-storey buildings

A building with more than five storeys is called a multi-storey

building. Unless there is solid rock just below it, a tall building needs deep foundations to stop it sinking, slipping sideways or being blown over in a gale. Most tall buildings are supported by *piles*. These are often huge steel or reinforced-concrete girders that are hammered deep into the ground.

The core walls of the building are built first. They are made by pouring concrete into wooden casings (shutterings). The core contains the main water and

electrical installations, such as lifts and lavatories. On top of it, at roof level, is the plant room which houses the lift and air-conditioning machinery.

A steel or concrete framework, which supports the concrete floor, is built around the core. Next the cladding panels are bolted on. These can be made of brick, metal (usually steel or aluminium), glass or concrete. Cladding that is bolted onto the outside of the frame is called *curtain walling*.

• Cement is made by burning a mixture of clay and limestone at such high temperatures that it melts. When cool, it forms small lumps, called clinkers, which are ground to a fine grey powder. Cement is mixed with water and crushed stone or sand to make concrete. The wet cement binds all the materials together to make a strong, hard-wearing material.

◄ The framework of huge modern buildings is often made from concrete reinforced with steel rods or bars. You can clearly see the steel rods in this building under construction in Thailand.

find out more
Bridges
Materials
Towers

Calculators

A calculator is a machine which does arithmetic. We use simple calculators to help us with mathematics at school, or checking bills at home. Scientists, engineers and accountants use more advanced calculators which can do very complicated sums. Today's calculators are electronic ones containing a tiny silicon chip to work out the calculations.

A simple calculator can add and subtract, multiply and divide, and work out percentages. Inside its electronic 'brain', numbers are represented by tiny electric circuits being switched on or off. The 'brain' works using the binary system of numbers, which has only the digits 0 (off) and 1 (on), instead of the digits 0 to 9 in the decimal system. Any number that you enter into the calculator is changed into binary, and calculations in binary are changed back to decimal so that you can see the results in the display.

Basic pocket calculators can do simple calculations, and have just a few keys. Most have

- A shop till is a type of calculator. It adds together prices and prints out a list of them with a total. Most supermarket tills read prices automatically from the barcode printed on each item.

- A calculator's 'brain' can only add and subtract. It does multiplication and division by doing additions or subtractions over and over again.

- The components inside some pocket calculators are so tiny that they will fit into a credit card-sized case or a wrist-watch.

find out more
Computers
Electronics
Information technology

▲ This Japanese office worker is using an abacus. The abacus was probably the first calculating device. It was invented over 5000 years ago, and is still used in some countries. Sums are done by sliding wooden beads along wires held in a wooden frame. Beads represent different units, for example 1s, 10s, 100s, and so on.

a simple eight-digit display, and a memory for storing numbers. They are powered either by small batteries or by a solar panel.

Calendars

A calendar is a way of grouping days so as to help people organize their lives. It is needed for planning farming, business, religion, and domestic life. Western countries use the Gregorian calendar, which was proposed in 1582 by Pope Gregory XIII.

The solar year (the time it takes the Earth to complete its orbit around the Sun) is actually 365 days, 5 hours, 48 minutes and 46 seconds long. The Gregorian calendar is based on the solar year. An extra day, 29 February, is put in the calendar every four years (called *leap years*). This helps to keep the calendar in step with the seasons, but there is still a small difference that adds up over many years.

The word 'month' comes from the name Moon. The Gregorian calendar is divided into 12 months with 30 or 31 days (28 or 29 in February). The Moon actually takes about $29\frac{1}{2}$ days to go through its phases as it orbits the Earth, so the months do not quite keep in step with the Moon's phases.

Other societies and communities use different calendars, often based on the Moon. The Jewish calendar has 12 months of 29 or 30 days. An extra month is put in seven times in a 19-year period. The Islamic calendar has 12 lunar months of 30 or 29 days and does not keep in step with the seasons.

Days of the week

People have organized days into blocks of seven, called

weeks, for a very long time. The Romans named the days of the week after the Sun, the Moon and the planets, which were themselves named after the Roman gods. The Anglo-Saxons used their own versions of the names of the Norse gods.

- In the Chinese calendar, each year is named after one of 12 animals: rat, ox, tiger, hare, dragon, snake, horse, sheep, monkey, rooster, dog and pig.

◀ This French lunar calendar dates from 1680. By turning the two wheels and using the table of dates, the Moon's appearance on any given date could be worked out.

- A millennium is a period of 1000 years. 1 January of the year 2000 is the beginning of the third millennium in the Gregorian calendar.

find out more
Moon
Seasons
Time

Cameras

- Infrared cameras make pictures in the dark using the heat radiation given off by, for example, the bodies of animals.

- Digital cameras have no film. The picture is recorded by a special microchip and can then be viewed on a computer screen.

We use cameras to take photographs or record moving pictures. Cameras which make photographs range from disposable ones that fit inside your pocket, to the single-lens reflex cameras used by keen amateur and professional photographers. Other cameras, such as cine-cameras and camcorders, are used to re-create a moving scene.

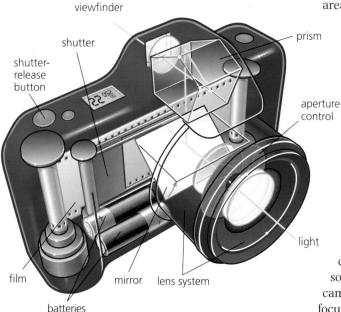

viewfinder
shutter
shutter-release button
film
batteries
prism
aperture control
light
mirror   lens system

▲ The main parts of a single-lens reflex (SLR) camera.

A camera's sturdy lightproof body protects the delicate parts inside, and stops light getting to the film. When you take a photograph, a *shutter* opens for a split second to let light hit the film. The *lens* collects light and focuses it on the film inside to make a small picture, or image. In most cameras the lens can be adjusted to make a sharp and clear image on the film. This is called *focusing*. Light-sensitive chemicals in the film record the image. Later, the film is processed to produce the finished photograph.

To take a good photograph, the camera must let just the right amount of light hit the film. This is called the correct *exposure*. Most cameras have an *aperture* (opening), which changes in size to let more or less light through the lens.

Developing and printing

After you have taken a photograph, the film has to be developed to make the image appear. Washing the film in chemical solutions changes it where it has been exposed to light. Usually the developed film is a *negative*. This means that areas that were light in the original image are dark on the film, while dark areas appear light. To make a positive image, light is shone through the negative onto a piece of light-sensitive paper. This is then developed to produce a *print* of the photograph.

Types of camera

All-plastic disposable cameras are the simplest and cheapest type of camera. The more sophisticated compact cameras have automatic focusing (autofocus), automatic exposure, motorized film wind-on, and an automatic flash unit. A zoom lens allows you to pick out a smaller or wider section of a scene.

Whatever you see in the *viewfinder* when taking a photograph appears in the final picture. Compact cameras have a viewfinder close to the lens, but in a single-lens reflex (SLR) camera you look through the lens itself.

Cine-cameras, TV and video cameras

A cine-camera takes 24 pictures (called frames) every second on a long strip of film. When the developed film is projected, the frames appear quickly one after the other. TV cameras change the picture into electrical signals. With video cameras and camcorders the pictures are stored or handled electronically.

► FLASHBACK ◄

The first proper camera was built by Frenchman Joseph Niepce in 1826. Another Frenchman, Louis Daguerre, invented the first practical camera in the 1830s.

▼ This photograph of a balloon bursting has been taken using high-speed photography. In this kind of photography the film may be exposed for as little as one-millionth of a second. It can be used to photograph rapid events such as explosions, or the flight of birds and insects.

find out more
Television
X-rays

Canals

find out more
Ships and boats

Most canals have been built for use by boats moving heavy loads. Other canals are built for irrigation or drainage.

Canals are usually built in places where there is no river, or where rivers flow too fast or are too narrow and winding for boats. The long thin boats that were used to carry large loads on the canals are called *narrow boats*. The early ones were pulled by horses led along the canal towpath, but narrow boats were later motorized. On wider waterways, large barges are used, some of them pushed or pulled by tugs. Some tow boats can pull up to 50 barges at a time carrying very heavy loads. This is such an economical form of transport that canals and waterways are likely to be used extensively in the 21st century.

Huge ship canals that join seas and oceans have dramatically reduced the time taken by ships to travel around the world. The Suez Canal links the Mediterranean and the Red Sea, allowing ships to travel from Europe to India and the East without having to sail around Africa. The Panama Canal allows ships to go from the Atlantic and Caribbean to the Pacific without travelling around the continent of South America.

Other canals link rivers and lakes. In North America, the St Lawrence Seaway allows large ships to sail from the Atlantic right through to the Great Lakes.

Locks

Canals cannot go up or down slopes. So, where a canal passes through hilly country, a series of locks is needed. A lock is a section of canal with watertight gates at each end. The water outside the two gates is at different levels. By altering the water level inside the lock, boats and ships can move from one water level to another. In this type of lock, which is called a *pound lock*, a boat can be raised or lowered by up to 9 metres.

▼ Barges carrying goods along a stretch of China's Grand Canal. Work on the canal began in the 6th century BC. In the UK, canal building started in about 1750.

Carbon

Carbon is an element found in countless different things. It is the black material you see on burnt wood or toast. Plants and animals are mainly made from materials containing carbon. Other things with carbon in them include vinegar, alcohol, plastics and disinfectants.

Pure carbon can exist in three very different forms: graphite, the black material used as the 'lead' in pencils; diamond, which is the hardest substance known; and a newly discovered group of materials called the fullerenes. Although all of these forms are made up only of carbon, the carbon atoms are arranged differently, so they look different and have different properties.

When foods and fuels are burnt, the carbon in them combines with oxygen to form a gas called *carbon dioxide*. When carbon combines with hydrogen, it forms a family of materials called *hydrocarbons*. These include natural gas, petrol, paraffin and diesel oil. Carbon also combines with hydrogen and oxygen to form foods like sugar and starch. These are called *carbohydrates*.

▼ Carbon is used again and again in a process called the *carbon cycle*. Plants take in carbon dioxide from the air through their leaves. Carbon is then transferred to animals, which release it back into the air as they breathe. When plants and animals die their bodies decompose (rot). Over millions of years they form fossil fuels, which we can burn as a source of energy.

find out more
Air
Elements
Greenhouse effect
Oil
Plants

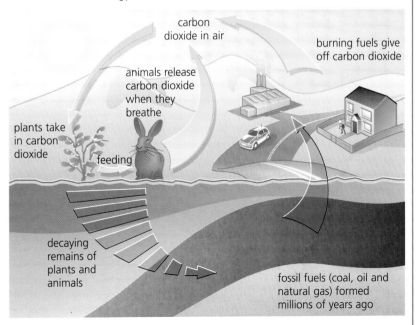

carbon dioxide in air

burning fuels give off carbon dioxide

animals release carbon dioxide when they breathe

plants take in carbon dioxide

feeding

decaying remains of plants and animals

fossil fuels (coal, oil and natural gas) formed millions of years ago

Cells

Cells are the building blocks of life. Some very simple plants and animals have only one cell, but most living things are made of huge numbers of cells. A newborn baby has about 5 million million cells in its body, and an adult has over 10 times that number. Most cells are so tiny that they can be seen only by using a powerful microscope.

Cells can look different, but most have the same basic parts. They are each surrounded by a cell membrane which holds them together and controls which substances can enter or leave. Inside this membrane, the cell is divided into two parts: the nucleus and the cytoplasm.

The *nucleus* contains the body's genes. Genes control what features a plant or animal will have. They contain a chemical, DNA, which forms a kind of code or blueprint setting out how the cell will develop. Genes are arranged in groups on structures called *chromosomes*. When a cell divides, each chromosome makes an exact copy of itself so that the new cell has a complete blueprint.

The *cytoplasm* surrounds the nucleus and contains food and many other substances. It is a kind of chemical factory where the materials needed for living, growing and changing are produced. The nucleus controls what goes on in the cytoplasm by sending chemical messages to it. The cytoplasm contains a number of structures called *organelles*, each surrounded by its own membrane.

Different organelles have different tasks. The *endoplasmic reticulum* makes various chemicals that the body needs and breaks down waste materials. The *mitochondria* are the powerhouses of the cell. Here, the cell uses oxygen to break down glucose from food to provide energy. In plant cells, organelles called *chloroplasts* contain the green pigment chlorophyll, which traps the energy of sunlight. This is used to build up sugars for food from carbon dioxide and water.

Not all cells contain a nucleus. In very simple cells, such as those of bacteria, the DNA is free in the cytoplasm. Instead of chromosomes, there is a single circular strand of DNA. These cells do not have organelles either.

Tissues and organs

Tissues are groups of similar cells that work together to perform a particular function. For example, muscle tissue is made up of cells called muscle fibres. These contain protein fibres which can shorten (contract) in response to nerve signals. Nerve tissue consists of cells with long, thin nerve fibres and a cell membrane that can transmit electrical nerve impulses.

Organs are groups of different kinds of tissue, containing different types of cell, which work together to carry out a particular function. For example, the heart contains muscle tissue for pumping, nerve tissue for controlling the pumping, and blood vessels for supplying the other cells with food and oxygen.

• The oldest forms of life are microscopic, single-celled organisms, such as bacteria and certain algae. Over time, groups of single-celled organisms began to cluster together in colonies. Some simple animals, such as sponges, are in some ways like masses of colonial cells living in a single co-operative structure.

find out more
Animals
Biotechnology
Genetics
Human body
Living things
Plants

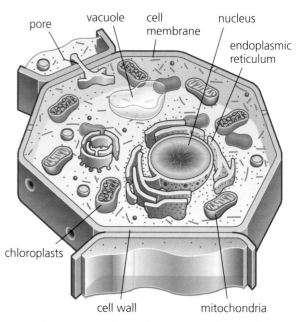

▲ A typical animal cell. Animal cells have a faint outline when seen under a microscope, because they are enclosed only in a thin cell membrane.

▲ A typical plant cell. Plant cells are clearly visible under a microscope because they have a thick cellulose cell wall outside the cell membrane.

Chemistry

Chemistry is the science that looks at substances. Chemists study how substances differ from one another – for example, one substance may burn easily, while another does not. They also study how different substances react together.

The most basic kinds of substance are called *elements*. These are substances made of only one kind of atom. But atoms can also join together, through chemical bonds, to form new substances called *compounds*. Water is a compound: it is made up of two atoms of hydrogen joined to one atom of oxygen.

When two or more substances react together, the chemical bonds between them change. When coal burns, for example, carbon atoms in the coal join up with oxygen from the air to make carbon dioxide. All chemical reactions involve making or breaking chemical bonds.

There are chemical changes going on around us all the time. Burning gas in a fire or a cooker is a chemical process. Boiling an egg until it goes hard is a chemical change. And a battery produces electricity by chemical changes.

The chemical industry develops processes by which quite simple chemicals can be made into useful products such as plastics and synthetic fibres, medicines, batteries and fertilizers.

◀ A chemist carrying out a titration. This is a method for finding out how much of one substance there is in a solution by adding a measured amount of another substance. If the chemist knows how the two substances react, and how much of the second substance he has added to the mixture, he can work out how much of the first substance is in solution.

• Chemists use letters for different elements: carbon, for example, is C, oxygen is O, and hydrogen is H. Compounds can be written using these letters: water is H_2O.

• *Organic chemistry* is the study of compounds of carbon, many of which are found in living things. *Inorganic chemistry* is the study of chemicals that do not contain carbon.

find out more
Atoms and molecules
Elements
Matter

Clocks and watches

People have kept time for many thousands of years. Before the invention of mechanical clocks, people used instruments such as sundials, hourglasses and water clocks to tell the time.

On a sundial you can read the time by seeing where a shadow falls on a dial. You can tell the time from hourglasses (which are like egg-timers) and water clocks by seeing when all the sand or water from one container has poured into another container.

The first mechanical clocks were made in the 14th century. They did not have hands or a dial, but made a bell ring every hour. They were powered by weights, which were attached to cogwheels. As the weights moved down, the cogwheels turned.

The first pendulum clocks were made in the 17th century. A clock pendulum consists of a rod with a weight on the end, which is free to swing to and fro. A pendulum of a given length always swings at the same rate. This is what enabled pendulum clocks to keep such accurate time.

The first accurate watches were also made in the 17th century. They used a small balance spring to keep time.

The first clocks powered by electricity were made in the 19th century. Today, many clocks and watches are powered by batteries. They use the natural vibrations (100,000 per second) in a quartz crystal to keep time. Many are built like small computers, and show the time on a digital electronic display.

• Pocket watches became possible after the invention, in about 1500, of the mainspring (a tightly wound coil) to give the power.

• The first electric clock was invented in 1843 by Alexander Bain.

◀ The most accurate clocks today are atomic clocks. They use vibrations in (certain) atoms to control their beat, and gain or lose less than a millionth of a second every year.

find out more
Calendars
Time

Colour

We live in a world full of colour. A rainbow arching its colours across the sky is a beautiful sight. The pictures we see on our television screens are filled with colour. Even the light from the Sun or an electric light bulb contains a mixture of colours – all the colours of the rainbow. How do we see all this colour?

All light travels like the ripples across a pond when you drop a stone in. The distance between the top of one ripple and the top of the next is called the *wavelength*. Light of different colours has different wavelengths. Red light has the longest wavelength and violet the shortest. The wavelength of the light makes us see different colours, although our brain also has an important part to play. Nobody knows exactly how we see all the shades of all the different colours.

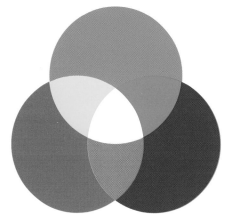

▲ When mixing light beams, only the three primary colours – red, green and blue – are needed to make all the other colours. When the three colours are mixed together they produce white, because they contain all the colours in the spectrum.

White and coloured light

Although the light from the Sun seems colourless, it is made up of all the colours of the rainbow. We call this spread of colours a *spectrum*. Whenever our eyes receive this mixture of colours, we see it as white light.

To make beams of light of different colours, you can put sheets of transparent coloured plastic (filters) in front of a torch beam of white light. A red filter gives you a red light beam. A green filter gives you a green light beam. If you shine the red beam and the green beam onto a sheet of white paper, you will see yellow where they overlap! When light is added together in this way, only three basic colours – red, green and blue, each in different proportions – are needed to

make all other colours. Scientists call these three basic colours the *primary colours* of light. Television uses only these colours to produce colour pictures.

Paints and inks

Mixing paints or inks gives different colours from mixing beams of light. When you mix paints, colours are taken away. The paint on the walls of a room absorb most of the colours in white light. So when you see blue walls, for example, you are seeing only the colours in the blue part of the spectrum. All the colours in the red part of the spectrum are absorbed by the paint.

The primary colours of paints, inks and dyes are different from those for light: they are red, blue and yellow.

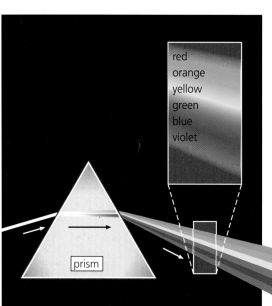

red
orange
yellow
green
blue
violet

prism

▲ A glass prism splits white light into the colours of the spectrum. We can see the invisible light rays because they are bouncing off specks in the glass or smoke particles in the air.

▲ If you mix the three primary paint colours – red, blue and yellow – together in equal amounts, you make black.

▼ Raindrops can act like tiny prisms, splitting sunlight into different colours. Only one colour from each raindrop reaches our eyes, but because there are thousands of drops we can see the whole rainbow. When a beam of sunlight goes into a raindrop, it is refracted (bent) and split up. It is then reflected from the back of the drop and is split up even further as it comes out.

Comets

Comets are icy objects which travel through the Solar System. A bright comet in the night sky looks like a hazy patch with a long wispy tail. The most famous comet, Halley's Comet, can be seen from the Earth every 76 years.

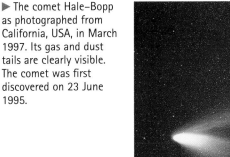

▶ The comet Hale–Bopp as photographed from California, USA, in March 1997. Its gas and dust tails are clearly visible. The comet was first discovered on 23 June 1995.

find out more
Gravity
Solar System
Sun

Comets travel in orbits through the Solar System. They evaporate gas and dust and grow long tails when they are near enough to the Sun's heat and light. The tails are caused by the light and streams of atomic particles from the Sun.

Comets that are bright enough to be seen easily by the unaided eye are quite rare, but astronomers using telescopes find 20 or 30 comets every year. When a comet comes near Earth, it gets brighter over a few weeks. A check from night to night shows that it moves slowly among the stars. Then it gradually fades and disappears.

Most comets are seen only once. They are pulled towards the Sun by the force of its gravity, then they vanish into distant space. Others get trapped by the gravity of the Sun and planets and keep moving around the Sun in long oval orbits.

Halley's Comet

Halley's Comet is named after the astronomer Edmond Halley. He observed a bright comet in 1682, and realized that it had appeared at least twice before. Halley predicted that it would reappear in 1758, although he did not live to see it.

Compact discs

Compact discs (CDs for short) have many different uses. You can listen to recorded music on audio CDs. You can look up an encyclopedia entry or play a game on a CD-ROM, which stores computer programs and other data. Almost any sort of information can be recorded on a CD.

Compact discs are made of plastic, about 1 millimetre thick, and normally measure 12 centimetres across. On a CD, information is coded as binary numbers (just the digits 0 and 1). Groups of 0s and 1s represent larger numbers, which in turn represent sounds, pictures, letters and so on. The first CDs were developed in the early 1980s.

Recording on a CD

A laser beam makes a recording by burning pits into the surface of a compact disc. A master disc is made from this. The master disc stamps the pits into transparent plastic discs. The pitted side is coated with aluminium and a layer of lacquer, and then the label is put on. On the underside of the disc, the reverse of the pits comes out as a pattern of 'steps' and 'flats' (no step). A flat represents a 1 in binary, and a step represents a 0.

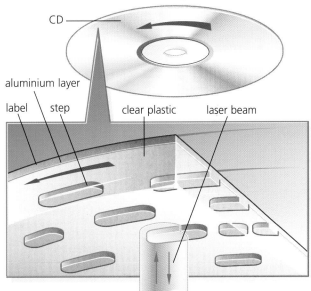

CD

aluminium layer

label   step   clear plastic   laser beam

find out more
Computers
Electronics
Information technology
Lasers
Recording

● The steps on a CD are extremely narrow – you could fit 200 of them across a human hair.

● Each 0 or 1 stored on the CD is called a bit. A normal CD can store millions of bits. The track is 5 km long.

◀ Inside a CD player, a laser beam reads the pattern of steps and flats on the underside of the CD. Electronic circuits turn this pattern into electrical signals, which are used to form the sounds you hear or the words and pictures you see on the screen.

Computers

Computers are electronic machines that can be programmed to do a huge number of different tasks. In homes, schools and offices, they are used to produce documents, create designs, make calculations, store lists and search for information. In factories, computers operate tools and robot arms. There are even computers inside washing machines and microwave ovens.

Computers work by processing *data*. Data is information. It can be numbers, words, pictures, sounds – in fact, almost any sort of information. As the computer operates, it follows instructions stored in its electronic memory. These instructions are called a *program*. The reason a computer can do so many different jobs is that the program can be changed easily. This means that the same computer can be a word processor, an encyclopedia, or a powerful mathematical calculator.

Hardware and software

A computer system is made up of two parts, the hardware and the software. The hardware is the actual computer itself – the electronic parts, the screen and the keyboard. Software is the programs and data that the computer uses. *Systems software* is software that the computer needs to do basic jobs, such as sending words and pictures to the screen. *Applications software* is software that allows the computer to do different jobs – word-processing, storing information, doing calculations or playing games.

Inside a computer

At the heart of every computer is a tiny microchip, a small slice of silicon imprinted with an extremely complicated electronic circuit. This is the *microprocessor*. It is the part of the computer that does all the calculations and carries out the instructions it gets from programs. The computer also has a set of memory chips for storing programs and data. There are two types of memory – RAM (Random Access Memory) and ROM (Read-Only Memory). RAM is the computer's short-term memory, where it stores data it needs quickly. Everything stored in the RAM is lost when the computer is turned off. ROM is where the computer stores data it will need again and again. It takes longer to read or to store data in the ROM, but the data is not lost when the computer is turned off.

The microprocessor carries out programs stored in the memory. As the microprocessor follows the program instructions, it gets pieces of data from the memory, does something with them, such as adding them together or multiplying them, and then stores the results. A microprocessor understands only a few dozen simple instructions. But when these instructions are combined in a program, it can do very complicated calculations and tasks.

▲ A computer's power is measured by how many instructions it can carry out each second. Today's personal computers (PCs) operate at around 300 MIPS (millions of instructions per second), but supercomputers like this CM-5, which is as tall as a wardrobe, can operate at over 10,000 MIPS. Instead of using a single microprocessor, like a PC, it can use up to 1024 processors.

• Computer circuits recognize only two numbers, 0 and 1. These are called *binary numbers*. Binary numbers are based on two. This means that the number one is written as 1, but two is 10 (one 2 and no 1s), three is 11, and so on. Computers store and process data using binary numbers.

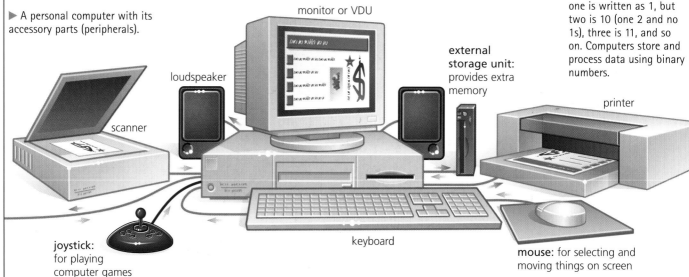

▶ A personal computer with its accessory parts (peripherals).

monitor or VDU

loudspeaker

external storage unit: provides extra memory

printer

scanner

joystick: for playing computer games

keyboard

mouse: for selecting and moving things on screen

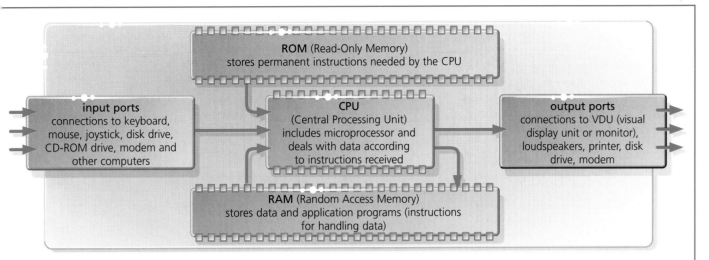

ROM (Read-Only Memory)
stores permanent instructions needed by the CPU

input ports
connections to keyboard, mouse, joystick, disk drive, CD-ROM drive, modem and other computers

CPU
(Central Processing Unit) includes microprocessor and deals with data according to instructions received

output ports
connections to VDU (visual display unit or monitor), loudspeakers, printer, disk drive, modem

RAM (Random Access Memory)
stores data and application programs (instructions for handling data)

Peripherals

Peripherals are devices attached to a computer, which send it data and receive data from it. *Input devices* are used to get data into the computer. The most common input device is the keyboard. Others include a mouse, CD-ROMs, scanners (which copy pictures into the computer), microphones and digital cameras. *Output devices* are used to get information out of the computer. The most common output devices are monitors, which display words and pictures, and printers, which print out data. Loudspeakers and earphones are also output devices.

Some peripherals are both input and output devices. Disk drives are the most common of these. Disk drives store data on magnetic disks (floppy disks). They can write data from the microprocessor onto a disk, or they can read data from the disk and send it back to the microprocessor. A modem is an input/output device that can send information from one computer to another through the telephone network.

▶ FLASHBACK ◀

In the mid-1830s, before scientists fully understood electricity, a British mathematician called Charles Babbage designed a mechanical computer called an analytical engine. Unfortunately it was far too complicated to build in his lifetime.

▶ Technicians changing the wiring of ENIAC (the Electronic Numerical Integrator And Calculator). ENIAC was completed in 1946 and was one of the first electronic computers. Changing the wiring created different circuits between ENIAC's 18,000 valves, and so changed its 'program'.

The first electronic computers were developed in the 1940s. Instead of microchips, they used thousands of electronic valves, which looked rather like light bulbs and were about the same size. These huge computers were not as powerful as today's small portable computers. In the 1950s electronic valves were replaced by transistors, which were much smaller – about the size of a pea – and computers became smaller and more powerful.

In 1972 the first microchips were made. In the late 1970s and early 1980s the first personal computers (PCs) were produced. Since then, microprocessors have become more and more powerful and computers have become cheaper. Today, computer scientists are experimenting with computer systems called *neural nets*, which can solve problems by learning for themselves.

▲ Flow diagram showing how data is processed in a computer.

• The amount of information a computer or a disk drive can store is measured in *bits* and *bytes*. One bit of memory stores either a 0 or a 1. One byte is eight bits: enough to store one letter of the alphabet.

find out more
Calculators
Compact discs
Electronics
Information technology
Internet

Copernicus, Nicolas

Born 1473 in Poland
Died 1543 aged 70

Nicolas Copernicus was the first person to work out that the Sun is at the centre of our Solar System, and all the planets orbit around it.

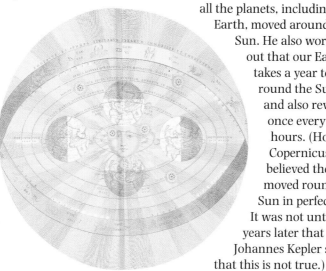

▶ This map of the Solar System was published by Copernicus in about 1530. In it he demonstrates how the Earth orbits the Sun, and how its position in relation to the Sun at different times of the year affects its climate and creates the seasons. He also shows the orbits of Saturn, Jupiter and Mars.

find out more
Astronomy
Galilei, Galileo
Solar System

When Nicolas Copernicus started studying astronomy, everyone believed that the Earth was at the centre of the Universe, and that the Earth did not move. Copernicus, however, realized that this picture did not agree with astronomical observations. He believed that all the planets, including the Earth, moved around the Sun. He also worked out that our Earth takes a year to travel round the Sun, and also revolves once every 24 hours. (However, Copernicus also believed the planets moved round the Sun in perfect circles. It was not until 50 years later that Johannes Kepler showed that this is not true.)

Copernicus set out his Sun-centred theory in a famous book, *De revolutionibus*. This was printed in 1543, just a few weeks before he died. His ideas were considered very controversial. They challenged views about the Solar System which had been held since the times of the ancient Greeks. They also challenged the Church's belief that God created the Earth at the centre of the Universe.

Copernicus's book was regarded as a source of evil ideas, and in 1616 it was put on the 'Index', a list of books that Roman Catholics were not allowed to read. Copernicus's theory was the subject of a famous trial in 1633, when the great astronomer Galileo was forced against his will to declare that the Earth did not move at all.

Crystals

We may think of a crystal as a clear, sparkling object like a diamond. But to a scientist, the word has a very different meaning. Any solid in which the atoms are arranged in a regular pattern is a crystal.

If you look at salt grains through a magnifying glass, you will see that each grain is a tiny crystal. The salt crystals are always the same basic shape – a cube. Like all substances, salt is made from millions of tiny atoms. In salt, there are two types of atom, sodium and chlorine, arranged in a regular formation. The cubic shape of the salt crystals is a result of this regular arrangement.

Pure crystals of a particular substance always have the same basic shape, because the atoms of that substance always arrange themselves in the same way. However, crystals of different substances can be different shapes and sizes. Some substances form large crystals. Quartz, for example, can form crystals as big as a person. Other substances, such as metals, are made up of very tiny crystals, too small to see.

Forming crystals

Large crystals only form under certain conditions. For example, if a substance is dissolved in water, crystals will form if the water evaporates. They can also form if a liquid cools down and solidifies. You can see crystals formed in this way on a cold morning, when water on the outside of a window cools down and forms patterns of ice crystals on the panes.

▲ This photograph of the surface of the metal palladium has been magnified many times to show the tiny crystals that make up the metal.

◀ The cubic shape of salt crystals can be seen in this photograph.

Growing salt crystals
To grow your own salt crystals, add some salt to a little warm water and stir until it dissolves. Pour the liquid (called salt solution) into a saucer and leave on a windowsill for a day or so. As the water slowly evaporates, salt crystals will appear.

find out more
Atoms and molecules
Matter
Metals
Rocks and minerals

Curie, Marie

Born 1867 in Warsaw, Poland
Died 1934 aged 66

Marie Curie was a physicist who spent her life studying radioactive materials. She invented an instrument to measure radioactivity. With her husband Pierre, she discovered the element radium.

Marie Curie grew up in Warsaw, the capital of Poland. Her name was then Marya Sklodowska. Women could not go to university in Poland at this time, so Marya went to study in Paris, France, where she changed her name to Marie. In 1894 she married a chemist called Pierre Curie, who, realizing that his wife was a great scientist, began to work as her assistant.

Marie Curie devoted her life to the study of radioactive substances. She discovered that a substance called pitchblende – the ore from which uranium is extracted – was a thousand times more radioactive than the uranium itself.

To find out what was making the pitchblende so radioactive, the Curies tried to separate out the tiny quantity of unknown radioactive material from several tonnes of pitchblende. Some years later they ended up with a pinch of a highly radioactive element which they called radium. They also discovered a second radioactive element, called polonium. In 1903 the Curies received the Nobel prize for physics.

The dangers of radioactivity were not properly understood at that time, and as a result of her work, Marie died from leukaemia – a type of cancer that can be caused by radiation.

• When she was a student in Paris, Marie Curie was so poor that she sometimes fainted with hunger during her classes. However, she still managed to come top of the class in the exams.

find out more
Atoms and molecules
Elements
Radiation

▼ Marie and Pierre Curie at work in their laboratory in Paris. Pierre was killed in an accident in 1906, but Marie carried on with her work and in 1911 received a second Nobel prize, this time for chemistry.

Darwin, Charles

Born 1809 in Shrewsbury, England
Died 1882 aged 73

Charles Darwin was a scientist who came up with the revolutionary idea that plants and animals evolve (change) over time by a process called natural selection.

Darwin did not pursue his interest in plants and animals seriously until he became friends with the cleric and botanist John Stevens Henslow at Cambridge University. On Henslow's recommendation, he was invited to join the naval survey ship, HMS *Beagle*, as naturalist and gentleman companion for the captain. He set sail on 27 December 1831.

For Darwin, the most important part of the five-year voyage was visiting the Galapagos Islands, west of Ecuador. He noticed that the finches on the different islands were closely related, yet the finches from any one island were different from all the others. Also, they all looked similar to a type of finch that lived on the South American mainland. Darwin decided that some of the finches must have first reached the islands accidentally and then evolved separately on each island.

Darwin concluded that, over many generations, living things evolve and adapt to their environment through a process of natural selection. This means that only the best-adapted survive and produce offspring. In 1859 Darwin published his theories in his book *The Origin of Species*. It was very unpopular because it went against the belief that all kinds of plants and animals were created by God and had not changed since. Today few people doubt the logic of Darwin's arguments.

• Darwin became ill a year or so after his return from the *Beagle* voyage, and his health gradually declined. For the last 40 or so years of his life he was an almost permanent invalid, but he continued his scientific work until his death.

find out more
Evolution
Genetics
Living things

▶ Darwin is shown here studying plants in a conservatory.

Earth

The Earth is one of the nine planets in the Solar System. It is a huge rocky ball whose surface is two-thirds water and one-third land. The layers of air that surround the Earth make up its atmosphere. The atmosphere contains oxygen, which is essential to living things. The Earth is tiny compared with some of the other planets, or with the Sun. Jupiter and Saturn are hundreds of times bigger than Earth, and the Sun is over a million times bigger.

The Earth is constantly moving. It spins round in space like a top, and at the same time it travels around the Sun in an orbit (path) that takes one year to complete. Satellite photographs taken from space

▲ An eruption of Krafla, a large, active volcano in Iceland. The lava (molten rock) in a volcanic eruption comes from deep within the Earth.

show the Earth as a blue ball covered with masses of swirling cloud. Closer views can show its surface features, such as the shapes of the continents, the oceans, the great snow-covered mountain ranges, and even large rivers and cities.

Inside the Earth

We live on the outer part of the Earth, which is called the *crust*. It is made up of hard rocks and is covered with water in places. The crust is about 5 kilometres thick under the oceans and up to 30 kilometres thick under the land.

Beneath the crust lies a ball of hot rock and metals. The inside of the Earth is extremely hot, and below about 70 kilometres the rocks are molten (melted). This molten rock comes to the surface when a volcano erupts. The deeper below the surface, the hotter and denser (thicker) the rock becomes. The main inner layer of molten rock, immediately below the crust, is called the *mantle*. It surrounds the hot

metallic centre, which is called the core. The core is partly solid and partly liquid metal.

How the Earth was made

The Sun, like other stars, developed from huge spinning clouds of gas, called nebulas. The Sun is thought to have formed about 5000 million years ago. When it first formed, a broad disc of dust and gas swirled around the Sun. Some of the dust and gas collected together to form larger lumps of material, which became the planets of the Solar System. One of these planets was Earth.

When it was first formed, about 4600 million years ago, the Earth is thought to have been a ball of molten rock. The surface was probably as hot as 4000 °C. It took many millions of years for the surface to cool down enough for a solid crust to form.

▼ A cross-section of the Earth shows the different layers beneath the outer layer, or crust. Scientists find out about the inside of the Earth by measuring the speed at which the waves from earthquakes travel through the layers.

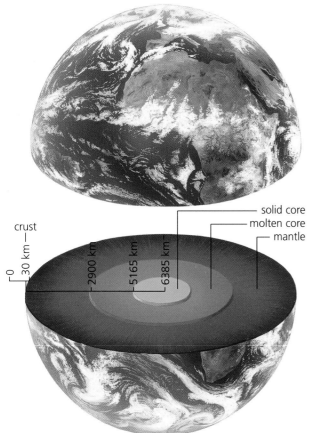

crust

30 km
0

2900 km
5165 km
6385 km

solid core
molten core
mantle

Eclipses

We see an eclipse when the Earth, the Moon and the Sun line up in space. If the Moon moves between the Earth and the Sun, there is an eclipse of the Sun. If the Earth is between the Sun and the Moon, we see an eclipse of the Moon.

The Moon goes round the Earth once a month, but it only goes directly in front of the Sun a few times each year. Although the Sun is very much bigger than the Moon, it is also a lot further away. By chance, the Moon and the Sun look about the same size when seen from Earth, so the Moon sometimes just covers the Sun to make a total eclipse. When this happens, the sky goes dark and the Sun's corona, a faint halo of glowing gas, can be seen around the black disc of the Moon. Even then, a total eclipse can be seen only from places along a narrow strip of the Earth's surface, just a few kilometres wide. In any one place, total eclipses of the Sun are rare. Partial eclipses, when the Moon covers just part of the Sun, are seen much more frequently.

Eclipses of the Moon are easier to see because they are visible from all the places where the Moon has risen. During an eclipse, the Moon looks a lot darker and reddish, but it does not disappear completely.

Total eclipses of the Moon
21 January 2000
16 July 2000
 9 January 2001
 9 November 2003
16 May 2003

Total eclipses of the Sun
21 June 2001
 4 December 2002
23 November 2003

find out more
Moon
Sun

▼ Eclipses of the Moon last for several hours while the Moon passes through the Earth's shadow.

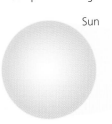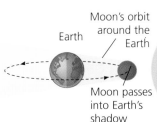

Sun

Earth

Moon's orbit around the Earth

Moon passes into Earth's shadow

▼ Total eclipses of the Sun last for a few minutes while the Moon covers the Sun.

Sun

Moon

Moon's shadow on the Earth

Ecology

Ecology is the science that studies how plants and animals live together, and how they affect, and are affected by, the world around them. Scientists who study ecology are called ecologists.

There are many complicated links between plants, animals and their environment. For example, thrushes eat the berries of trees like the mountain ash. The seeds inside the berries pass through the gut and come out in the thrush's droppings. The seeds then grow into new trees, which produce more berries. In bad summers, the trees produce few berries and the thrushes cannot feed so many young, so the number of thrushes falls. The trees therefore depend on the thrushes, and the thrushes depend on the trees, and both are affected by the weather.

Ecologists often need to make careful measurements as part of their study. So, in the example above, they might count the number of thrushes, measure the quantities of berries that are available for the thrushes to eat, count the number of seedlings that begin to grow, and record careful details of the weather. Putting all these measurements together, they can begin to understand the processes that control the numbers of the different plants and animals.

Living spaces

Ecology also shows how plants and animals depend on all the features that make up their surroundings, called their *environment*. So cacti and rattlesnakes, for example, are adapted (designed by nature) to live in the desert environment, and this is described as their *habitat*. To survive there, they must have ways of saving water, keeping cool, coping with the shifting sands

▼ The thrush and the mountain ash depend on each other. The thrush needs the tree's berries for food, while the mountain ash needs the thrush to spread its seeds.

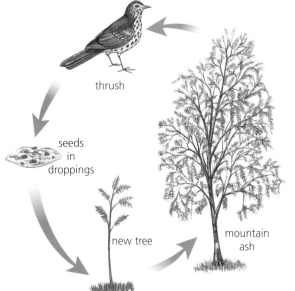

thrush

seeds in droppings

new tree

mountain ash

and avoiding their enemies. The spines of the cacti, for example, are there to stop them being eaten by animals, while rattlesnakes have a special way of moving over the hot ground. The lives of all the plants and animals in any habitat depend on each other and on their surroundings. The living system that ties them all together is called an *ecosystem*. Deserts, rainforests and coral reefs are examples of ecosystems. Even a small pond can be an ecosystem in itself.

Energy and food

Ecologists also study how energy flows through living systems. All living things need energy to stay alive. They get this energy from their food. Green plants make their own food, using water, carbon dioxide from the air, and the energy from sunlight. Animals cannot do this. They have to get their food either by eating plants or by eating other animals. So the plants and animals which live in an area are all connected to each other by the way that they get their food.

When green plants use sunlight to make their food, they are storing some of the Sun's energy. Plant-eating animals (*herbivores*) get this energy directly from the plants, by eating them. The herbivores are eaten in turn by flesh-eating animals (*carnivores*), which may themselves be eaten by other carnivores. But even for these animals, the energy in their food comes originally from plants.

▶ A food web. In many meadows, field voles eat grass, and kestrels often hunt and kill the voles, making a simple food chain (red arrows). Other kinds of animals (herbivores) also feed on grass. They, in turn, are eaten by carnivores.

Food chains

The plants and animals which live in an area are all linked together by energy and food, forming a food chain. In a garden, caterpillars may eat a cabbage plant. Some of the energy stored in the cabbage is passed to the caterpillars. If a thrush then eats a caterpillar, some of the energy is passed to the thrush. Cabbage, caterpillar and thrush are all links in the food chain.

There may be only two links in a food chain, for example when a horse eats grass. If large carnivores feed on smaller carnivores, there may be three or more links in the food chain. If we use our original example, a fox may kill and eat the thrush. Then the food chain has four links.

Scavengers and *decomposers* add further important links to most food chains. Scavengers are animals such as vultures, hyenas and some kinds of beetle. They feed on dead plants and animals. Decomposers are certain types of bacteria and fungi, which break down the

remains of dead animals. This puts minerals back into the soil and helps new plants to grow.

Food webs

In real life, food chains are rarely quite so simple. Many different food chains may interconnect to form a food web. All living things are linked together in food webs. A change in the numbers of animals or plants in one part of a food web (for example, as a result of pollution) can affect all the other parts of the web. Human activities often disrupt natural food webs, putting the whole living system (the ecosystem) out of balance. The result is difficult to predict, but often damaging to us and to other living things.

▲ In a few food chains, a plant is the carnivore rather than an animal. The Venus fly-trap grows in soils that are short of certain minerals that the plant needs for growth. It gets the extra minerals by catching and digesting insects in its specially adapted 'fly-trap' leaves.

find out more
Animals
Energy
Living things
Plants
Pollution

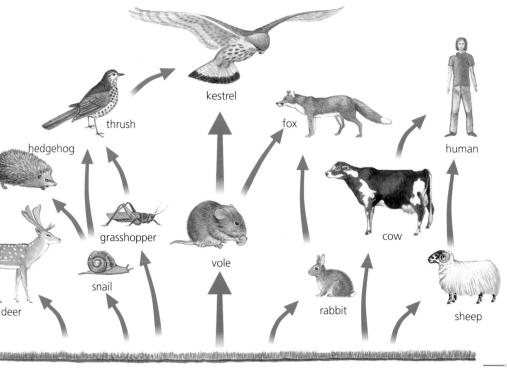

Edison, Thomas

Born 1847 in Ohio, USA
Died 1931 aged 84

Thomas Edison was one of the greatest inventors of all time. He patented (registered with the government) over 1000 inventions, including the electric light bulb.

From the age of 7, Thomas Edison was taught at home by his mother, who encouraged his interest in science. By the time he was 10, he had made his own laboratory and was starting to do his own experiments.

One of Edison's most important inventions was the world's first machine for recording sounds, the phonograph. The whole of our modern recording industry, which includes music, film, television and video, developed from this invention.

Edison also helped to invent the electric lamp. The one he designed consisted of a wire, or filament, inside a glass bulb from which all the air had been taken out to create a vacuum. His breakthrough came when he eventually found the right material from which to make the filament.

While he was experimenting, Edison found that a current could also flow across the vacuum to a plate inside the bulb. He did not understand why, but we know today that it is due to electrons escaping from the filament: it is known now as the Edison effect. This discovery led to the invention of the electronic valve (used before transistors and microchips were invented), and was really the beginning of the whole of our modern electronics industry.

• In 1869 Edison was offered a large sum of money for his design of a telegraph device. With this money he set up a research laboratory, which he called his 'invention factory'. He used to boast that this laboratory made a small invention every 10 days and a big one every six months.

find out more
Electronics
Inventors
Light
Recording

▶ This photograph of Thomas Edison was taken in 1888 after he had worked continuously for five days and five nights to improve his latest invention, the phonograph (shown beside him).

Einstein, Albert

Born 1879 in Württemberg, Germany
Died 1955 aged 76

Albert Einstein was a scientist who revolutionized physics in the 20th century. Without his radical ideas, lasers, television, computers, space travel and many other things that are familiar today might never have been developed.

▶ This portrait of Albert Einstein was made in 1921. This was the year in which he was awarded the Nobel prize for physics.

• Although Einstein's scientific ideas were used to develop nuclear weapons, he himself was a prominent campaigner for world peace.

find out more
Atoms and molecules
Physics

Albert Einstein was unhappy at school and his teachers thought he was not very clever. However, despite this poor start, it was not long before he became really interested in mathematics and started studying seriously. After spending some time in Italy, he went to Switzerland, and there his skills as a mathematician and scientist were recognized. In one year, when he was only 26, Einstein published several scientific papers that completely changed the way scientists think.

In 1914 he moved back to Germany. His scientific work made him world-famous and he was awarded the Nobel prize for physics in 1921. However, the rise of the Nazi Party meant he suffered abuse because he was Jewish. Eventually he had had enough, and in 1933 he went to the USA, where he lived for the rest of his life.

Einstein's scientific ideas were so unusual that at first people found them difficult to understand. He developed theories about time and space (relativity) and about how very tiny particles such as electrons and protons behave (quantum theory). Now his theories are essential to the way scientists think about atoms and the Universe.

Electricity

• At very low temperatures (–200 °C or less) some materials become *superconductors*. These are perfect conductors which do not need a battery to keep a current flowing through them.

▼ Special symbols are used for drawing circuits. These are the ones that would be used in a diagram of the circuit below.

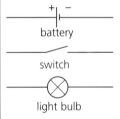

battery

switch

light bulb

Electricity makes cling-film stick to your hands, and sparks jump through the air. It is also one of the most useful forms of energy we have. It can power torches, TVs, tumble-driers and trains. It can come from batteries, or from massive generators hundreds of kilometres away.

Electricity is lots of tiny particles called *electrons*. These come from inside atoms. Everything is made of atoms, so there is electricity in everything. But you do not notice its effects until something makes the electrons move from their atoms.

Rubbing can make electrons move. When cling-film rubs on your hand, it pulls electrons away from atoms in your skin. The atoms try to pull the electrons back again, so the cling-film sticks to your hand. Scientists say that the cling-film has electric charge, or *static electricity*, on it.

Batteries and generators can push electrons through wires. The electrons flow between the atoms of metal that form the wire. The flow is called an electric *current*.

Conductors and insulators

Materials that let current flow through are called *conductors*. Metals, such as copper and aluminium, are good conductors. So is carbon.

Materials that do not let current flow through are called *insulators*. They include rubber, and plastics such as PVC.

In most electric cables, the wires are made of copper, with PVC insulation around them to stop the current passing from one wire to another – or into anyone who touches the cable.

Some wires, especially thin ones, warm up when a current flows through them. In an electric cooker, the current makes the metal element red-hot. In a light bulb, a filament (thin wire coil) gets so hot that it glows white.

Using circuits

To make a small bulb light up, it can be connected to a battery. This has two terminals, one positive (+) and one negative (–). If these are linked by a conductor, such as a bulb and connecting wires, electrons flow from the negative terminal round to the positive. The complete loop through the wires, bulb and battery is called a circuit. With a switch in the circuit, you can turn the current on and off. Switching off pulls two contacts apart and breaks the circuit.

A circuit like this could also be used to run an *electromagnet* – a magnet that can be

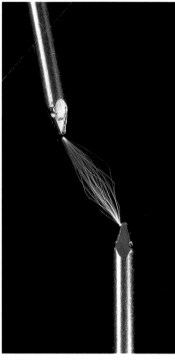

▲ Air is normally an insulator. But with 10,000 volts or more, it can be made to conduct … in a flash.

switched on and off. This is an iron bar with a coil of wire wound round it. When a current flows through the coil, it produces a magnetic field which is made stronger by the iron. The magnetic effect of a current is also used in electric motors and loudspeakers.

Many circuits run on mains electricity rather than on batteries. Mains electricity comes from huge generators in power stations. When you plug in a kettle, for example, you are connecting it to the big mains circuit.

Generating electricity

Generators, or *dynamos*, produce electricity when turned. The dynamo on a bicycle is turned by a small wheel which presses against the tyre. Inside the dynamo, a magnet is rotated close to a coil of wire. As the magnetic field moves through the coil, a current is generated. It flows backwards and

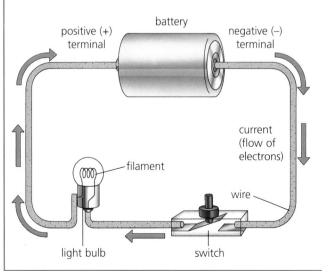

positive (+) terminal

battery

negative (–) terminal

current (flow of electrons)

filament

wire

light bulb

switch

◄ In an electric circuit the battery pushes the electrons from the negative (–) terminal through the wire to the positive (+) terminal. The bulb lights up as the electrons flow through its filament (thin wire coil). The switch turns the current on and off by pulling the contacts apart and so breaking the circuit.

Amps, volts and watts

Scientists measure current in amperes ('amps'). The higher the current, the more electrons are flowing every second.

The *voltage* of a battery or generator tells you how hard it pushes out electrons. A 1.5-volt battery is safe to touch, but a 12-volt car battery would give you a nasty shock. A 230-volt mains socket pushes electrons so hard that the flow through your body might kill you if you touched a wire inside.

Electrons carry energy from a battery or generator. When the electrons pass through a bulb, the energy is spent as heat and light. The *power* of the bulb is measured in watts. The higher the power, the more energy is spent every second, and the more heat and light are produced every second.

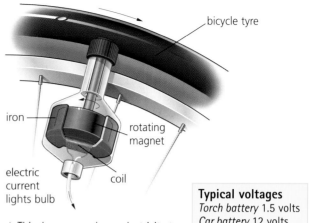

▲ This dynamo produces electricity to run the lights on a bicycle. It is turned by the bicycle tyre. Inside the dynamo, a rotating magnet generates current in a fixed coil.

forwards, as first one end of the magnet and then the other sweeps past. Current like this is called *alternating current* (AC). The generators that produce it are known as *alternators*. (The 'one-way' current from a battery is called *direct current*, or DC.)

The huge generators in power stations are alternators. The moving magnet is a powerful electromagnet, and the generator is turned by turbines driven round by the force of high-pressure steam, gas or water.

Mains electricity

At a power station, current from the generator is passed through a *transformer*. This steps up the voltage before the power is carried across country by overhead transmission lines. Increasing the voltage reduces the current. The electrons are pushed harder, so fewer are needed to carry the energy, and thinner lines can be used.

Typical voltages

Torch battery 1.5 volts
Car battery 12 volts
Mains supply
230 volts (UK), 110 or 220 volts (Canada and USA)
Underground train
600 volts
Lightning flash
100 million volts

▼ Large power stations can generate 2000 megawatts of electricity (1 megawatt equals 1 million watts). At substations more transformers reduce the voltage, and cables carry power to homes, schools, shops, offices and factories.

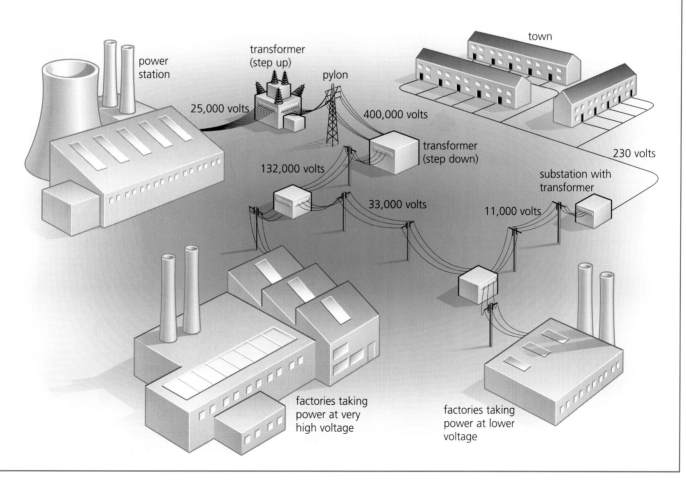

factories taking power at very high voltage

factories taking power at lower voltage

Electronics

Electronics help us in many ways in our daily lives. TVs, telephones, computers, CD players, watches – all these devices use electronics.

Electronic circuits work by using changing electric currents called *signals*. These signals can carry information, such as sound, pictures, numbers or instructions. They can produce sounds from loudspeakers or pictures on a TV, send messages across the world, or control the flight of an airliner.

Analogue and digital

There are two main types of electronic circuit – analogue and digital. In an *analogue circuit*, the electric current changes smoothly. For example, when you speak into a microphone, it produces an electric signal that changes smoothly in the same pattern as the sound waves. In a *digital circuit* the current is either on or off. Digital circuits send signals as long strings of 'ons' and 'offs'. These represent strings of numbers, each one measuring the strength of the signal at one particular moment.

▼ A microchip resting on a person's finger.

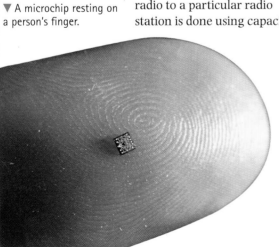

Electronic components

Electronic circuits are built from a few basic parts, called components. *Transistors* are the most important components. They can be used to amplify (boost) the strength of a signal, or to switch other circuits on or off. *Resistors* reduce the flow of electricity through a circuit. They make sure that all the other components get the right amount of current. *Diodes* work as electronic valves. They let the current flow in one direction but not in the other. *Capacitors* can store electricity, to smooth out the flow of current. They can also be used to pass on one signal but not others. Tuning a radio to a particular radio station is done using capacitors.

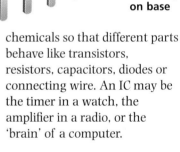

a single transistor

aluminium (for electrical connections)

layers of treated silicon form circuit components

silicon wafer

electronic circuits

▶ The structure of an integrated circuit (IC) or microchip.

whole microchip

microchip

plastic base

connector pins

microchip on base

What circuits do

In an electronic circuit, different components are joined together to perform different jobs. One of the most common circuits is an *amplifier*. Electronic signals are often weak. In an amplifier, transistors use the small, changing current of the original signal to regulate a much stronger current from another power source. The powerful current thus becomes a much stronger 'copy' of the original weak signal.

Another common circuit, used particularly in computers, is the *adder*. This can take two digital signals, corresponding to two numbers, and add them together.

Most of today's electronic devices use *integrated circuits* (ICs), or *microchips*. An IC is a circuit with thousands of parts, formed on a single chip of silicon. The chip is treated with chemicals so that different parts behave like transistors, resistors, capacitors, diodes or connecting wire. An IC may be the timer in a watch, the amplifier in a radio, or the 'brain' of a computer.

▶ FLASHBACK ◀

Ambrose Fleming invented the diode valve in 1904. It did the same job as a modern diode, but looked rather like a light bulb, and was about the same size. In 1906 the triode valve, which did the same job as a modern transistor, was developed. Valves were used in radios and other equipment for over 40 years. Then in 1947 three scientists invented a transistor made out of a piece of silicon. It was about the size of a pea. In 1958 the first integrated circuit was produced. It could fit hundreds of transistors onto a single silicon chip.

Elements

The elements are the basic materials that everything on the Earth and in the whole Universe is made of – including us. About 90 different elements are found in nature. Scientists have given each one a name and a chemical symbol. Oxygen and silicon are the most common elements on Earth.

Each element contains only one kind of atom, so it cannot be split up into different materials. The atoms of an element all behave in the same way. However, most familiar materials are not pure elements but *compounds* (combinations). To make a compound, the atoms of two or more elements join together to make a completely different material. Water is a compound. It is made from hydrogen and oxygen.

Hydrogen and oxygen are both gases, and water is nothing like either. Sugar is another compound. It is made from hydrogen, oxygen and carbon.

New elements

Scientists have made new elements by shooting tiny atomic particles at some heavy elements. So far they have made at least 11 new elements, though tiny amounts of two of these were later found in nature.

The periodic table

At the end of the 19th century, a Russian chemist, Dimitri Mendeléev, arranged all the chemical elements into a pattern called the periodic table. In it, all the elements are arranged in a continuous pattern of horizontal rows in order, starting with the lightest atoms and ending with the heaviest. Each vertical column makes up a group of elements with similar properties.

◀ Drops of the element mercury. It is a metal, but unlike other metals mercury is liquid at room temperature. It is extremely poisonous to humans and other animals.

• About 99% of the Earth is made of just eight elements.

• At ordinary temperatures most elements are solids. Only 2 elements (bromine and mercury) are liquids and 11 are gases.

find out more
Atoms and molecules
Chemistry
Matter
Metals
Oxygen

▼ The periodic table.

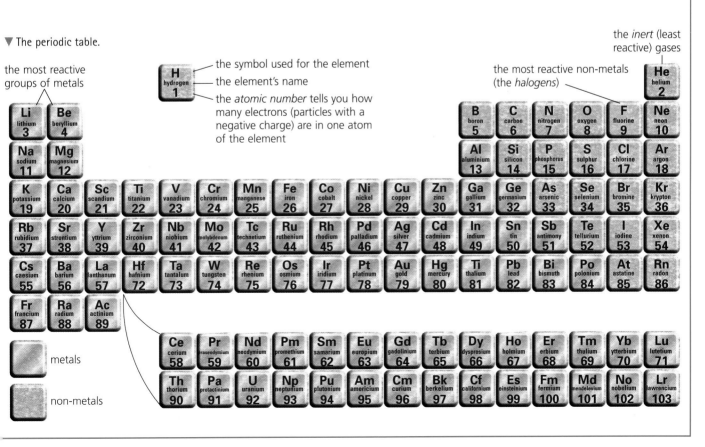

the most reactive groups of metals

the symbol used for the element
the element's name
the atomic number tells you how many electrons (particles with a negative charge) are in one atom of the element

the most reactive non-metals (the *halogens*)

the *inert* (least reactive) gases

metals

non-metals

Energy

Our bodies depend on energy, as do our homes, vehicles and factories. On Earth, the Sun is the source of nearly all of our energy. Without energy, nothing would live, move or change.

It is hard work pedalling uphill or moving heavy objects about. To scientists, *work* is done whenever a force makes something move. The greater the force and the further it moves, the more work is done.

If something has energy, it means that it is capable of doing work. An engine uses the energy in its fuel to move a car along. A battery can store the energy needed to turn an electric motor. And some winds carry enough energy to blow trees over. Hot things also have energy. In any material, the tiny particles (atoms) of which it is made are always on the move. Heating the material makes its atoms move faster.

Scientists measure energy in joules (J). A litre of petrol stores about 35 million joules. But this energy is not a 'thing'. It is just a measure of how much work can be done. The energy can be used to produce motion that you can see (such as a car speeding up) or tiny movements that you cannot see (like the atoms moving more quickly when something gets hot).

Changing forms

Energy can exist in many different forms. Things that are moving, such as cars and winds, have *kinetic* energy. Springs or other stretched or compressed materials have *potential* energy. So does any-thing in a position where it can fall. When hot materials cool down, they give off heat, or

thermal energy. Foods, fuels and batteries store *chemical* energy – their energy is released by chemical reactions. Light and sound are types of *radiant* energy. Electric currents carry *electrical* energy. And energy that comes from the nucleus (centre) of an atom is called *nuclear* energy.

Energy can change from one form to another. When you kick a ball, your muscles change chemical energy from your food into kinetic energy. As the ball moves through the air and across the ground, friction slows it down and its kinetic energy is changed into thermal energy (heat).

Scientists have discovered that, although energy can change into different forms, it cannot be made or destroyed. People may talk about 'using energy', but in fact it never gets used up. It just gets passed on in another form. Eventually, most

The energy that radiates from the Sun's surface as heat and light is the source of almost all the energy we use.

Green plants use the energy in sunlight falling on their leaves to produce their own food from water and carbon dioxide.

Weather systems are driven by heat radiated from the Sun. Hot air rising above the Equator causes belts of wind around the Earth. Heat and wind lift water vapour from the oceans and so bring rain and snow.

Solar panels use the energy from the Sun to heat water. Solar cells use sunlight to produce small amounts of electricity.

Coal, oil and natural gas are formed from the remains of plants and animals that lived millions of years ago. We extract them from the ground and burn them to get energy. This energy is used to power engines, to make electricity and for heating.

We get energy from the food we eat. The food may be from plants or from animals that feed on plants.

For centuries people have been using the power of the wind to move ships, pump water and grind corn. Today, huge wind turbines are used to turn electrical generators.

▲ How the Sun provides the Earth's energy.

• Lifting this book 5 cm takes about 1 joule (J) of energy.

• An average 11-year-old needs about 10,000 kilojoules (kJ) of food energy a day. (1 kJ equals 1000 joules.)

of it ends up as heat, but it is so spread out that it cannot be detected or used.

Energy from fuels

Industrial societies need huge amounts of energy to run their homes, vehicles and factories. More than 80 per cent of this energy comes from burning coal, oil and natural gas. These are called *fossil fuels*, because they formed from the remains of plants and tiny sea creatures that lived on Earth many millions of years ago. They include fuels made from oil, such as petrol, diesel and fuel for jet planes.

Most large power stations burn fossil fuels. The heat is used to boil water and make steam. The force of the steam turns turbines which drive generators.

There are two main problems with burning fossil fuels. First, their waste gases pollute the atmosphere. These gases include carbon dioxide, which traps the Sun's heat and may be causing global warming. Second, fossil fuels cannot be replaced. Supplies will eventually run out, so we must find alternatives.

Nuclear fuel, used in nuclear power stations, does not burn. Instead, its energy is released as heat by nuclear reactions. Nuclear power stations produce no waste gases, but they are expensive to build, and produce dangerous radioactive waste which must be stored safely for centuries. Nuclear accidents are rare, but when they do occur, radioactive gas and dust may be released. These cause cancer. They may contaminate the local area and be carried thousands of kilometres by the wind.

In developing countries, wood is the main fuel for 2 billion people. Unlike fossil fuels and nuclear fuel, wood is a *renewable* energy source, because new trees can be grown. At present, however, not enough trees are being planted to replace those cut down for timber, papermaking and fuel.

Alternative energy

To reduce our use of fossil and nuclear fuels, alternative energy sources are needed. There are many possibilities. *Hydroelectric* schemes generate electricity using the flow of water from a lake behind a dam. *Solar panels* use the Sun's radiant energy to heat water, while *solar cells* use it to generate electricity. In *wind farms*, generators are turned by giant wind turbines (windmills). *Biofuels* are made from plant or animal matter. In Brazil, for example, many cars run on alcohol made from sugar cane. Gases from sewage, dung and rotting waste can be used as fuels, and some power stations burn rubbish as their fuel.

All of these alternative energy sources are renewable, but none can be used without affecting the environment in some way. For example, creating a lake for a hydroelectric scheme changes the landscape and destroys habitats for wildlife. Also, none

▲ Hydroelectric power uses fast-flowing water to turn generators which produce electricity. This energy source is renewable because the water is constantly resupplied through rain.

of these sources can yet provide enough energy to meet our present demands.

For these reasons, many people think that we should find ways of being less wasteful with our energy. These could include greater use of public transport and bicycles instead of cars, better insulation in our homes, manufacturing goods that last longer before they are thrown away, and recycling more of our waste materials.

▼ This solar-powered car, called *Sunraycer*, has been developed by the giant US car manufacturer General Motors. Rows of solar cells on the back and sides of the car use sunlight to charge the batteries that run its electric motor.

- Power, measured in watts, tells you the rate at which energy is being spent. A power of 1 watt (W) means that 1 joule of energy is being spent every second.

- The Sun runs on nuclear energy. It has enough stored to keep it shining for another 5000 million years.

- Seven million tonnes of household rubbish contains the same amount of energy as 2 million tonnes of coal.

Typical powers
Light bulb 60 watts (60 joules per second)
TV set 120 watts
Hotplate 1500 watts
Small car engine 45 kilowatts (45,000 joules per second)

find out more
Atoms and molecules
Electricity
Engines
Forces and pressure
Greenhouse effect
Heat
Oil
Pollution
Power stations
Sun

Engines

Engines produce the power to drive vehicles and machines. Engines are themselves machines that burn fuel and turn the resulting heat into motion.

Steam engines, which mostly use coal as fuel, were the first successful engines. Until the beginning of the 20th century steam engines powered trains, ships and many machines. Over the last 100 years they have largely been replaced by internal-combustion engines, fuelled by petrol or diesel oil. Most airliners and military aircraft are powered by jet engines, which burn kerosene.

Many machines and some vehicles, especially trains, are powered by electric motors. Electric motors are not usually regarded as 'true' engines, since they do not produce motion directly from heat.

Steam engines

The first really practical engine was a steam engine built in 1705 by Thomas Newcomen. It pumped water from deep mine shafts. Newcomen's engine was very inefficient, but in 1765 the design was improved by James Watt. The first steam-powered railway locomotive was built in 1803 by Richard Trevithick.

In a steam engine, heat from a burning fuel (usually coal) heats water to make steam. The steam pushes on a piston to produce movement. The piston can be used to turn a wheel, which may then drive a locomotive or power a pump.

Many power stations and some ships are powered by modern steam engines called *steam turbines*. A turbine is a kind of fan or propeller, with many blades. When high-pressure steam pushes against the turbine blades, they spin round very fast.

▲ A large steam engine designed by James Watt, and built in 1788 by the Boulton and Watt Company.

Petrol and diesel engines

Cars, motorcycles, trucks and buses are all powered by *internal-combustion engines*. Most of these use petrol or diesel oil as their fuel. In this type of engine, fuel is exploded inside a closed cylinder. The force of the explosion pushes out a piston inside the cylinder. The movement of the piston pushes round a crankshaft, which is fixed to a heavy

• The biggest jet engines produce as much power as 500 large car engines. The steam turbines in large power stations produce as much power as 5000 large car engines. But most powerful of all are the rocket engines that lift spacecraft into orbit. They produce as much power as 500,000 large car engines, but only for a few minutes at a time.

▶ A single cylinder of a petrol engine, showing how it works. The engine is called a four-stroke engine because the piston goes through a series of four movements, or strokes. The heavy flywheel helps to keep the crankshaft and piston moving after the power stroke. Most petrol engines have four or more cylinders, so that each cylinder is on its power stroke at a different time.

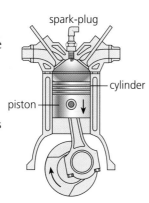

spark-plug · cylinder · piston

Power stroke
A mixture of petrol and air is exploded in the cylinder by a spark from a spark plug. The expanding hot gases push the piston out.

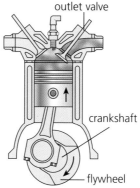

outlet valve · crankshaft · flywheel

Exhaust stroke
The outlet valve opens as the piston moves in again. The piston pushes the burnt gases out of the cylinder.

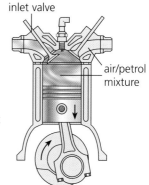

inlet valve

Induction stroke
The inlet valve opens as the piston moves out once more. A mixture of petrol and air is sucked into the cylinder.

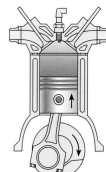

air/petrol mixture

Compression stroke
Both valves close as the piston moves in, compressing the petrol/air mixture. The cylinder is ready for the next power stroke.

Environment *see* Ecology *and* Pollution

Engines

▶ Technicians making final adjustments to two Formula 1 racing engines. Each engine has 10 cylinders, arranged in two rows of five. Extra-light materials and special fuels help to make these engines much more powerful than normal engines of a similar size.

• On a flight from London to Hong Kong a Boeing 747 jumbo jet with four jet engines uses enough fuel to fill a car's petrol tank 3500 times. This much fuel would take a car over 2 million km.

flywheel (the flywheel helps to keep the crankshaft turning smoothly). The turning of the crankshaft drives the wheels of the vehicle.

Most trucks and buses, and some cars, use four-stroke diesel engines. In a diesel engine, air drawn into the engine is compressed so much that it becomes very hot. Diesel oil is squirted straight into the cylinders. It starts to burn as soon as it meets the hot air, so the engine does not need spark-plugs. Diesel engines are less powerful and more expensive than petrol engines of the same size, but they use less fuel and last longer.

Jet engines

Jet engines are very powerful engines, used mainly to drive aircraft. They have fewer moving parts than internal-combustion engines, and they need less looking after. The first jet engine was designed by Frank Whittle in 1937.

In a basic jet engine (*turbojet*), air is sucked in at the front, then compressed and forced into a combustion chamber. Fuel is added and burnt in the chamber. This produces very hot gases, which

shoot out of the back of the engine. As the gases escape, they drive the aircraft forward. They also push round a turbine, which turns the compressor that draws in air at the front of the engine.

Turbofan engines are quieter than turbojets and use less fuel. Most large airliners use turbofan engines. In a *turboprop* engine, the hot gases are used to drive a propeller. Turboprops are often used in helicopters.

Rocket engines

All the engines described so far burn a mixture of fuel and air. The oxygen in the air is vital to combustion; without it, the fuel will not burn. Rocket engines do not need air, because they carry their own oxygen supply with them. This means that they work in space.

A simple firework rocket is a tube open at one end and filled with gunpowder. One of the chemicals in gunpowder contains oxygen, so it does not need air to burn. As the gunpowder burns, hot gases rush out of the tube and shoot the rocket into the sky.

Some spacecraft engines use a solid fuel rather like the gunpowder in a firework. Other rockets have two liquid fuels – liquid hydrogen and liquid oxygen. The hydrogen and oxygen are fed to the engine's combustion chambers, where they mix and burn.

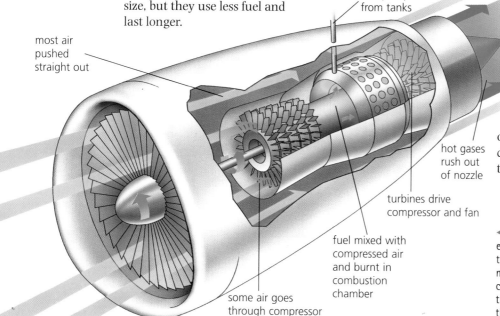

fuel pumped in from tanks

most air pushed straight out

hot gases rush out of nozzle

turbines drive compressor and fan

fuel mixed with compressed air and burnt in combustion chamber

some air goes through compressor

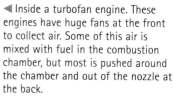

◀ Inside a turbofan engine. These engines have huge fans at the front to collect air. Some of this air is mixed with fuel in the combustion chamber, but most is pushed around the chamber and out of the nozzle at the back.

Evolution

Evolution is the way new kinds of plants, animals and other living things come into being as a result of many small changes over a long period of time.

Evidence from fossils in ancient rocks shows that over millions of years new kinds of creature have appeared. At the same time some of the old forms, such as the dinosaurs, have become extinct (died out).

In the 19th century the biologists Charles Darwin and Alfred Russel Wallace proposed a theory to explain how evolution takes place. The theory of *natural selection* (sometimes called the 'survival of the fittest') argues that the offspring of an animal or plant that are most likely to survive are those best suited to the present conditions and best able to compete for the things they need, such as food, water, light and space. These 'fit' individuals are also more likely to produce offspring, which in turn will inherit the special characteristics that made their parents fit. In a few generations that kind, or species, of plant or animal will contain more fit creatures and will gradually change. This may eventually lead to the development of a new species.

find out more
Animals
Darwin, Charles
Genetics
Living things
Plants

▶ Darwin's theory of evolution can explain the development of the pterosaur, an ancient flying reptile that lived over 150 million years ago. It began as a four-footed lizard (1). Over millions of years, small folds of skin developed between its feet, which enabled it to glide from tree to tree (2). Over many more generations the folds, and the bones and muscles supporting them, grew to form wings (3).

1

2
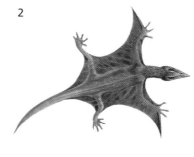

3

Explosives

Explosives are used in bombs, missiles and other weapons. They are also found inside fireworks and the flares set off by people lost at sea or in mountains. Explosives are more widely used for peaceful jobs like demolishing buildings and breaking up rocks in quarries and mines.

The high-pressure gas given off by an explosive expands violently to produce a noisy explosion. All explosives have a fuel, which burns rapidly, and a chemical that provides oxygen for burning.

Gunpowder and the explosives used in shells, guns and some rockets are *low explosives*. They can be set off by heat or even an electric spark. They are tightly packed inside a container so that the gas pressure can build up rapidly. Inside a firework container an explosive mixture, which includes gunpowder, burns, and pressure builds up. This forces out showers of sparks or sends a rocket up into the air.

High explosives such as dynamite and gelignite explode so fast that they shatter everything around them. They are used in bombs and for rock-blasting. They are set off by a small explosion from a detonator. *Plastic explosive*, a high explosive that can be moulded into shape, is used by terrorists because it is easy to hide and difficult to detect.

▶ **FLASHBACK** ◀

As early as the 9th century AD the Chinese made fireworks using gunpowder, the first explosive to be discovered. It was first used for firing guns in 14th-century Europe. Dynamite was invented in 1866 by the Swedish chemist Alfred Nobel, who later developed other high explosives, including gelignite.

• Always be careful with fireworks; their heat and explosive power can burn, blind and even kill.

find out more
Atoms and molecules
Mining
Rockets
Weapons

▶ Fireworks behind Sydney Harbour Bridge in Australia. The beautiful colours of fireworks are produced by chemicals (compounds) containing certain metals. Calcium or strontium compounds produce red, sodium produces yellow, copper or barium makes green, and potassium makes violet.

Faraday, Michael

Born 1791 in London, England
Died 1867 aged 75

Michael Faraday was one of the greatest scientists of all time. His most important achievements were the invention of the transformer, a vital part of most modern electrical equipment, and of the electric generator.

Faraday's research covered many subjects in both chemistry and physics. He was especially interested in the effect of electric currents on chemicals, and the way electric currents are produced from chemicals in cells (batteries). He also studied how gases turn to liquids at low temperatures, and how to make new kinds of glass for the lenses of microscopes.

Faraday knew that the French physicist André-Marie Ampère had shown that when electricity flowed in a coil, the coil behaved like a magnet. Faraday thought that if electricity could produce a magnet, then a magnet could produce electricity.

His experiments proved that this idea was right: when a piece of iron inside a coil becomes magnetic, an electric current flows in the coil. Faraday had, in fact, discovered the transformer. By moving a magnet in and out of a hollow coil, a current flowed in the coil and Faraday had discovered the principle of the generator.

▼ Michael Faraday giving one of his famous Royal Institution Christmas Lectures for young people, which he started in 1826. They have been held every year since, except for three years during World War I, and are now watched by millions of people on television.

find out more
Electricity
Magnets

Fax machines

▶ How a fax machine works.

● With some personal computers, you can send documents directly to a fax machine. You can also receive faxed documents on the computer. They appear on the screen and can be stored or printed out.

● The idea of fax originated in Germany in 1902. For many years newspaper offices used fax to receive pictures quickly from around the world.

A fax machine sends a copy of pages of text and pictures to another fax machine. It also prints copies of text and pictures sent by other fax machines. The word 'fax' is short for facsimile, which means 'exact copy'.

Office fax machines first became popular in the early 1980s. Some have a telephone handset for talking to the person operating the other machine.

Sending and receiving a fax

Once the sending machine has dialled the receiving machine and the receiving machine has answered, it begins to scan the document. It changes the pattern of light and dark in the pages of text and pictures (the document) into electrical signals, then sends these signals over the telephone network to the receiving machine.

The receiving fax machine takes the signals from the sending machine one line at a time. It sends them to a line of tiny heating elements. Where the original document was

0s and 1s sent as digital signals, one line at a time, through the telephone network.

light sensors

Light sensors change blacks and whites of image into electrical 0s and 1s.

sending fax

heating elements

Heating elements turn the line of 0s and 1s into a series of hots and colds.

Heat-sensitive paper turns black where it is heated.

receiving fax

dark, the heating element is turned on, and where it was light, the element is turned off. Heat-sensitive paper moves past the heating elements, and where the elements are on, the paper turns black. Gradually, the pattern of light and dark on the original document is drawn line by line.

find out more
Information technology
Photocopiers
Telephones

Forces and pressure

'Force' is the word we use for a push or a pull. A force will make a still object move. It will make a moving object travel faster, more slowly, or in a different direction. Together, two or more forces can make something stretch, squash, bend, twist or turn.

Gravity is a force of attraction – it tries to pull things together. There is a gravitational attraction between all objects. The more mass things have, and the closer they are, the stronger is the gravitational pull between them. The force of gravity between you and the Earth is strong enough to keep you on the ground.

Friction is the force which tries to stop one material sliding over another. If you throw a ball, the ball has to 'slide' through the air. This causes a type of friction called *air resistance*. For cars and other vehicles, air resistance is a nuisance. However, parachutists use air resistance to slow their descent.

If you stretch a rubber band, you feel a force called *tension*. Tension forces support climbers on ropes and goods in shopping bags. They are very useful. They even hold up your clothes! *Compression* (squashing) forces are the opposite of tension forces. They are produced when you lie on a bed, sit on a chair, or just stand on the ground. Without compression forces nothing could ever support your weight.

Scientists measure force in newtons (N). It takes a force of about 5 newtons to switch on a light, and 20 newtons to open a canned drink.

Different kinds of force

Scientists think that there are several kinds of force in the Universe: gravitational, magnetic, electric and two types of nuclear force. You feel a

---

Pressure

Pressure tells you how concentrated a force is. If the same amount of force is spread across two areas, one large and one small, the pressure acting on the smaller area will be greater than that on the larger area. Pressure is measured in newtons per square metre (N/m^2), also called pascals (Pa).

Pressure from gases like air pushes out in all directions. In liquids like water (and in gases), the pressure gets greater as you go deeper down in the liquid. If divers go too deep under the sea, the water pressure will crush them.

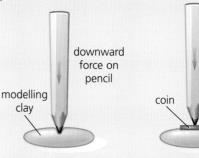

downward force on pencil

modelling clay

coin

▲ When force is applied to a pencil, the point will sink easily into a lump of modelling clay.

▲ The force applied to the pencil here is spread by the coin. The pressure on the modelling clay is less and so it is squashed only a little.

---

magnetic force if you hold a magnet close to a piece of iron or steel. You can see the effects of an electric force if you pull a comb through your hair and then hold it close to some tiny pieces of paper. Electric and magnetic forces are in fact parts of a single electromagnetic force.

▼ This sequence of events shows just some of the forces involved when playing on a tree. (1) The boy is using the *tension* in the rope to help him climb the tree. (2) The boy is exerting a *compression* force by standing on the branch. (3) The boy uses *friction* to help him hold onto the branch as he swings. (4) The boy's hands slip, and *gravity* pulls him down to the ground.

Galaxies

Our Sun and all the stars you can see in the night sky belong to a giant family of stars that we call our Galaxy. It contains around 100,000 million stars. The view we have of the Galaxy from inside it is known as the Milky Way. Beyond our own Galaxy, there are countless other galaxies scattered all through the Universe.

An image of the Whirlpool Galaxy, which is around 13 million light years away from Earth.

If you could go far out in space to look at our Galaxy, you would see a flat, circular shape with a bulge in the middle and a pattern of spiral arms. Between the stars there are giant clouds of gas and dust, some of them shining brightly and some dark.

On a dark night, the Milky Way looks like a hazy band of light stretching across the sky.

You can look at it through binoculars or a small telescope on a clear night, and see that it is the light from vast numbers of faint stars.

Our Galaxy is a *spiral galaxy*, which measures about 100,000 light years across. (One light year is equivalent to 9.5 million million kilometres, the distance that light travels in a year.)

Many large galaxies have beautiful spiral shapes. *Elliptical galaxies* are just flattened balls of stars. Another kind of galaxy is irregular, and has no particular shape.

Many of these galaxies send out strong radio waves that can be picked up by radio telescopes. Galaxies tend to cluster together in space. Our own Galaxy belongs to a cluster called the Local Group.

The nearest galaxies to Earth are the two Magellanic Clouds. They are about 180,000 light years away. One of the biggest galaxies that astronomers have studied is the elliptical M87. It is 1 million light years across and 50 million light years away.

• A quasar (quasi-stellar radio source) is something that sends out radio waves and looks like (but is not) a star. Quasars are embedded in galaxies. The most distant ones are more than 10 billion light years away. They shine so brightly that they swamp the fainter light of their parent galaxy.

find out more
Astronomy
Black holes
Stars
Telescopes
Universe

Galilei, Galileo

Born 1564 in Pisa, Italy
Died 1642 aged 77

Galileo Galilei (or simply Galileo, as he is usually known) was one of the leading figures of the Renaissance. This was a period of exciting change in Europe, when many discoveries in science and the arts were made.

Galileo was supposed to study medicine at university, but he was much more interested in mathematics and physics. He abandoned medicine and, at the age of 25, became professor of mathematics.

In 1609 Galileo heard news of the invention of the telescope in the Netherlands, and he set about building a small one for himself. When he used it to study the sky, he soon made some very important discoveries. He saw four moons circling the planet Jupiter, craters on the surface of the Moon, spots on the Sun, and rings around Saturn.

From his studies of Venus, he became convinced that all the planets, including Earth, moved around the Sun. This went against the thinking at the time, which was that all the planets and the Sun travelled around the Earth. The Christian Church believed God had created the Earth at the centre of the Universe, and punished anyone who said otherwise. When the astronomer Copernicus had published his ideas about the Sun-centred Universe 20 years before Galileo was born, his book was officially banned by the Church.

Galileo's views on the subject and the books he wrote landed him in serious trouble with the Church. He was forced to say he did not agree with Copernicus in order to avoid torture or even execution. But, even though he said this in public, he never changed his real belief.

◄ It was not until 1992 that the Church finally acknowledged that it had been wrong to condemn Galileo for his theories about the Solar System.

find out more
Astronomy
Copernicus, Nicolas
Moon
Solar System
Telescopes

Genetics

The young of all living things are similar to their parents. A mother rabbit always has baby rabbits; apple seeds always grow into apple trees. Children inherit characteristics from their parents. Genetics is the study of how these characteristics pass from one generation to the next.

▼ Identical twins (below) look very alike because they have the same genetic material. They both grow from a single egg that splits after it has been fertilized. Non-identical twins look less alike: they grow from different eggs and do not have the same genetic material.

Different kinds of animal or plant are obviously different from one another. But there are also smaller differences between animals or plants of the same kind. Pansy flowers, for example, can be many different colours, while female spiders are bigger than males. Some of these differences are due to *heredity*. Heredity is the inheritance of characteristics from our parents.

Environmental influence

Not all of an individual's characteristics are inherited. Some things about us are purely the result of our environment and upbringing. Reading and writing, for example, are things that we learn. We also have characteristics that result from a combination of both inheritance and environment. Our body shape is partly due to heredity, but how much we eat can have a major influence on it.

Chromosomes and genes

Characteristics are passed on from parents to their offspring through structures called *chromosomes*. These are found inside the cells that make up the body. Each cell carries inside it a complete blueprint of the whole plant or animal.

There are a number of chromosomes in a cell, and they are arranged in pairs, one from each parent. Different animals and plants have different numbers of chromosomes – humans, for example, have 46 chromosomes arranged in 23 pairs.

Arranged along the length of each chromosome, like beads on a necklace, are units called *genes*. Each gene carries information about a particular characteristic of the plant or animal. A human gene, for example, might carry information about eye or hair colour. More complicated features such as body shape are the result of many genes working together.

Every chromosome in a cell is different. But the chromosomes of a pair carry genes for the same characteristics. So for each characteristic we have two genes.

Genes produce the different characteristics of an animal or plant by controlling the making of proteins. There are thousands of different proteins, each with an important job in the body. Each gene controls the making of one or a small number of these proteins. Which genes your cells have influences which proteins are produced.

Passing on genes

A new animal or plant is made by the joining together of two special cells, called *sex cells*, one

Sex chromosomes

The difference between males and females is in their chromosomes. One particular pair of chromosomes is responsible for deciding the sex of a plant or animal. In humans, this sex chromosome can be either X or Y. A person with two X chromosomes will be female; someone with an XY chromosome pair is male.

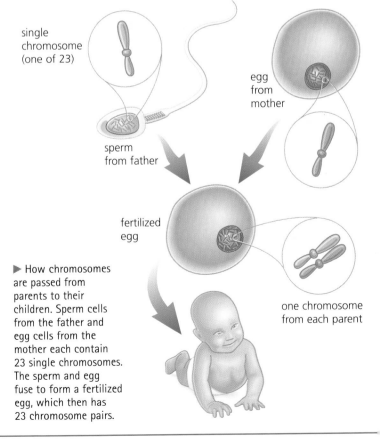

▶ How chromosomes are passed from parents to their children. Sperm cells from the father and egg cells from the mother each contain 23 single chromosomes. The sperm and egg fuse to form a fertilized egg, which then has 23 chromosome pairs.

single chromosome (one of 23)

sperm from father

egg from mother

fertilized egg

one chromosome from each parent

◀ Genes are made from a chemical called *DNA*. Each gene is one section of an enormously long DNA molecule. DNA is like a long ladder, twisted into a spiral. The 'rungs' of the ladder carry coded information that body cells can use to make proteins.

- - - ➤ genes from wrinkled seed

- - - ➤ genes from round seed

from each parent. Sex cells are different from all other cells in the body, in that they do not have a complete set of chromosomes. Each sex cell contains only half the normal number of chromosomes, one from each chromosome pair. When two sex cells join, the resulting cell (which becomes the new animal or plant) has the normal number of chromosomes – half from the mother and half from the father.

▲ Breeding wrinkled-seed pea plants with round-seed pea plants. The offspring from these plants produce only round seeds. But if two of the offspring plants are bred together, they produce a mixture of round and wrinkled seeds, with about three times as many round seeds as wrinkled seeds. The symbols inside the peas show the gene pairs in the plants in each generation. The round-seed gene, R, is dominant over the wrinkled-seed gene, w.

Dominant genes

The characteristics we inherit are passed on through pairs of genes. But if we have two genes for each characteristic, which one does the body use? Or does it use both?

Of the two genes we inherit for any characteristic, one of them is usually *dominant* over the other. For example, in pea plants, there is a gene that controls whether the pea seeds are round or wrinkled. A plant with a round-seed gene from each parent will have round seeds, and a plant with a wrinkled-seed gene from each parent will produce wrinkled seeds. But the round-seed gene is dominant over the wrinkled seed gene. So if a plant inherits a round-seed gene from one parent and a wrinkled-seed gene from the other, it will produce only round seeds.

This dominance of one gene in a pair over another means that animals and plants carry within their chromosomes many 'hidden' genes. These do not show as characteristics because they are masked by a dominant gene.

Genetic engineering

Scientists' improved understanding of genetics has made it possible to 'engineer' living cells to give them useful properties. For example, microbes (tiny, single-celled creatures such as bacteria and yeasts) can be modified (changed) to produce medically useful vaccines, hormones and other chemicals that are normally made only in the human body.

Genetic engineering has many important uses, but many people are worried by it. They do not like the idea that one day babies may be 'designed' to have specially chosen characteristics.

find out more
Animals
Biotechnology
Cells
Plants

▶ Dolly the sheep, born in 1997, was the first large animal to be cloned from an adult. A cell from a Dorset sheep (Dolly's mother) was injected into an unfertilized sheep's egg that had had its nucleus removed. The two cells were fused using a spark of electricity. The new cell was placed in the womb of a third sheep, where it grew into Dolly. Dolly has exactly the same genetic material as her mother.

Glass

Window panes, tumblers, ornaments, cooking vessels and windscreens are just a few of our everyday uses of glass. Special glass is used for lenses, telescope mirrors and furnaces. There is even bulletproof glass to resist machine-gun fire.

Much of the glass used today is produced by heating a mixture of sand, soda ash and limestone in a large furnace at a temperature of 1500 °C. Before the ingredients are added, some broken glass is put in to speed up the process.

As the mixture melts, any impurities rise to the surface and are skimmed off. The molten glass is allowed to cool until it looks like thin, sticky toffee. It is then moulded or rolled into sheets.

The cheapest kind of glass, used for windows, is *sheet glass*. The molten glass is lifted from the furnace and passed through rollers to form a flat sheet. *Plate glass* is made by flattening molten glass into sheets. The sides are then ground and polished by machine. In 1952 Alastair Pilkington invented a method to make *float glass*, which has a smooth, polished finish. Car windscreens are made by combining layers of float glass and plastic material to make *laminated glass*.

• Some high-quality glass products are still blown by hand today. The glass-blower blows down a hollow iron tube which has been dipped into molten glass.

find out more
Lenses

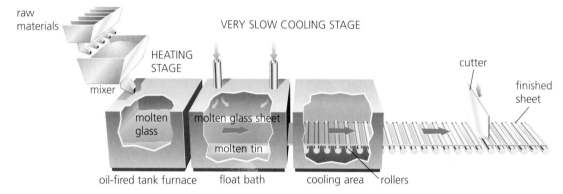

raw materials
HEATING STAGE
mixer
VERY SLOW COOLING STAGE
molten glass
molten glass sheet
molten tin
oil-fired tank furnace
float bath
cooling area
rollers
cutter
finished sheet

◀ In the float-glass method, a thin layer of molten glass is floated on the perfectly flat surface of a tank filled with molten tin. The glass formed has a clear, smooth surface.

Gold

Pure gold is a soft yellowish metal. It has been a valuable material since ancient times – gold coins were first made by King Croesus of Lydia in about 600 BC. Because gold does not react with other chemicals in its surroundings, it does not corrode (wear away).

Gold is generally hardened by alloying (mixing) it with copper or silver. The gold content of alloys is measured in *carats*. Pure gold is said to be 24 carats; an alloy of equal parts of gold and, say, silver is said to be 12-carat gold; 18-carat gold is 18/24 pure gold (75% gold).
 Gold is widely used to make jewellery, ornaments and other precious objects. Dentists use gold for filling and capping

teeth, while gold or alloys of it are used to make electrical contacts for the electronics industry.

Mining gold

Most gold is obtained from mines. Rock containing veins of gold is blasted out with the help of explosives and then crushed by heavy machinery. The

powdered rock is treated with chemicals to extract the gold. Around 100 tonnes of gold-bearing rock have to be mined to produce 1 kilogram of gold.
 Shallow metal pans are used to collect grains of gold found in sand or gravel on some river-beds. The sand is washed over the pan edge while the gold sinks to the bottom.

• South Africa produces three-quarters of the world's gold, after which come the USA and Australia. South Africa still makes gold coins, called krugerrands, but they are for investment purposes.

◀ Inside a gold refinery, hot molten gold is carefully poured into a mould.

find out more
Elements
Metals
Mining

Gravity, weight and mass

Gravity is the pulling force that holds us all down onto the Earth's surface. In fact, everything has a gravitational pull towards everything else; even two people attract each other. The more massive the object, the larger the pull, so the pull of the Earth drowns out the tiny pulls that we have on each other.

The force of gravity pulling us towards our planet gives us our weight; it makes us feel heavy. Our weight depends on where we are because the pull of gravity gets less if we move further away from the centre of the Earth. A man standing on top of a high mountain would weigh very slightly more if he came down to sea level.

Other planets, smaller than the Earth, have a weaker gravitational pull, so we would weigh less on them. On a more massive planet we would weigh more, even though the mass of our bodies stays exactly the same as on Earth. Your weight on Earth is about six times more than it would

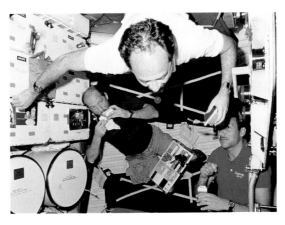

be on the Moon, while on the planet Jupiter you would weigh about three times as much as you do on Earth.

Gravity and the Universe

The pull of the Earth's gravity holds the Moon in its orbit circling round us, and the Sun's gravity keeps the Earth and the other planets in their orbits. Gravity also holds the Sun and 100,000 million other stars in a gigantic group called the Galaxy. In fact, the Sun and the planets would not exist at all if gravity had not pulled together particles of gas and dust to make them.

◀ Everything in space floats around because the effects of gravity are tiny. Things become weightless. This floating astronaut on board the Space Shuttle *Discovery* is weightless, as is the bubble of strawberry drink he is trying to catch.

● People often use the word 'weight' when they really mean 'mass'. Mass is the amount of matter in something. Weight is the force of gravity pulling us towards our planet. The more matter there is in something, the more strongly gravity acts on it and the heavier it is.

find out more
Forces and pressure
Newton, Isaac
Solar system
Universe

Greenhouse effect

Some of the gases in the Earth's atmosphere act naturally like the glass in a greenhouse. They trap heat from the Sun to help keep the surface of the Earth warm. However, human activities have increased the amounts of these greenhouse gases in the atmosphere and they are now trapping too much heat. Scientists believe that this greenhouse effect is causing the world to become warmer.

The atmosphere is a mixture of gases, but our modern lifestyle is upsetting the natural balance of these gases. Exhaust gases from vehicles and power stations add about 6 billion tonnes of carbon dioxide (the main greenhouse gas) to the atmosphere each year. The destruction of huge areas of forest leaves fewer plants to absorb the gas. Methane, another greenhouse gas, is released by animal waste, swamps, paddy-fields, and oil and gas rigs. Nitrous oxide comes from car exhausts and fertilizers. Chlorofluorocarbons (CFCs) are used in refrigerators, aerosols and foam packaging. They are present only in small quantities in the atmosphere, but they are

10,000 times more effective than carbon dioxide at trapping heat.

Scientists believe that we can slow the greenhouse effect if we produce less greenhouse gases. We could burn fewer fossil fuels, like petrol, oil, natural gas and coal, if we develop more efficient heating systems and engines, design buildings which waste less heat, and create transport systems with fewer vehicles.

find out more
Atmosphere
Energy
Pollution
Power stations

▼ How greenhouse gases trap energy from the Sun.

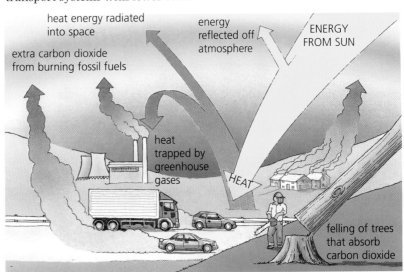

heat energy radiated into space

extra carbon dioxide from burning fossil fuels

energy reflected off atmosphere

ENERGY FROM SUN

heat trapped by greenhouse gases

HEAT

felling of trees that absorb carbon dioxide

Heat

When hot things cool down, their temperature drops and they give off energy. Scientists call this thermal energy, or heat. Heat can travel through solids, liquids, gases, and even through empty space.

• As something becomes colder, its atoms or molecules move more slowly. Eventually, they reach a point at which they can lose no more speed. This happens at −273 °C, or *absolute zero*. It is the lowest possible temperature. The Kelvin scale measures temperatures using absolute zero as its starting point. On this scale water freezes at 273 kelvins.

All materials are made up of tiny particles, called atoms and molecules. These are constantly on the move. For example, in a solid object such as an iron bar, the atoms are not still. Each one is vibrating. If the bar is heated up, its atoms get more energy and vibrate faster. With enough heat, they may vibrate so much that they start to break free. At this point the solid melts.

Conduction

If you put one end of a metal spoon in a hot drink, the heat eventually reaches the other end. Heat flows through the metal by conduction, which means that fast-moving atoms at the hot end gradually pass on their energy to slower-moving ones at the colder end. Metals are good *conductors* of heat. Poor conductors of heat are called *insulators*. Air is one example. Wool, feathers and plastic foam all insulate well because they trap air.

Convection

Air is a poor conductor, but it can carry heat in another way – by convection. If air is heated, it rises, and cooler air flows in to take its place. When the hot air cools down again, it sinks. As a result, a circulating current – called a *convection current* – is set up in the air. This is how the air in a room is warmed up by a fire or a radiator. Convection can also take place in liquids.

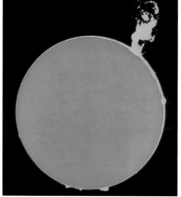

▲ Radiation from the Sun travels millions of kilometres through empty space to heat the Earth.

Radiation

Between the Sun and the Earth, there is empty space. Yet heat from the Sun still reaches us. This is because the heat energy is carried by the Sun's radiation. It travels through space as invisible waves. All hot things lose heat by radiation. The hotter they are, the more they radiate.

Temperature

Temperature tells you how hot something is. It is measured using a thermometer, which has a scale marked on it to show the degree of hotness. Most countries use the Celsius scale (sometimes called the centigrade scale). On this scale water freezes at 0 °C and boils at 100 °C. Temperatures below 0 °C are given minus numbers.

Temperature is not the same as heat. The amount of heat needed to make an iron wire red-hot, for example, would hardly raise the temperature of an iron frying pan at all. Also, different substances need different amounts of heat to change their temperature. For example, it takes more heat to raise the temperature of a kilogram of iron by 1 °C than it does to raise the temperature of a kilogram of aluminium by the same amount.

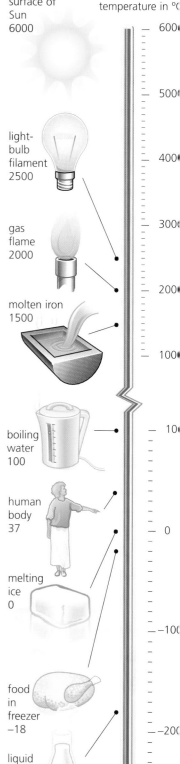

▼ A range of temperatures on the Celsius scale.

temperature in °C

surface of Sun 6000

light-bulb filament 2500

gas flame 2000

molten iron 1500

boiling water 100

human body 37

melting ice 0

food in freezer −18

liquid oxygen −180

absolute zero

600
500
400
300
200
100
10
0
−100
−200
−273

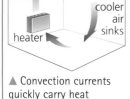

hot air rises

cooler air sinks

heater

▲ Convection currents quickly carry heat around a room.

Human body

Like the bodies of all animals, the human body is made up of billions of tiny cells. Particular kinds of cells are grouped together to form tissues, and these in turn are organized together into organs such as the heart and the lungs.

Some groups of organs and tissues work together in *systems* to perform particular jobs. There are eight main systems in the human body.

The *skeleton* is a system of bones and joints that supports the soft parts of the body and provides a framework for muscles to attach to. *Muscles* make the limbs and organs of the body move.

In the *digestive system* food is broken down into a liquid form from which nutrients that the body needs can be absorbed into the blood. The *excretory system* is the body's waste disposal unit. It is made up of the kidneys and the bladder.

The windpipe (trachea) and the lungs are the *respiratory system*. This system enables us to take in oxygen, which our bodies use to produce energy from our food. The *circulatory system* is made up of the heart, the blood vessels and the blood. The blood carries nutrients and oxygen to all the body tissues, and takes away waste materials.

The *nervous system* is made up of the brain, the spinal cord and a network of nerves. It is the body's communication and control system. The *reproductive systems* of males and females work together to produce new human beings.

find out more
Animals
Cells
Genetics

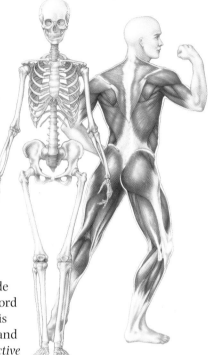

◄ The skeleton and the muscular system.

Hydrogen

Hydrogen is a very light, invisible gas that burns easily. It is also the commonest element in the Universe. However, nearly all of the Earth's hydrogen is locked away in other substances.

Hydrogen atoms are the lightest of all atoms. They stick together in pairs to form molecules of hydrogen gas. When hydrogen gas burns, it combines with oxygen in the air to form water. Each water molecule is made up of two hydrogen atoms joined to one oxygen atom. (The chemical formula for water is H_2O.)

Nearly all of the Earth's hydrogen is combined with other elements in substances such as water, oil and natural gas. Industry gets most of its hydrogen from natural gas. Hydrogen can also be extracted from sea water. Passing an electric current through the water splits it into hydrogen and oxygen atoms.

find out more
Atoms and molecules
Balloons and airships
Elements
Matter
Oxygen
Rockets
Water

◄ The fuel tank in this experimental car is being filled with liquid hydrogen, which produces no pollution. However, liquid hydrogen is expensive to produce and must be stored at extremely low temperatures.

Uses of hydrogen

The chemical industry uses hydrogen in the manufacture of ammonia, soap and plastics. The food industry uses it to turn oils into margarine.

Being so light, hydrogen floats in air. At one time, airships and balloons were filled with hydrogen. But in the 1930s there were terrible accidents when airships caught fire. Today, airships are filled with helium gas.

Hydrogen is used as rocket fuel. One day it may be widely used as a fuel in cars and trucks. Hydrogen-powered engines are non-polluting and produce only water vapour (extracting hydrogen in the first place causes some pollution).

Our Sun is mainly hydrogen. It gets its heat and light by releasing the nuclear energy in hydrogen atoms.

Information technology

When you write a story on a word processor, take money out of the bank, buy food at a supermarket, or program a microwave oven to cook a meal, you are using information technology (IT for short). IT includes all the uses of computers, from controlling industrial robots to playing games.

Businesses, schools, banks and individuals all use computers to store huge amounts of data (information), such as names and addresses, wages, exam results, or details of bank accounts. This data can be called up on a screen instantly, changed, printed on paper, or sent to another computer. Today, with an ordinary personal computer, you can use the Internet to link up with computers all around the world.

You can see IT at work when you visit a supermarket or shop. At the till, the assistant uses a laser scanner to read the barcode on each item. The barcode tells the shop's computer what the item is, and the computer tells the till the name and price of the item. If a shopper pays with a plastic card, the till operator 'swipes' the card through the till. The till reads the data stored on the card's magnetic strip, for example the shopper's bank account number. It then sends the data, and the price of the goods, along a telephone line to the bank's computer.

Creative computers

Scientists and engineers use computers to work out very complicated calculations that would have been impossible to do before they had computers. For example, they can create

Inside the cockpit of an aircraft flight simulator. Its five computers can re-create the movements, sounds and views of a real flight between any of 20 different airports. Simulators like this are used to train new airline pilots.

computer models of buildings to check if they will stand up to hurricanes or earthquakes. Designers use CAD (computer-aided design) to look at a design, for example of a new car, from all angles on the computer screen. Using high-speed supercomputers, graphic artists can produce a full-length animated film from just a few drawings.

Keeping control

One of the most common uses of computers is to control everyday machines, such as washing machines and video recorders. The computers send out signals to turn motors, pumps or switches on and off, and receive signals from electronic sensors telling them what the machine is doing. In factories, computers control larger machines, for example machine tools such as lathes and drills, and robots programmed to do everything from packing boxes to painting and welding. They make sure that parts are made accurately every time, and that the whole product is put together correctly and efficiently.

Schoolchildren in the UK using computers to access the Internet. Today children are beginning to use the Internet as a part of their learning. They can connect to sites all around the world to find up-to-date information about a huge range of subjects. They can also communicate with children in other schools by e-mail.

IT terms

ATM *(automatic teller machine):* a machine that reads the information from the magnetic strip on a credit or debit card when the card is 'swiped'.

On-line shopping: with a computer linked to the telephone network or the Internet, you can order and pay for goods. The goods are delivered later.

Smart card: a credit card-sized plastic card with a microchip embedded in it. The chip can hold far more information than the magnetic strip on a normal card.

find out more
Aircraft
Calculators
Compact discs
Computers
Electronics
Fax machines
Internet
Robots
Telephones
Virtual reality
Word processors

Internet

The Internet ('the Net' for short) is a huge computer network that connects millions of computers. It is a fast and efficient way of sending information around the world. Any two computers connected to the Internet, wherever they are, can exchange information.

To join the Internet, you need a personal computer, a modem and a telephone line. You can use the Internet to send electronic messages to other users (this is called *e-mail*), hold electronic conversations, transfer computer files, or find information on thousands of different subjects. The number of people connected to the Internet, and the amount of information passing through it, are increasing rapidly. Some experts think that the Net will change how we work and live.

The fastest growing area of the Internet is a system called the *World Wide Web* ('the Web' for short), which allows you to look at information stored on the Internet. To look at this information (text, pictures, sounds and video clips), you need a program called a *Web browser*. It finds the information on a *Web site*, and displays it on your screen.

The Internet works by linking together many small computer networks belonging to organizations such as businesses, universities and government departments.

▶ Most computers belonging to individuals, schools and small organizations that are linked to the Internet are connected through an Internet service provider (ISP).

Internet jargon
Surfing the Net Browsing through information on the Internet.
Netiquet The unwritten rules of good behaviour for Net users.
Snailmail Net users' word for normal mail.

find out more
Computers
Information technology

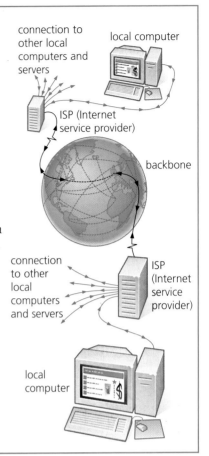

connection to other local computers and servers

local computer

ISP (Internet service provider)

backbone

connection to other local computers and servers

ISP (Internet service provider)

local computer

Inventors

An inventor is someone who makes something new or who finds new ways of using old ideas. What they make is called an invention.

◀ Alexander Graham Bell invented the telephone in 1876. In this photograph, taken in 1892, he is making the first phone call from New York to Chicago.

We usually think of inventions as objects such as cars, washing machines and rockets, but they can also be processes like making paper or canning food. Everything made by people has an inventor. Hundreds of inventors are remembered by name because of the impact that their invention has had on our lives. Examples of such inventors include Marconi (radio), Baird (television), Edison (electric light) and Bell (telephone). Sometimes the invention takes the name of the inventor: Biro pens, Hoovers, Diesel engines. Most modern machines are so complex that they are invented by teams of people, rather than by a single person.

Famous inventors	see article on
Archimedes	Archimedes
Babbage, Charles	Computers
Baird, John Logie	Television
Bell, Alexander Graham	Telephones
Brunel, Isambard Kingdom	Ships and boats
Daguerre, Louis	Cameras
Diesel, Rudolf	Engines
Edison, Thomas	Edison, Thomas
Faraday, Michael	Faraday, Michael
Ford, Henry	Motor cars
Gutenberg, Johann	Printing
Marconi, Guglielmo	Radio
Montgolfier brothers	Balloons and airships
Newcomen, Thomas	Engines
Stephenson, George	Railways
Trevithick, Richard	Railways
Volta, Alessandro	Batteries
Watson-Watt, Robert	Radar
Watt, James	Engines
Whittle, Frank	Engines
Wright Brothers	Aircraft
Zworykin, Vladimir	Television

Invertebrates *see* Animals • **Ions** *see* Atmosphere

Iron and steel

find out more
Elements
Metals

▶ FLASHBACK ◄

Iron was first made by heating a mixture of iron ore and charcoal over a fire. While it was still hot, the iron was beaten into shape with a stone to make knives and axes.

The introduction of the blast furnace to England at the beginning of the 16th century allowed pig iron to be made continuously. The first cheap method of making steel used the Bessemer process, invented in England in 1856 by Henry Bessemer.

Iron and steel are used for making buildings, cars, ships, trains and many other things. There are many different kinds of iron and steel. Most of the iron produced is used to make steel. Steel is a mixture of iron and other products.

Iron comes from the ground, sometimes in its pure form but mostly combined with rocky materials in the form of ores. The commonest iron ore is called haematite. These ores are heated in a blast furnace to make iron.

Making iron

Iron is made in a *blast furnace* – a tall oven made of steel and lined with fireproof bricks. A mixture of crushed iron ore, coke and limestone is fed into the furnace and heated by a continuous blast of hot air.

The three substances react together inside the furnace to form iron and a waste material called *slag*. These are drained separately through tap holes at the bottom of the furnace while they are still molten. When the slag solidifies, it is sold for road-building. Some of the iron solidifies in moulds to form a rather brittle kind of iron, called *cast* or *pig iron*. Most of the molten iron is turned into steel.

Steel-making

To make steel, excess carbon and unwanted impurities in the iron are removed in an oxygen furnace. Molten iron is poured into the furnace. Scrap steel may be put in as well. Then some quicklime is added and a jet of oxygen is turned on. The impurities burn away, leaving a small amount of carbon in the iron so that it is hard but not brittle. Other metallic elements may then be added to the molten steel to make an alloy (metal mixture) which has special properties. Stainless steel, for example, is an alloy of steel and chromium which, unlike ordinary steel, does not rust.

Steel can also be made in electric-arc furnaces. A large electric current is carried into the furnace to produce the heat needed to melt the scrap and solid iron inside. This process produces both steel and slag (waste material).

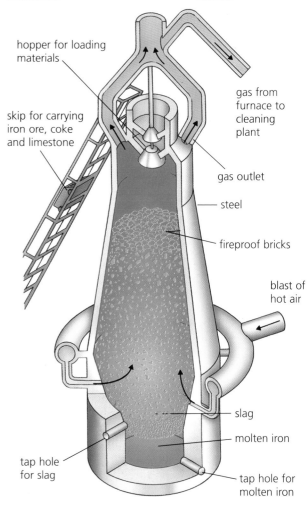

▼ Making iron in a blast furnace.

hopper for loading materials

skip for carrying iron ore, coke and limestone

gas from furnace to cleaning plant

gas outlet

steel

fireproof bricks

blast of hot air

tap hole for slag

slag

molten iron

tap hole for molten iron

Lasers

Lasers produce a narrow beam of bright light. Ordinary light is a mixture of colours, but laser light is just one pure colour. Lasers are used in a wide range of everyday situations – to read bar codes at supermarket tills, to play compact discs, to carry telephone signals over long distances and to make 3D pictures called holograms.

A laser beam is much narrower than that of an ordinary lamp. Laser light is different in other ways as well. First, it has a single wavelength, which explains why it is a single pure colour. Second, the light waves move exactly in time with each other. Waves of ordinary light are sent out in disorganized bursts.

How lasers work

Some lasers have a crystal in them. Others have a tube containing gas or liquid. An electrical discharge or flash of bright light gives extra energy to the atoms in the laser material. A few atoms lose this energy by giving out light. These trigger other atoms into losing energy and sending out light waves, and so on.

Mirrors at each end of a laser send the light to and fro so that more and more atoms are triggered into sending out light. One of the mirrors is only partly reflecting. Light escapes through it, either as a steady beam or as a sudden pulse, depending on the type of laser.

Using lasers

Some supermarket tills use lasers to 'read' the bar codes on the things you buy. The laser beam is reflected from the bars

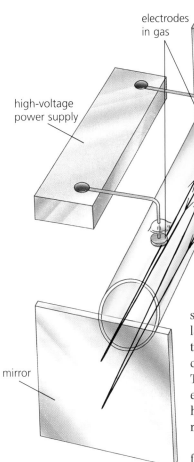

electrodes in gas

high-voltage power supply

laser beam

◀ Inside a helium–neon gas laser.

mirror letting out some light

mixture of helium and neon gas in tube

mirror

in pulses which are changed into electrical signals. Doctors use lasers to burn away birthmarks and some cancer cells. Military lasers guide missiles to their targets, and factories use powerful lasers to cut through metal, glass and cloth for clothing.

Holograms

The special single-colour light from a laser is used to make a hologram. Unlike an ordinary flat picture of an object, the picture stored in the hologram has depth, so you can see round the sides of the object as though it were solid and really there.

▶ Doctors use lasers to perform delicate eye surgery. If the retina (the part of the eye that contains light-sensitive cells) becomes loose, a laser can be used to stick it back in place. The laser beam is sent to the patient's eye in a series of pulses.

To see the picture stored in some holograms a beam of laser light is shone on them, but the holograms used on credit cards work with reflected light. They give a 3D image which is easy to see if you place the hologram upright under a reading lamp.

Holograms are used in factories to show up small differences in machines and parts which should be exactly the same. Holography has been used on the Space Shuttle to show which of its protective tiles have become loosened during flight.

• LASER stands for Light Amplification by Stimulated Emission of Radiation.

• DANGER! Never look directly down a laser beam. It could damage your eyes and even make you blind.

Lenses

The lenses in spectacles are specially shaped pieces of glass or plastic that bend a beam of light as it goes through them. Lenses range from tiny ones found in microscopes to huge ones, over one metre wide, used in astronomical telescopes. The lenses we use most often are the ones in our eyes.

There are two types of lens. A *convex* lens is thicker in the middle. A magnifying glass is a convex lens. A *concave* lens is thinner in the middle. Spectacles worn by short-sighted people have concave lenses.

Looking through lenses

If you hold a lens above a newspaper, you will see that a convex lens makes the words look bigger and a concave lens makes them look smaller. If you hold a convex lens in front of a sheet of card facing a window, the lens makes a small, upside-down picture of the window on the card. We call this picture an *image*. The lenses in our eyes help make an image of what we are looking at, inside our eyes. In the same way, a camera lens makes an image on the film inside the camera.

We use magnifying glasses to make things look larger and clearer. Stronger magnifying glasses have fatter lenses which magnify more. However, a thick lens will only make a clear picture near the middle of the lens. Near the edges, where the lens is thinner, the picture will be blurred.

We look through the lenses of microscopes, binoculars and telescopes to see things that are too small or too far away to be seen with our eyes alone. These lenses vary in size, from under 2 millimetres in a microscope to over 1 metre in the biggest astronomical telescopes. In all these instruments each 'lens' is really several lenses joined together. These make clearer pictures than single lenses, which produce pictures with blurred or coloured edges.

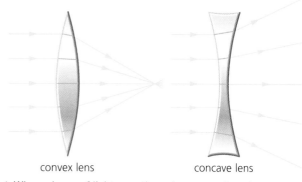

convex lens   concave lens

▲ When a beam of light goes through a convex lens, it narrows down to a point as the lens focuses the light. A concave lens spreads out a beam of light.

find out more
Cameras
Light
Microscopes
Telescopes

Light

Light is a type of radiation. It comes from the Sun, a lamp, or anything that glows. Light can pass through glass or water, but it bounces off materials that look solid. We need light to see, but we can also use it to communicate with each other.

▼ A dentist using ultraviolet light to cement braces onto a young girl's teeth. The UV light causes a chemical reaction in the cement, which hardens it. Although UV light itself is invisible to the eye, the light source gives out some visible light.

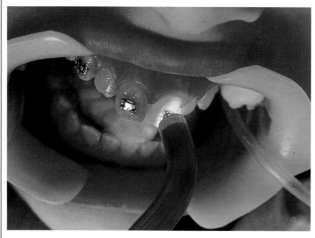

The Sun, lamps, TVs and fires give off their own light. But most things do not. We only see them because they reflect light into our eyes. White surfaces reflect most light and look bright. Black surfaces reflect hardly any light. Mirrors reflect in a regular way. The light bounces off in the same pattern as it arrives. As a result, your eyes see an image in the mirror.

Light normally travels in straight lines. If it is blocked, a shadow forms where the light cannot get through. When light passes into glass, water or other clear material at any angle other than 90°, it bends. This effect is called *refraction*. It occurs because the light travels slower in the clear material than it does in the air. Refraction tricks the eye by making a straw leaning in a glass of water look bent.

Colours and waves

White light is a mixture of all the colours of the rainbow. When white light passes through a prism (a triangular piece of glass), the colours are bent by different amounts and a range of colours called a *spectrum* is formed.

Light is lots of tiny waves, which travel through space rather like ripples travelling across the surface of a pond. The waves are extremely small – more than 2000 of them would fit across a pinhead. The distance from one 'peak' of a wave to the next is called the *wavelength*. Different colours have different wavelengths. Red light waves are the longest, and violet waves the shortest.

The light that we can see is just one member of a whole family of *electromagnetic waves*. Others include infrared,

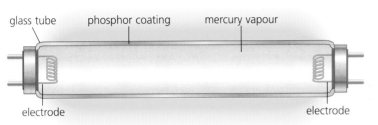

glass tube　　phosphor coating　　mercury vapour

electrode　　　　　　　　　electrode

ultraviolet, radio waves and X-rays. All these waves travel through space at the same speed: about 300,000 kilometres per second. Nothing can travel faster than this. If you could travel at the speed of light, you could go round the Earth more than seven times in one second!

Lamps and lighting

If a material is heated to more than about 700 °C, it starts to glow. The Sun, candles and many lamps give off light because they are hot. In most light bulbs there is a tiny filament (thin wire) made of tungsten metal. This glows white-hot when an electric current is passed through it.

Electricity can be used to produce light in other ways too. Many street lamps are filled with sodium vapour. Passing a current through the vapour makes it glow yellow. Similarly, a tube filled with neon gas glows red. In a fluorescent light, the current makes mercury vapour give off invisible ultraviolet radiation. The inside of the tube is coated with a special powder that glows when it absorbs the ultraviolet light. Fluorescent paints use the same effect. They give off extra light when they absorb the ultraviolet radiation that is naturally present in sunlight.

Light signals

Flashing lamps have long been used to send signals across land or between ships at sea. Now, telephone calls, TV pictures and

▲ In a fluorescent light, an electric current flows between the electrodes at either end of the tube. The current causes the mercury vapour inside the tube to give off invisible ultraviolet light. This ultraviolet radiation makes the phosphor coating on the inside of the glass tube glow white.

computer data can be carried thousands of kilometres by sending flashes of laser light along *optical fibres*. These fibres are hair-thin strands of glass. A beam of laser light put in at one end cannot escape from the sides and comes out of the other end. High-speed electronic circuits flash the laser on and off millions of times a second. The flashes are digital signals, which means that they stand for numbers. At the far end, more circuits can turn these signals back into sounds or pictures.

▶ FLASHBACK ◀

Lamps that burn animal or vegetable oils have been used since prehistoric times. The first candles were made in Egypt about 2000 years ago. Gas lamps became available in the early 19th century, but they flickered badly and were not very bright. These problems were solved by covering the flame with a mantle – a cloth bag coated with chemicals that glow with a brilliant-white light when hot.

The first electric filament bulbs were made by Joseph Swann and Thomas Edison in the late 1870s. The filament bulbs that we use today were developed from these. They are

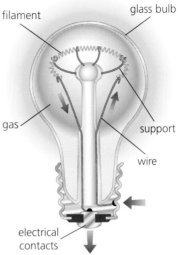

filament　　　　　　　glass bulb

gas

support

wire

electrical contacts

cheap, but produce more heat than light. Low-energy bulbs use small fluorescent tubes. They give as much light as a filament bulb but use only one-fifth of the amount of electricity.

◀ In a filament light bulb, an electric current heats a coil of thin wire, the filament, making it glow white-hot. The hot filament would burn up in air, so the bulb is filled with argon gas to stop this from happening.

find out more
Colour
Edison, Thomas
Electricity
Lasers
Lenses
Radiation
Telephones
Waves

▼ A lamplighter lighting a gas lamp in a city street in the early 1900s. Around this time, electric street lights were starting to replace gas lamps in many cities.

Living things

Human beings are living things, as are whales and mosquitoes, oak trees and mosses, even bacteria. Despite their differences in size and appearance, living things have several things in common: they are able to grow for part or all of their lives; they are able to reproduce (to make a new generation of young); and they are able to react to changes in their surroundings.

This reaction to change can take many different forms. A plant may react to a change in the weather by losing its leaves or opening its flowers. An amoeba (a single-celled animal) might move towards a smell that may mean food. Larger, more complex animals behave in still more complicated ways.

An example of classification

Kingdom Animalia	All animals belong to the kingdom Animalia.
Phylum Chordata	All animals that have a stiffening rod in their backs in the early stages of their lives belong to the phylum Chordata (chordates).
Subphylum Vertebrata	All animals that have backbones belong to the subphylum Vertebrata (vertebrates).
Class Mammalia	All animals that breathe air, are hairy and feed their young on milk belong to the class Mammalia (mammals).
Order Perissodactyla	All animals that are hoofed and have an odd number of toes – including horses and their relatives – belong to the order Perissodactyla.
Family Equidae	All horse-like animals, from about 60 million years ago to the present day, belong to the family Equidae.
Genus Equus	All single-toed horses, from about 5 million years ago – including horses, donkeys and zebras – belong to the genus Equus.
Species Equus caballus	The domestic horse belongs to the caballus species. The scientific name for any animal species combines its genus and species names, so the domestic horse is properly known as Equus caballus.

Classifying life

Ever since ancient times, human beings have tried to improve their understanding of the natural world by classifying (grouping together) similar living things. Today, plants, animals and other living things that are similar in structure are classified under a system developed over 200 years ago by a Swede, Carolus Linnaeus.

The basic unit of the Linnaean system is the individual. Although no two individuals are exactly the same, some are clearly very alike. They belong to the same *species*, a group that is able to breed successfully in the wild. Similar species belong to the same *genus* (plural: genera). They cannot breed together. Genera are grouped into *families*, which consist of clearly related animals or plants. For instance, all cats belong to one family; all dogs to another.

Families are put together into *orders*. Cats and dogs both belong to the same order, along with bears and weasels among other flesh-eaters. Orders are grouped into *classes*. All mammals belong to one class. A number of classes together make up a *phylum* (plural: phyla). A phylum includes living things with basic similarities, though these are often masked by adaptations to a particular way of life. Finally, the phyla are grouped into five *kingdoms* – animals, plants, fungi, Protoctista and Monera.

THE FIVE KINGDOMS

Bacteria and blue-green algae (kingdom **Monera**): about 4000 species

Protozoa and algae (kingdom **Protoctista**): about 80,000 species

Fungi (mushrooms, moulds): about 72,000 species

Plants: about 270,000 species

Animals: about 1,320,000 species

heliozoan

amoeba

fly agaric mushroom

moss

tulip

Scot's pine

spore-producing

flowering

cone-bearing

invertebrates

vertebrates

lugworm

rat

spider

swallow

sea anemone

frog

shark

▲ Living things can be divided into five kingdoms.

• More than 1.75 million different species of living thing have been identified, and more are being discovered all the time. The total number could be in the region of 13 million! The numbers of identified species belonging to the Monera and Protoctista kingdoms are probably only a tiny proportion of the total numbers that exist.

find out more
Animals
Ecology
Evolution
Genetics
Plants

Machines

Machines are devices that make work easier. A machine can be as simple as a door handle, or as complex as a computer. Most machines, even big and complicated ones like railway engines or printing presses, are made up of five simpler machines: the wedge or ramp, the lever, the wheel and axle, the screw and the pulley. These simple machines can be joined together to do a complex job.

A *wedge* or *ramp* is used to raise a heavy weight (the load) a small amount. By moving the load up a slope, less effort is needed but the load has to move further. The powerful sideways force of a wedge (an axe) is used to split wood. A *wheel and axle* is another way of moving a heavy load easily. The wheel's turning action can become a strong turning force at the axle (rod), as when a spanner turns a bolt. All motor vehicles and many other machines have wheels and axles.

Power is transmitted from one part of a machine to another in different ways. Gears, belts and chains are three common devices for transmitting power and for making parts of a machine run faster, slower or in different directions. Fast and complex machines are often controlled by electronic devices. Electrical sensors can tell when it is time to switch on other parts of the machine and check that everything is running smoothly and safely.

• A screw moves with great force. It turns round many times to move only a short distance. A screw-jack produces enough force to lift a car.

find out more
Engines
Forces and pressure
Robots

Gears and belts

Gears are used inside machines to transmit power in different directions or at different speeds. Most gears are made up of an axle and a wheel with teeth around the outer edge. A small gearwheel will turn a larger one more slowly, but with more force and in an opposite direction. The teeth of the two wheels are meshed (locked together) to make this possible. *Belts* and *bands* drive household machines like washing machines, food processors and video recorders. When you connect two wheels with a belt (a *pulley*), both wheels turn in the same direction. Different sizes of pulley turn the machines faster or slower.

Chains

If a belt has to transmit too much power, it will slip. A *chain* overcomes this problem because it fits over teeth, called sprockets, on the gearwheels. The pedals on a bicycle turn a big gearwheel, called a chain wheel. The bicycle chain turns a little gearwheel, called a sprocket wheel, which is connected to the back wheel. Some bikes have several chain wheels and sprocket wheels. When you change gear, you move the chain so that it fits over the gearwheels which are best for the job. You use the smallest chain wheel and the biggest sprocket wheel for steep hills, and the biggest chain wheel and the smallest sprocket wheel for speed on the flat and for downhill.

The lever

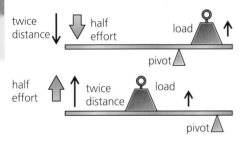

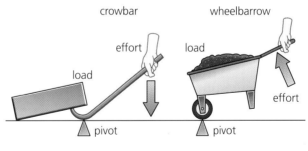

◀ A *lever* moves a heavy load easily. The pivot of the lever can be in different places. The pivot on a crowbar is closer to the load than to you, so a small effort lifts a large load. In a wheelbarrow, the load is between you and the pivot.

▶ A *pulley* lifts heavy loads by making it possible to pull downwards, which is easier than pulling upwards. Pulleys magnify the pulling force. Big pulley systems have many sets of wheels. With a pulley system called a chain hoist, one person can lift a motor car engine.

The pulley

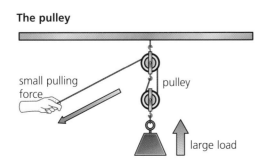

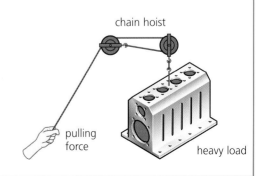

Magnets

• The space around a magnet, where it attracts or repels, is called the *magnetic field*.

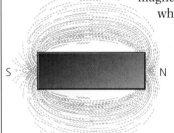

▼ The forces from a magnet seem to come from two points near its ends, called poles. One is a north pole, the other is a south pole. Iron filings show the lines of force in a magnet.

Magnets are all around you in your home. Some hold refrigerator and wardrobe doors shut. Others are hidden, for example in the doorbell and the telephone.

Magnets attract iron, nickel, cobalt and most types of steel. But there are many metals they do not attract, including copper, aluminium, brass, tin, silver and lead.

If you put a steel needle next to a magnet, it too becomes a magnet and stays magnetized when you take the magnet away. An iron nail also becomes magnetized near a magnet, but it loses its magnetism when the magnet is removed. Magnets that keep their magnetism are called permanent magnets. Most are made of steel or alloys (metal mixtures).

How magnets work

Scientists think that, in materials like iron and steel, each atom is a tiny magnet. Normally the atoms point in all directions and their magnetic effects cancel. But when a material is magnetized, its atoms line up, and it becomes one big magnet.

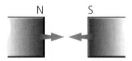

like poles repel each other

opposite poles attract each other

▼ The disc-like object hanging from this scrapyard crane is an *electromagnet*, a type of magnet that can be switched on and off. The magnet has an iron core which only becomes magnetized when an electric current passes through it. The electromagnet is used to separate and lift heavy objects from among the waste.

Materials

Materials are the substances that things are made of – from the concrete and steel used for buildings and bridges, to the paper and ink used to make this book. All materials come originally from substances such as rocks, oil, plants or animals.

Many of the materials that are around us have been used for hundreds or thousands of years. They include wood and paper from trees; cotton from cotton plants; leather from animal skins, wool from sheep; and materials such as pottery, stone, concrete, slate, glass and many metals, which are made from substances that have been dug out of the ground.

Traditional materials

Before metals began to be widely used around 5000 years ago, the most common materials used by humans were stones such as flint that could be sharpened. Bone and wood were also important materials. Wood is strong and hard-wearing, but can be cut and carved easily.

It is still used for making all kinds of things, and for building.

Another material that has been used for thousands of years is clay. Objects made from baked clay are known as pottery. Pottery is the oldest known technology using fire. Clay looks and feels like mud, but it has special qualities. When it is wet, it can be shaped. When it is baked, it changes into a permanent solid material.

• Liquid crystals are unusual materials that change colour when heated, or when an electric current is passed through them. They are used to make displays for calculators and portable computers. They can also be used to make fabrics that change colour as they get warmer or colder.

◄ Pots are made all over the world. This potter is working on a wheel-made pot in a village in Indonesia. The pots are made of local clay and decorative patterns are cut into them by hand.

Bricks are made in a similar way to pottery, and have been used for building for thousands of years. Cement is also made from clay. The clay is mixed with limestone and then heated until it melts. When cool, it forms grey lumps, which are crushed into a powder. Cement mixed with sand and water makes mortar, which is used for sticking bricks together. Cement mixed with water and crushed stone or sand makes concrete. Although we may think of concrete as a modern building material, it was actually also used by the ancient Romans.

Modern materials

Traditional materials still have many uses. But countless new materials have been developed that can be lighter, stronger and cheaper than traditional ones.

Plastics are probably the most important modern materials. They can be hard or soft, rigid or flexible, transparent or coloured. They can be moulded easily, and they are hard-wearing and long-lasting. Most plastics are not strong enough to be used for building, and they melt or burn at quite low temperatures. However, some new plastics are much stronger. Kevlar, for example, is stronger and lighter than steel, and can resist high temperatures. Most plastics do not rot, but they can be recycled.

Many new types of metal have been created by making *alloys*. An alloy is a combination of two metals, or a metal with a small amount of another substance. Alloys can be made with many different properties. For example, new steel alloys can be used at much higher temperatures than ordinary steels, and alloys that combine aluminium and titanium are extremely light and strong.

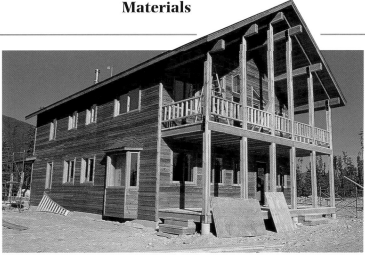

At very high temperatures, even the best metal alloys become too soft to be useful, and *ceramic materials* must be used. Ceramics are materials that are made by baking at high temperatures. They do not lose strength at these temperatures and they insulate (keep heat in) well. However, they break easily under stress, rather than bend. Some special kinds of ceramic can work as superconductors at very low temperatures. Superconductors are materials which conduct electricity so well that they do not need a battery to keep a current flowing through them.

Composites are mixtures in which fibres, pieces or sheets of a strong material are surrounded by another, less rigid material. The fibres make the material strong, while the surrounding material stops the fibres from breaking. Composites such as carbon-reinforced plastics are used to make aircraft wings, helicopter rotor blades and some sports equipment. Composites can also be made with fibres that are embedded in metal or a ceramic material, rather than plastic. These composites are very expensive, but can be used at high temperatures.

Many other materials have been developed for particular purposes. These include metals developed for storing radioactive waste, which will remain stable for hundreds of years, and materials that can be used inside the body for making heart valves and artificial hip joints.

◀ In parts of the world that are heavily forested, such as Scandinavia and North America, wood is often an important building material. Today many forests in these parts of the world are carefully managed, and more trees are planted than are cut down.

find out more
Building
Glass
Iron and steel
Metals
Mining
Oil
Paper
Plastics
Rubber
Textiles

▼ The underside of the Space Shuttle gets extremely hot as it drops through the atmosphere on landing. Ceramic tiles are used to protect the metal skin of the craft from the heat.

Matter

'Matter' is the scientific word for what everything is made of. There are three types (called states) of matter – solid, liquid and gas. The three states seem very different, but substances can change from one to another when heated or cooled.

Every material is made from tiny particles, called atoms and molecules. The way in which these particles stick together and move determines whether something is a solid, a liquid or a gas. Each state has its own special features.

The states of matter

At the temperatures and pressures normally encountered on Earth, most substances are found in one particular state. Iron, for example, is a solid, while oxygen is a gas. However, iron can be heated in a furnace until it becomes a liquid, and oxygen can be made liquid at low temperatures and high pressures.

A *solid* has shape and strength. You can pick it up and turn it around. If you stretch, squash or twist a solid, it resists the forces that are trying to change its shape. It behaves like this because its particles (atoms or molecules) are held together by strong forces of attraction. The particles move, but only by vibrating. The hotter the solid, the faster its particles vibrate.

A *liquid* does not have shape or strength like a solid. It flows and takes up the shape of its container. It offers little resistance to stretching and twisting, but it does resist squeezing. For example, you cannot force a cork into a bottle that is filled to the brim. A liquid behaves like

▼ The particles in any substance move around in all directions. In a solid they stay fairly close together. In a liquid the particles move around more freely, and in a gas they move around even more than in a liquid.

▶ At room temperature carbon dioxide is a gas, but if compressed it can be turned into a liquid. If the liquid is then allowed to expand, it freezes to a snow-like powder called *dry ice*. At room temperature the dry ice sublimes (turns directly from a solid to a vapour). The vapour is heavier than air, so it pours, like water.

this because its particles, although close together and vibrating, are free to tumble over each other, like grains of rice in a sack.

A *gas*, such as air, does not have shape, strength or a fixed volume. It completely fills whatever container it is in. It behaves like this because its particles have enough speed to escape from the forces trying to hold them together. They whizz around, constantly knocking into each other and the container walls. These collisions put pressure on the container. If you heat a gas, its pressure increases. The particles move faster, so their collisions have a stronger effect.

Ice, water and steam

Water is the only substance that is commonly found as a solid, a liquid and a gas. Below 0 °C, it takes the form of solid ice, with its molecules held together in a rigid pattern. When heated, the molecules begin to break free from each other, and the ice melts to become liquid water. Once liquid, the water starts to *evaporate* – faster molecules escape from its surface to form a gas called water vapour. When water is heated to 100 °C, under normal atmospheric conditions, it evaporates so rapidly that big vapour bubbles form in it – the water boils.

Floating
Different substances have different *densities* – a certain volume of one substance has a different weight from the same volume of another. A litre of oil, for example, weighs less than a litre of water. One substance can float on another if it is less dense. This is why oil and wood float on water.

● Most substances expand as they are heated. This means that if a substance melts it has a greater volume (takes up more space) than it did as a solid. And if it is heated more and turns into a gas, it takes up even more space. However, water behaves unusually. It expands when it freezes – ice has a greater volume than liquid water. This is because of the way ice crystals are made.

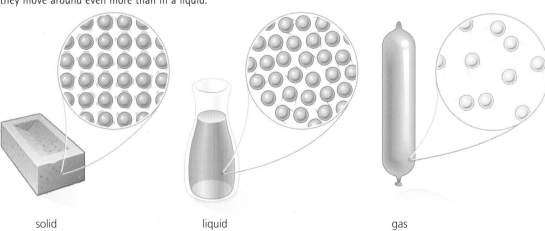

solid   liquid   gas

find out more
Air
Atoms and molecules
Crystals
Forces and pressure
Heat

Measurement

How tall are you? How much do you weigh? How long does it take you to walk to school? The answers to all these questions are measurements.

Measurements are numbers that give us information about the world around us. We use them to buy and sell things, to build roads, to design machines, to cook meals, to do experiments and to plan our lives.

Making measurements

All measurements, whether simple or complicated, are written with a number and a unit of measurement. For example, you might be 1.5 metres tall and weigh 45 kilograms. To make measurements like these, you need measuring instruments.

Lengths can be measured with rulers and tapes. Surveyors use accurate tapes which give measurements on a digital read-out. For longer distances instruments that use pulses of infrared radiation or laser beams can be used. Using a micrometer gauge, lengths as small as one millionth of a metre (less than one hundredth the thickness of a hair) can be measured accurately.

Masses and *weights* are measured with scales and balances. Weight can be measured using a spring balance. The amount the spring stretches indicates the object's weight. A set of balancing scales compares an unknown mass with a known one.

Time can be measured with watches and clocks. It is now possible to buy a clock that has a radio link to an atomic clock, and is accurate to within 1 second in 1.7 million years.

Temperatures are measured with thermometers. A digital thermometer has an electrical sensor and displays the temperature on a digital display.

Measuring systems

Scientists and others who make measurements must agree standard values for basic units of measurement. Everyone has to agree, for example, how long a metre is, otherwise measurements made in different places cannot be accurately compared. The set of standards for different kinds of unit together make up a *measurement system*.

Early standard units for length were based on parts of the body. For instance, an inch was the width of a man's thumb, and a yard was the distance around his waist. But people's thumbs and waists vary in size, and more reliable standards were needed.

Today, the *metric system* or *SI* (*Système Internationale*) is used in many parts of the world. In this system the basic measure of length is the metre, while mass is measured in kilograms. All other measures of length and mass are found by multiplying or dividing these basic measures. A millimetre, for example, is a thousandth of a metre.

The standard metre in the metric system was first defined as one ten-millionth of the distance between the North Pole and the Equator. But as scientific measurements became more accurate, a better standard was needed. So since 1983 the metre has been defined as a certain fraction of the distance that light travels in a vacuum in one second.

▲ The metric system was first introduced in France in around 1800. This illustration shows some of the units of measurement they used at that time. They are the litre (volume), the gram (weight), the metre (length), the are (a unit of area, equal to 100 square metres), the franc (currency) and the stère (a unit for solid measures, equal to one cubic metre).

◄ This surveyor is using a *theodolite* to measure the angle between the point where he is standing and the rule in the foreground. Accurate measurements of angles, combined with a single accurate length measurement (the baseline), can be used to calculate distances that could not easily be measured directly.

• Once the basic units of a measuring system have been agreed, then units for all the different quantities we wish to measure can be made up from them. For example, area can be measured in square metres, volume in cubic metres, and speed in metres per second.

• For many years the imperial system of measurement was used in the USA, the UK and some other countries. Its measures of mass and length were based on the pound and the yard. A pound is just under half a kilogram; a yard is slightly less than a metre.

Medicine

find out more
Human body
Lasers
Radiation
Scanners
X-rays

Medicine is the practice of detecting, treating and preventing disease. Medicine has improved people's health in countless ways. It has also helped people to live longer.

Doctors today know a lot about how the human body works. They also use many different kinds of instruments and machines to help them in their work.

Finding out what is wrong

If you are ill, the first thing the doctor will do is ask you detailed questions. They may also look closely at different parts of your body. And perhaps they will use a *stethoscope*, a tube for listening to your heart and breathing.

Doctors can now see inside your body using a number of techniques. X-rays are particularly useful for looking at the hard parts of your body, such as the bones. Machines called *scanners* show much more detail than X-rays. Other machines can pick up signals from the heart and brain, to see how well they are working. The doctor can also insert a thin tube called an *endoscope* into various natural openings in your body. Through the endoscope the doctor can actually see what is going on.

Doctors may also examine your blood or your urine to find out what is wrong with you. Germs that cause disease can be seen through a microscope. Doctors may also carry out chemical tests to check for other diseases.

▼ A nurse attends to a patient in an intensive care unit. The ventilator monitor to which the patient is connected keeps a check on the oxygen and carbon dioxide levels of the air he breathes out. It is equipped with an automatic alarm system.

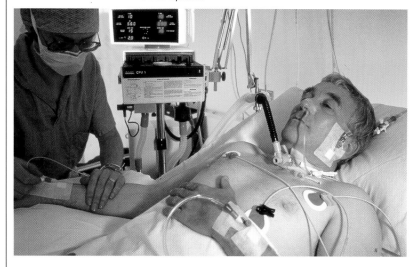

▲ Modern medicine is so advanced that we can discover whether an unborn child (fetus) is developing normally. This laboratory technician is checking sample cells from the fluid that surrounds the fetus to discover whether the fetus has a genetic disorder.

Treatment

Thousands of drugs are now available to help in the treatment of illnesses, and scientists are developing new ones all the time. But drugs cannot cure everything. Sometimes it is necessary to cut open your body in an operation, to repair or remove a damaged part. Many operations can now be carried out using *keyhole surgery*, in which only a tiny cut is needed. The surgeon looks through an endoscope, and carries out the operation using very fine instruments. Surgeons also sometimes use lasers to carry out safer and more precise operations.

Surgeons can replace a damaged organ such as a heart with a healthy organ taken from someone who has just died. Sometimes an artificial part can be made instead. Such 'spare parts' include artificial legs and arms, and replacements for various parts of the heart.

Prevention

In medicine, prevention is better than cure. We can all help to prevent illness by eating more sensibly and taking more exercise. Another important way of preventing disease is *vaccination*. Vaccination involves injecting you with a harmless form of a disease. From this, your body learns how to fight the disease, so that even if you are infected with the harmful form of the disease, you will not become ill.

It is now also possible to discover some serious diseases before you actually start to feel ill. This is called *screening* and it means that doctors can start to treat you very early in the development of the disease.

Metals

The Earth is made of about 90 different basic substances, called elements. Of these, about three-quarters are metals. For thousands of years, people have been making use of metals. Today they are used for everything from needles to bridges.

Although there are many different metals, they all have certain properties in common. Except for mercury, which is a liquid, metals are all solids at room temperature, and pure metals are shiny when polished. Metals are good conductors of electricity and heat. Most are fairly strong, and can withstand crushing or stretching without breaking. However, they are also *malleable*, which means that they can easily be shaped by hammering or rolling. Many metals are also *ductile* – they can be drawn out into wires.

From ore to metal

Only metals such as copper, silver and gold, which do not easily combine with other materials, are found in a pure state in nature. Most metals are found in the ground as *ores* – rocks that are particularly rich in one type of metal. Some ores are much more common than others. Gold, silver and platinum are very rare. Aluminium, by contrast, is the most abundant metal on Earth. It is found mostly as *bauxite*, a mixture of aluminium oxide with materials such as sand and iron oxide.

Once an ore has been dug out of the ground, it is usually crushed to a powder, which allows many of the larger impurities to be either floated or washed away. Next, the pure metal has to be extracted. Some ores (for example iron and tin)

▲ A bronze mirror from Egypt. Bronze, a mixture of copper and tin, was probably the first alloy to be made.

▼ The properties and uses of some metals.

Metal	Properties	Uses
Aluminium	Light and strong, especially in alloys. Good conductor of electricity and heat.	Principal building material for aircraft. Used for parts of cars, trains and ships, and in all kinds of machines. Soft-drink cans, doors and window-frames, saucepans, electric cables.
Copper	Reddish-yellow, quite soft, easily shaped. Very good conductor of heat and electricity.	Electrical wires and cables; also for water pipes and sometimes roofing. Important alloys include bronze and brass.
Gold	Yellow, shiny metal. Excellent conductor of electricity.	Main use as a precious metal in jewellery and coinage. Also used for electrical connections in electronics.
Iron	Pure iron greyish, malleable, easily magnetized. Alloys have wide range of properties.	Most widely used metal, mostly as its alloy, steel. Used for making huge range of products, from bridges, cars and machinery of all kinds, to needles and paper clips.
Lead	Soft, easily shaped. Does not rust. Very heavy. Poisonous.	Used for small, heavy weights, for example in yacht keels, and for waterproof joins on roofs. Also for plates in car batteries, shielding around radioactive materials, and in some kinds of petrol.
Magnesium	Light, silver-white metal. Burns with brilliant white flame.	Makes strong, light alloys with aluminium that are used in aircraft and cars. Pure metal used in fireworks.
Mercury	Silvery-white; liquid at room temperature. Good conductor of electricity. Poisonous.	Used in some electrical switches and long-life batteries. Used to be widely used in thermometers and barometers.
Nickel	Silvery-white, hard metal. Magnetic.	Thin layer of nickel on steel can prevent rust. Used in iron and steel alloys, for example stainless steel. Also used in coins.
Silver	White, shiny metal; easily shaped. Best conductor of heat and electricity.	Used as a precious metal in jewellery, ornaments and coins. Chemicals made from silver form the light-sensitive coating on photographic film.
Tin	Soft, silvery-white, does not rust or corrode.	Mainly used in tin-plating. Tin alloys include solder, pewter and bronze.
Tungsten	One of heaviest, hardest, stiffest metals. Highest melting-point of all metals.	Main use is for the filaments of light bulbs. Added to special hard steels used for the cutting edges of drills and saws.
Uranium	Heavy, yellowish metal; radioactive.	Used as a fuel in nuclear reactors.
Zinc	Bluish-white, brittle metal; does not rust.	Used to galvanize steel: thin coating of zinc on steel prevents rusting. Used for diecast metal parts such as car door handles. Important alloys include brass and solder.

▲ A coppersmith in Marrakesh, Morocco, finishing a large bowl. Copper is soft and easy to work, even when cold.

are purified by *smelting*, which involves heating them fiercely in a furnace with coke or coal. Other metals, such as aluminium, are purified by passing an electric current through the melted or dissolved ore. This process is known as *electrolysis*.

Shaping and alloying

Purified metals can be shaped in various ways. Hot metal may be rolled into thin sheets, or worked into shape by hammering while hot. Molten metal may be poured into a mould (cast), or it may be squeezed like toothpaste through a shaped hole to make bars, girders or wire.

Pure metals have relatively few uses. Much more useful are mixtures of metals, or metals mixed with small amounts of non-metals. Such mixtures are called *alloys*.

Alloys can have very different properties from the metals they are made from. Pure iron, for example, is fairly soft and stretches easily, but adding a small amount of carbon to it produces a form of steel called mild steel. This is hard and strong, and is used for buildings, bridges, car bodies and many other purposes. Brass is an alloy of copper and zinc, and bronze is made from copper and tin. Both are much harder and stronger than the metals from which they are made. More recently, alloys of aluminium have become important materials because of their hardness, lightness and strength.

Corrosion

Metals can be chemically attacked by air, water or other substances in their surroundings. This kind of damage is called corrosion. Rust, which forms on iron and steel, is the most common type of corrosion, but other metals also corrode. Copper and bronze get a green covering called verdigris, and a black tarnish forms on silver.

Various methods are used to prevent iron and steel from rusting. Usually these involve coating the metal with something to keep out air and water. Bridges and steel girders are painted with special anti-rust paint, while food cans are coated with a thin layer of tin, which does not rust and is not poisonous. Machine parts and tools are greased to stop rusting. Many alloys that do not corrode have also been developed.

▶ FLASHBACK ◀

The first metals to be used were gold, silver and copper, because they sometimes occur in the pure state. Copper was first used before 6000 BC in western Asia. About 4000 BC, in Egypt, people first learned to make copper from copper ore. The first alloy to be developed was bronze. Iron is thought to have been widely used in the Middle East from about 1200 BC.

During the Middle Ages, our knowledge of metals was advanced by alchemists, who were trying to turn other metals into gold. In the 16th century various writers brought together most of the existing knowledge about making metals and alloys. By the 18th century the development of the blast furnace for smelting iron, and the use of coke instead of charcoal in the smelting process, meant that iron could be made in much larger quantities then previously. A series of advances in the 19th century made it possible to produce large quantities of steel cheaply. In the late 19th century the modern process of electrolysis was developed, and aluminium became available in large quantities for the first time.

▼ Rusty cars in a scrapyard. The orange powdery rust is iron oxide, a chemical formed when iron reacts with oxygen in the air.

Metamorphosis *see* Animals

find out more
Atmosphere
Earth
Moon
Solar System

Meteors and meteorites

On a dark, clear night you might see a meteor as a sudden streak of light flashing across the sky. Meteors are the hot glowing gases which are created when pieces of rock and dust from space plunge into the Earth's atmosphere. When the pieces of rock are big enough to fall right to the ground, we call them meteorites.

▼ This crater in Arizona, USA, was made by a meteorite about 25,000 years ago. The crater measures 1.2 km across and is 200 m deep.

The common name for meteors is 'shooting stars', but they are not really stars. As the particles of dust and pieces of rock enter the Earth's atmosphere, most of them burn up completely. When they do this, we just see the red-hot flash that we call a meteor. As the Earth travels round the Sun, it sometimes passes through swarms of meteors. On these days we can see showers of meteors which all seem to come from a small area of the sky.

Meteorites

Meteorites are pieces of rock from space which are big enough to fall to the ground. About 500 largish ones strike the Earth each year. There are three main kinds of meteorite: some are stony, some are nearly all iron, and some are a mixture. They are different from the rocks the Earth is made of, so scientists like to find and study them.

A really large meteorite would make a big round crater in the ground. Meteorites made the craters on the Moon and planets. Long ago, when the Solar System first formed, there were many more large pieces of rock drifting in space but, fortunately, we think that nearly all of them have fallen onto the planets by now.

Microscopes

A microscope makes tiny things look much larger, and it lets us see things which are too small to see normally. We use microscopes in schools and in science laboratories. The most powerful microscopes, called electron microscopes, can magnify things several million times.

The most common type of microscope is the *optical microscope*. It has two lenses: the objective lens, which creates a magnified image of the specimen (the object you are looking at), and the eyepiece lens, which acts like a magnifying glass to magnify that image. The specimen is lit from underneath with sunlight or light from a lamp. It must be cut into a very thin slice and mounted on glass to support it and keep it flat. A simple optical microscope can magnify a specimen by about 100 times. So a hair, which is about one-tenth of a millimetre thick, would look 10 millimetres thick. The best optical microscopes can magnify up to about 2000 times.

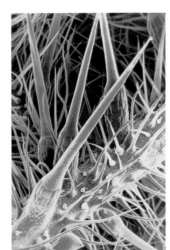

• There are two main types of electron microscope: the transmission electron microscope (TEM), which looks at thin slices of specimens, and the scanning electron microscope (SEM), which looks at the surface of specimens. The most powerful type – the scanning tunnelling microscope – can see individual atoms in a specimen.

find out more
Lenses
Telescopes

The *electron microscope*, a more powerful type of microscope, does not magnify with light. Instead, it fires a stream of tiny particles called electrons at the specimen, and detects how they pass through it or bounce off it.

▶ FLASHBACK ◀

The first microscope was probably made in Holland in about 1590. In the 17th century a Dutchman called Anton van Leeuwenhoek made many important discoveries about animal life with a simple, single-lens microscope. The first electron microscope was built in Germany in 1931.

◀ These hairs on the underside of a stinging nettle leaf are shown about 25 times bigger than their real size. The picture was taken by a scanning electron microscope, and the colours have been added by a computer.

Mining

Mining is the process of digging rocks and minerals out of the ground. (A mineral is any substance that can be mined from the ground.) Diamonds, coal and ores (minerals from which we extract metals) are just some of the materials that we mine. Many people think that mining always takes place far underground. In fact, although some mines are very deep, others are near or at the surface of the ground.

When materials such as coal, iron ore and aluminium ore lie near the surface of the ground, they are dug up by *opencast mining*. In this kind of mining, giant excavators strip off the surface soil. Power shovels and excavators then dig out the materials. Where a coal seam reaches the surface, miners tunnel horizontally into the seam. This is called *drift mining*.

Most gold is obtained by *underground mining*. Shafts are dug down to the level of the ore-bearing rock. Tunnels are then dug out from the shaft to that layer. The roofs of the tunnels are often held up with metal props. The ore is removed from the rock with explosives. It is then loaded onto railway wagons, taken to the shaft and lifted to the surface.

Underground coal is mined by tunnelling. Coal is quite soft, so it is often cut by machines. In mines that are not so highly mechanized, a gap is cut beneath the coal, and then the coal is brought down with explosives or by pneumatic drills. In all coalmines, steel props are used to support the roofs of the tunnels while the coal is being cut away.

Other forms of mining

Underwater mining is used to obtain tin ore. This kind of mining is called *placer mining*. Because tin ore is heavy, it tends to settle in the beds of streams or rivers. The ore is extracted by large floating dredges (a kind of scoop). Diamonds and gold, which are also heavy, are sometimes extracted by placer mining.

Stone or rock is dug out of a *quarry* (a pit or hole in the ground). In one type of quarry, large blocks of stone are cut and trimmed by special machines. The rocks quarried in this way include granite, marble, limestone, sandstone and slate. They are used for buildings and ornamental uses such as statues. Another type of quarry produces aggregate (broken stone) for road-making.

Mining dangers

Mining has always been one of the most dangerous jobs. Dusty mine air can damage miners' lungs, and explosives sometimes cause accidents. There is always the risk of poisonous gases, flooding, fire, or the roof of the mine collapsing.

• The gold-mines of South Africa are the world's deepest mines, going down over 3 km.

▶ Different methods of mining.

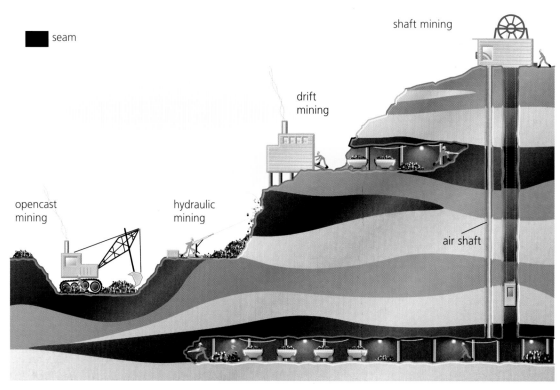

seam

shaft mining

drift mining

opencast mining

hydraulic mining

air shaft

Mirrors

Any polished surface which reflects light is a mirror. Most mirrors are made of smooth glass backed with a very thin layer of metal, often aluminium. As well as the mirrors we use in our homes and our motor vehicles, mirrors are found inside scientific instruments such as microscopes. Huge mirrors are used inside astronomical observatories and in solar power stations.

If you put an object (say, a mug) in front of a flat mirror, you see its image in the mirror. Light from the mug bounces off the mirror so that it seems to come from behind it. This is where the image appears to be. The image is reversed, but it is the same size as the mug, and as far behind the mirror as the mug is in front.

Not all mirrors are flat. *Convex* mirrors bulge outwards. They make things look smaller but give you a wider view. They are often used as driving mirrors in cars and security mirrors in shops. *Concave* mirrors curve inwards. They are sometimes used as make-up or shaving mirrors, because they magnify things which are close.

▶ These mirrors at a funfair have a curved surface. They produce a distorted image.

With distant things, they produce a tiny, upside-down image. In large telescopes they are used instead of a lens to collect and focus the light.

Kaleidoscopes

Kaleidoscopes use mirrors to make colourful five- or six-sided patterns. The mirrors are fixed at an angle to each other inside the barrel of the kaleidoscope. Tiny bits of coloured material move around as the barrel turns. They are reflected several times in the mirrors, creating a series of changing patterns.

find out more
Lasers
Lenses
Light
Telescopes

Moon facts
Distance from Earth
384,000 km
Diameter
3476 km
Mass
0.0123 of the Earth's
Surface gravity
0.165 of the Earth's
Surface temperature
120 °C maximum to
−163 °C at night
Time to orbit Earth
29.53 days

Moon

The Moon is the Earth's natural satellite. It travels round the Earth while the Earth travels round the Sun. The Moon is made of rock and looks like a small planet. It is just over a quarter of the Earth's size.

It takes the Moon about one month to orbit the Earth. In that time its shape as seen from Earth changes from a thin crescent to a Full Moon and back again.

The Moon does not give out any light of its own. It reflects some of the sunlight that falls on it. Half of it is lit by the Sun, and the other half is in darkness. At New Moon, the Moon cannot be seen because the dark side is facing the Earth. As the Moon moves on round the Earth, we see more and more of its sunlit part.

▲ A Full Moon viewed from a spacecraft. Dark plains, called *maria* ('seas'), are visible on the left. Many large craters can be seen on the right.

Nearly everywhere on the Moon there are craters. Most of them were made by huge lumps of rock (meteorites) that crashed into the Moon.

Until recently the Moon was thought to have no air or water. But in 1998 the space probe *Lunar Prospector* found ice at the poles. Lunar ice could provide water and rocket fuel for future space missions.

▶ In this diagram, the inner circle of Moons shows how the Sun always lights up half of the Moon. The outer circle shows how the Moon looks to us at each phase.

find out more
Eclipses
Meteors and meteorites
Satellites
Solar System
Space exploration

Gibbous Moon   First Quarter
Crescent Moon
Earth
New Moon
Full Moon
Crescent Moon
Gibbous Moon   Last Quarter

Motor cars

There are more than 500 million cars in the world today, and over 50 million new cars are produced each year. Cars come in a variety of shapes and sizes. Most have four wheels, though some have only three.

In most cars, only two of the wheels (front or back) are driven by the engine. However, in four-wheel drive (4 × 4) cars, the engine drives all four wheels. Four-wheel drive cars are designed for driving across rough terrain.

Designed for safety

Modern cars are designed with safety in mind. The passenger compartment is built so that it does not collapse in an accident, while the front and rear parts of the car's body are designed to crumple in an accident. This kind of design makes the impact of an accident less violent for the people inside the vehicle. Seat belts stop the driver and passengers from being thrown through the windscreen, and special locks stop the doors from bursting open. Car windows are made from safety glass, which has no sharp edges. Bars inside the doors protect passengers from sideways-on collisions. Anti-lock braking systems (ABS) help to prevent cars from skidding. Many cars are now fitted with airbags. In an accident, these inflate like balloons and cushion the car's occupants as they are thrown forwards.

Pollution

Motor cars give out exhaust gases, and some of these cause pollution. Carbon dioxide contributes to the greenhouse effect, while other exhaust gases damage people's health and cause smog. Petrol engines can now be fitted with devices called *catalytic converters*, which turn the harmful gases into carbon dioxide and water. Cars with diesel engines do not need catalytic converters, but their exhaust gases contain tiny particles that can damage human lungs. To reduce pollution, scientists are trying to develop cars powered by electricity, gas and solar power. But the best way to reduce pollution is for people to travel on foot or by bicycle, bus or train.

• The first vehicle powered by a petrol engine was a wooden motorcycle. It was built in 1885 in Germany by Gottlieb Daimler. In 1886 Karl Benz built a three-wheeler, which many people consider to be the first true motor car. In 1907 Henry Ford started to build cars in large numbers in the USA.

find out more
Engines
Greenhouse effect
Motorcycles
Pollution
Roads

▼ The different parts of a car.

The **engine** is the heart of the car. It runs on petrol or diesel fuel and provides the power to drive the wheels.

The **transmission system** takes the power from the engine via the gearbox to the wheels.

The **gears** allow the car to be driven at different speeds with the engine working efficiently.

The **cooling system** uses water (or sometimes air) to keep the engine cool.

The **exhaust system** carries waste gases from the engine to the air. The catalytic converter makes these gases less polluting.

The **steering-wheel** is used to control the car by turning the front wheels.

The **brakes** are used to slow the car down. They are attached to the wheels.

The **electrical system** uses a battery to power the starter motor and spark plugs when starting up. Once started the engine powers an alternator (a type of generator) which supplies electricity and recharges the battery.

The **suspension** joins each wheel to the body of the car. It uses springs to give the passengers a smooth ride.

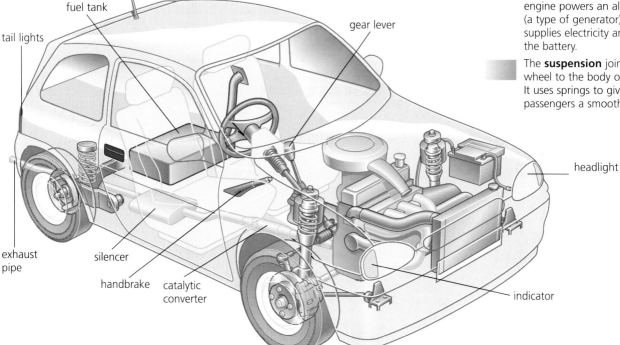

fuel tank

tail lights

gear lever

headlight

exhaust pipe

silencer

handbrake

catalytic converter

indicator

Motorcycles

A motorcycle is much stronger and heavier than a pedal bicycle. It is powered by a petrol engine. Motorcycles can transport one or two people. They are also used for sport and for leisure activities. Many people, such as police officers and delivery and messenger workers, ride motorcycles while doing their job. It is much easier to move through busy traffic on a motorcycle than in a car.

Motorcycles have a frame rather like that of a bicycle. The engine, gearbox, fuel tank, saddle and other parts are all bolted to this frame. The front and rear wheels have hydraulic dampers (shock absorbers) to stop the bike bouncing up and down too much. The engine is connected to a gearbox and turns the rear wheel, usually by means of a chain. Engines range in capacity from less than 50 cc (cubic centimetres) to over 1200 cc. Motorcycles with an engine capacity of 50 cc or less are called mopeds. Small motorcycles

▶ This motorcycle has an engine capacity of 650 cc. Its petrol engine is cooled by air.

generally have air-cooled, two-stroke petrol engines. Larger and more expensive machines usually have four-stroke engines and may also have water cooling.

The front brake, throttle, clutch, and lighting controls are mounted on the handlebars. The rear brake is applied by a foot pedal. Gear changes may also be made by foot. However, many motorcycles have automatic gearboxes.

• The first motorcycle with a petrol engine was made by Gottlieb Daimler in Germany in 1885.

find out more
Engines
Motor cars

twist-grip throttle
front brake
fuel tank
front fork with dampers and springs
engine
gearbox
rear brake
disc brake
chain drive to rear wheel

Motors

A motor is any machine that is capable of moving something. All engines are motors, but when people talk about a motor, they usually mean an electric motor. Electric motors are used in lots of the equipment we use every day, such as vacuum cleaners, food mixers, washing machines, video recorders and lawnmowers.

A simple electric motor has a coil which can spin between the poles of a magnet. When an electric current is passed through the coil, it becomes magnetized. This magnetic effect creates poles that are repelled by like poles on the magnet. The coil's north pole is repelled by the magnet's north pole, and the coil's south pole is repelled by the magnet's south pole. As a result the coil turns until its own north and south poles are next to the opposite poles of the magnet.

At this point, a device called a commutator reverses the direction of the current. This reverses the poles of the coil, so it is pushed round another half-turn. This cycle is continually repeated to keep the motor moving.

To run smoothly, real motors have several coils and the commutator has many sections to reverse the current for each coil. For a stronger turning effect, a powerful electromagnet is used instead of an ordinary permanent magnet. Many motors use alternating current (AC) instead of the 'one-way' direct current from a battery.

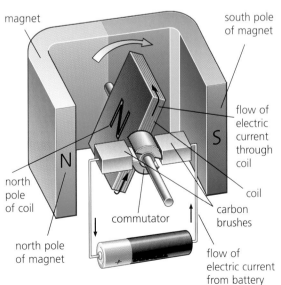

magnet
south pole of magnet
north pole of coil
flow of electric current through coil
coil
commutator
carbon brushes
north pole of magnet
flow of electric current from battery

◀ In a simple electric motor, the electric current magnetizes the coil. The magnetized coil turns between the poles of the magnet until its own poles are next to the opposite poles of the magnet. At this point the commutator reverses the direction of the current flowing through the coil, forcing the coil to make another half-turn.

find out more
Electricity
Engines
Magnets

Navigation

Navigation is knowing your position – at sea, on land or in the air – and where you will be a little while later. To do this, you need to work out your present position and you need to know your speed and the direction in which you are moving. The simplest way of navigating is with a magnetic compass. Today, more and more navigation is done by satellite.

A *magnetic compass* has a small magnetized needle that can turn freely. The Earth's magnetism pulls the needle so that it always points to the magnetic north pole, and from that you can work out your direction.

However, magnetic north is not in quite the same direction as true north, so ships and aircraft use a more accurate *gyrocompass*. It consists of a gyroscope (a heavy wheel that spins on its axis). Once it is spinning at very high speed, the gyroscope keeps pointing in the same direction. Other sensors detect any changes in motion so that a computer can work out how the position of the ship or aircraft is changing.

Lighthouses

The brilliant sweeping beam from a lighthouse helps passing ships to work out exactly where

they are. Each lighthouse has a distinctive code of flashing beams. In foggy conditions, some lighthouses also send out deep horn notes. Lighthouses usually mark locations that are dangerous to shipping, such as islands, rocks or reefs.

Most modern lighthouses are operated by computers from the mainland. Previously, up to three lighthouse keepers at a time used to keep the lighthouse working.

Navigation by satellite

Many walkers, climbers, sailors, pilots and motorists now navigate with the help of a network of satellites called the Global Positioning System (GPS). The GPS has a ring of satellites around the Earth in geostationary orbit – their motion matches the Earth's rotation so that they stay in fixed positions above the ground. The satellites transmit synchronized radio signals that can be picked up by a small receiver below.

▶ FLASHBACK ◀

Simple compasses using lodestone, a magnetic rock, may have been used in China in the 5th century BC. By the 12th century AD European sailors navigated with compasses made from lodestone.

The Pharos at Alexandria, in Egypt, was the first great lighthouse. Built in about 280 BC, it was one of the Seven Wonders of the ancient world. Torches in its windows guided ships into harbour. The same method was used for 1400 years, until oil lamps, and later electric lights, were used.

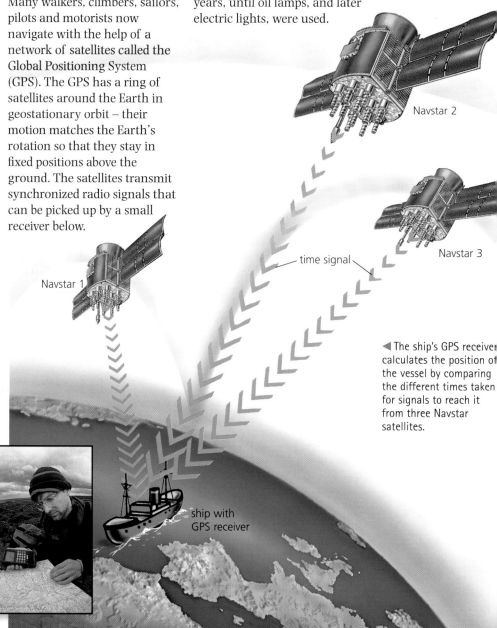

Navstar 2

Navstar 3

time signal

Navstar 1

◀ The ship's GPS receiver calculates the position of the vessel by comparing the different times taken for signals to reach it from three Navstar satellites.

ship with GPS receiver

▶ A walker checks his location with a satellite navigation receiver. Each GPS satellite sends out a signal with its identity and position and the exact time from an atomic clock. In the receiver, a tiny computer compares the arrival times of the signals from different satellites and uses the information to calculate its position to within 100 metres.

Newton, Isaac

Born 1642 in Lincolnshire, England
Died 1727 aged 84

• Despite being a brilliant scientist, Newton was renowned for being absent-minded. He could also be sensitive to criticism, and was very modest about his amazing achievements. He was knighted in 1702 for his great contribution to scientific understanding.

Isaac Newton was one of the greatest physicists and mathematicians that has ever lived. Today he is best remembered for discovering the law of gravity, and working out the three standard laws of motion.

find out more
Colour
Forces and pressure
Gravity
Light

Many people have heard the story of Newton sitting in an orchard and seeing an apple fall. He was only 23, but his studies at Cambridge University had started to make him think in a new way about the movement of the Earth, the Moon and the planets. He realized that, just as the force of gravity pulled the apple to Earth, so gravity also kept the Moon in its orbit. Without gravity, the Moon would fly off into space. Newton developed this idea into his theories of motion and gravitation.

Newton also made an important discovery while making a telescope. He noted

◀ Because he was master of the Royal Mint for nearly 30 years, Newton's portrait was chosen to be on the back of the last English one-pound note. This is the illustration on which the portrait was based.

that the bright images he saw through it had coloured edges. His determination to find out why this happened resulted in him being the first person to realize that white light is a mixture of all the different colours of the rainbow. He showed that a prism or raindrops in the air make a spectrum (rainbow) of colours by splitting up the white light.

Newton's greatest book, written in Latin and usually called *Principia* (1686–1687), included his three laws of motion. It has had an enormous effect on the way scientists have thought ever since. After the publication of *Principia*, Newton became active in public life. He was appointed master of the Royal Mint, and from 1703 until his death he was also president of the Royal Society.

Nitrogen

• Farmers often help crops to grow by spreading fertilizers containing nitrogen compounds (nitrates). However, using such fertilizers can cause large amounts of nitrates to build up in the soil. Rainwater may then wash them into water supplies, rivers and seas. High levels of nitrates in drinking water may cause illness.

The gas nitrogen makes up 78 per cent of the air we breathe, and it is found (combined with other elements) in all living things. Because nitrogen does not readily react with or attack other substances, it is often added to food packages, such as crisp packets. This method keeps the food fresh and stops it from spoiling.

Nitrogen is a chemical element, as are carbon and oxygen. When nitrogen combines with these and other elements, nitrogen compounds are formed. Some of these, especially amino acids and proteins, are essential to life.

Nitrogen can be separated out from air by cooling the air until the gases in it become

find out more
Air
Atmosphere
Ecology
Matter

liquid. Nitrogen becomes a liquid at a temperature of −196 °C. This very cold liquid is used to produce low temperatures, for example in rapidly freezing food to preserve it.

The nitrogen cycle

Although people and other animals breathe in nitrogen all the time, the nitrogen that they need enters their bodies in another way, as part of a constant movement of nitrogen called the nitrogen cycle. In this cycle, nitrogen moves from the air into plants and animals and back again, helping to sustain life as it does so.

The food that animals eat contains the essential nitrogen compounds. These compounds are present in plants, and people

and animals get them either by eating plants or by eating animals that have fed on plants. Plants absorb nitrogen compounds from the soil through their roots. These compounds come mainly from the decaying remains of dead plants and animals.

▼ Scientists use liquid nitrogen to store materials at very low temperatures. For example, cells from human beings, such as sperm and egg cells, are frozen and then thawed when needed.

Oil

Oil is one of the most important substances we use today, and it supplies more of the world's energy than any other fuel. Oil spills from tankers and rigs can cause widespread harm to the oceans and their wildlife. Also, the gases produced when we burn oil are damaging the Earth's atmosphere.

Oil is a fossil fuel, like coal and natural gas. It is the remains of tiny plants and animals which lived in the sea millions of years ago. When they died, they sank to the bottom and were covered by layers of mud and sand. Over the years, the mud and sand slowly turned to rock. Eventually, the weight of rock, combined with heat and the activity of bacteria, changed the animal and plant remains into oil (and natural gas). Deep down under layers of solid rock, the oil became trapped in the holes of porous rock, rather like water in a sponge. The geological name for this oil is *petroleum*.

The search for oil

Oil companies search for petroleum under the sea-bed or under land once covered by sea. After identifying areas where the rocks are most likely to contain oil, test drillings are made. At the drilling site, a framework tower called a *derrick* is erected. Under the derrick, a huge drill is turned by a diesel engine. As the drill hole deepens, the drill is lengthened by adding drill pipes from above. The cutting end of the drill is called the *bit*. It has hardened steel teeth, and there may also be diamonds on it for cutting very hard rock. To keep the bit cool, watery mud is pumped down the drill pipes and out through holes in the bit. If oil is found, it flows up through the drill hole. The hole then becomes an oil well.

Where oil is found under the sea-bed, the derrick and drilling equipment are built on an *oil rig*. Some rigs float, while others rest on legs on the sea-bed. Semi-submersible rigs are held down on the sea-bed by flooding their legs with water. The choice of rig depends on the sea-bed, the depth of water and the likely weather conditions. The rigs used for natural gas are similar to those used for oil.

Oil flowing from an oil well is called *crude oil*. After fitting valves to control the flow of crude oil, oil is pumped from the well and carried away by pipeline, tanker ship, rail or road to a refinery. Natural gas is produced from wells both on land and offshore. It is carried from the gas-producing areas by long-distance pipelines or as a liquid by tanker ships.

At the refinery

At the refinery, crude oil is separated into several substances, starting with a process called *fractional distillation*. This takes place inside a tall distillation tower. The crude oil is heated until most of its liquids boil and turn into vapours. These vapours rise up, cool, and become liquids again at different temperatures, so they flow out of the tower at different levels. The thicker heavier liquids are broken down further in a process called cracking, making more petrol and light oils.

find out more
Energy
Greenhouse effect
Plastics
Pollution
Rocks and minerals

• It is estimated that the world's supply of oil will only last for another 30 to 60 years.

▲ Workers on an oil rig are known as 'roughnecks'. They may have living quarters on the rig itself, although for safety reasons they often live on a separate platform.

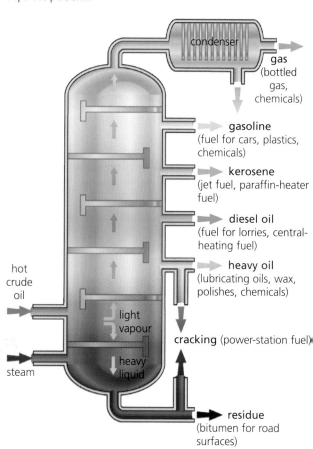

▶ At an oil refinery, crude oil is separated into different substances, called fractions, inside a distillation tower.

Oxygen

Oxygen is a gas which makes up one-fifth of the air we breathe. There is more oxygen on Earth than any other element, although most of the atoms of oxygen are combined with those of other substances. Oxygen atoms combine with atoms of hydrogen to make water.

When fuels such as oil and natural gas burn, they combine with oxygen and give out heat energy and carbon dioxide. This process is called

◀ Welders burn a mixture of oxygen and other gases in their torches. The mixture produces a flame with a very high temperature that can melt steel.

combustion. When materials combine with the oxygen in air, they 'oxidize' (this happens when iron rusts).

Living things need oxygen to release energy from their food. This process, which is called *respiration*, takes place in the cells of their bodies. As animals respire, they take oxygen from the air. Plants also respire and take oxygen from the air, but they give out more oxygen than they take in.

Fire

All fires require three things to burn: fuel, heat and oxygen. The fuel must be turned into a gas before it can burn. The burning gases combine with oxygen in the air to produce lots of heat. As the burning gases and tiny particles of soot stream upwards, they glow as red-hot or even white-hot flames.

▶ FLASHBACK ◀

Joseph Priestley, an English chemist, discovered oxygen (although he gave it a different name) in the late 18th century. Around the same time in France, Antoine-Laurent Lavoisier realized that air contains two gases: 'oxygen' and 'azote' (which we now call nitrogen).

Paints and dyes

Paints are coloured coatings put on houses, cars and other firm surfaces to make them look better, and to protect them from the weather. Dyes are chemicals that change the colour of materials.

The first paints and dyes were made from natural materials such as clays, rock ores and plants. Most modern paints and dyes are made from chemicals.

Paint consists mainly of a mixture of two types of substance – pigments and vehicles. The *pigments*, the coloured parts of paint, are usually in the form of fine powders. The *vehicles* get their name because they carry the pigment. They are liquids that dry to a tough film, binding the pigment to the surface. Most pigments and vehicles in modern paints are made artificially.

Paints are made in thousands of different colours and for all purposes. Paints for outdoor use need to be hard-wearing. They contain plenty of special oils, which make them slow to dry, but give a hard, glossy finish. Some indoor paints, such as those used on walls, consist mainly of water and contain no oil.

Dyes used to be made from plants and animals. For example, saffron, a yellow dye, comes from the crocus plant. Today, there are thousands of different-coloured artificial dyes. When cloth is dyed, special chemicals called *mordants* are used to help the dye penetrate the fabric and stay fixed.

• The vehicle used to make the first paints was animal fat. Later, gum arabic, gelatine, egg-white and beeswax were used to make paint.

◀ A scene inside a paint factory. The vats contain a yellow fluid that is to be used as a liquid pigment in the manufacture of paint. The yellow colour of the pigment comes from iron oxide.

Paper

Most of the paper that we use today has been made from wood pulp. The pulp comes mainly from coniferous trees such as pines and firs. We cut down millions of these trees each year to make paper, but most of them are specially grown for this purpose. We can also make perfectly good paper from waste paper, and many newspapers are now made from recycled paper.

The first stage in papermaking is to change the wood from the logs into wood pulp. They may be ground between heavy rollers or 'cooked' with chemicals to break the wood into fibres. These fibres are made into a thin slush, by adding water, and cleaned. 'Beaters' fray the fibres so that they will easily mat together. After this stage, chemicals and dyes may be mixed in.

At the 'wet end' of the papermaking machine, the liquid pulp goes onto a fast-moving belt of fine wire mesh. The water drains away or is sucked off. The remaining pulp, which still consists of about 80 per cent water, passes onto the rollers. They squeeze out even more water and press the fibres firmly together to form a 'web' of paper. It is dried by heated rollers before it finally emerges in a huge continuous roll.

• Some paper is moistened and passed through heated rollers to give it a glossy surface. Other papers are given coatings of china clay to make high-quality paper for art and for printing.

▼ At the paper mill, wood pulp is obtained from logs. The pulp is cleaned, beaten, drained, pressed and dried before it finally emerges as a huge continuous roll of paper.

Recycling paper

Paper can also be made from waste paper. When the waste paper is soaked in water, it breaks down into its original fibres. These can be used over and over again. At present only 25 per cent of the world's paper is recycled, but this amount could easily be increased to 75 per cent. For every tonne of waste paper collected and reused, at least two trees are saved. Waste paper is easy to collect, and many towns and cities have special paper banks where people can deposit their old newspapers and other waste paper. Many newspapers are printed on recycled paper which has been de-inked and cleaned.

▶ FLASHBACK ◀

In ancient Egypt, a form of writing material called papyrus was made from the stems of the papyrus reed. (The name 'paper' comes from papyrus.) Strips of reed were soaked in water to make them stick together. The sheet was hammered and dried, and then polished with ivory or a smooth shell.

True paper was first made in China about 1900 years ago. The Arabs learned the method from the Chinese in the 8th century, and Muslims took the industry to Spain. Paper was made in Europe during the Middle Ages, but it was rare and expensive. For centuries paper was made from plant fibres obtained from pulped cotton and linen rags. During the 19th century wood pulp replaced these plant fibres.

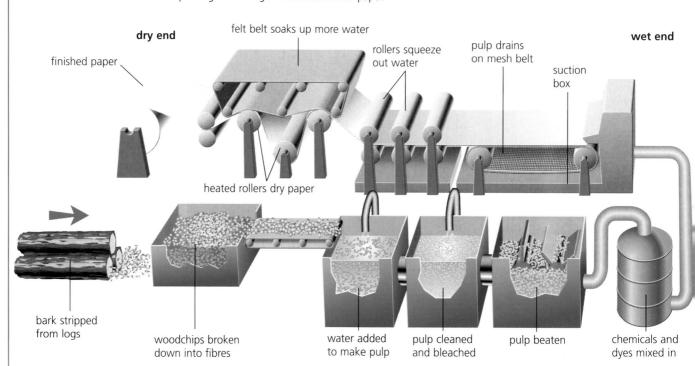

dry end

finished paper

felt belt soaks up more water

rollers squeeze out water

pulp drains on mesh belt

wet end

suction box

heated rollers dry paper

bark stripped from logs

woodchips broken down into fibres

water added to make pulp

pulp cleaned and bleached

pulp beaten

chemicals and dyes mixed in

Photocopiers

A photocopier is a machine that makes a copy of a document, for example a page of text, a drawing or a picture. The copy, which may be a black-and-white or a colour one, is called a photocopy.

Most photocopiers work by a process called *xerography* (pronounced 'zerography'), which uses light and static electricity. The drum inside a photocopier is charged with negative static electricity. When you press the copying button, a light shines onto the document to be copied. The white parts of the document reflect light onto the drum, knocking the negative charges off its surface. Dark parts of the document reflect no light onto the drum,

leaving the negative charges in place on these areas of the drum.

The ink particles in the photocopier toner are positively charged so that they are attracted to the negatively

charged parts of the drum. The toner then sticks to a clean sheet of paper that is pressed against the drum. The paper is then heated to melt the toner, and the copy is complete.

• Sophisticated photocopiers can make several copies of documents with hundreds of pages, and organize the pages in the right order. Some machines can make the original document bigger or smaller on the copy.

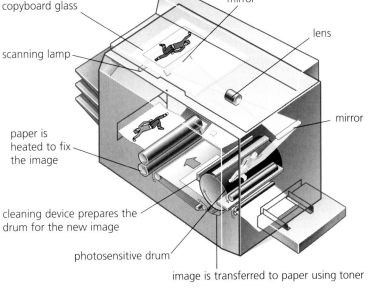

copyboard glass

mirror

lens

scanning lamp

paper is heated to fix the image

mirror

cleaning device prepares the drum for the new image

photosensitive drum

image is transferred to paper using toner

◀ A photocopier uses the process of xerography. The pattern of light and dark on the document being copied becomes a pattern of charge or no charge on the drum's surface.

find out more
Electricity
Fax machines
Paper
Printing

Physics

Physics is the part of science concerned with discovering the basic forces and laws of the Universe. Physics tries to explain how matter and energy behave. Physicists try to understand everything, from the tiniest particles inside atoms to the creation of the whole Universe.

Physicists are interested in what happens to matter when it is cooled to almost absolute zero, or heated to the temperature at the centre of a star. They study how electrons move inside the materials used to make computer chips, how liquids flow, and how energy is transformed from one form to another.

The first scientist we would now call a 'physicist' was Galileo Galilei. His ideas and experiments helped Isaac Newton to develop his laws of motion and his theory of gravity. During the 18th century physicists gained a better understanding of heat and light, and also began to experiment with the mysterious forces of electricity and magnetism. The basic laws of electricity and magnetism were discovered in the

19th century by Michael Faraday, James Clerk Maxwell and others. In the late 19th century radioactivity and subatomic particles were observed for the first time.

The early 20th century saw some remarkable new ideas, including Einstein's theories of relativity. These gave a new understanding of time and space. The theory of quantum mechanics, developed by Max Planck and others, explains how matter behaves at the scale of the atom. Quantum theory made possible the incredible progress in electronics which led to the computer age.

find out more
Atoms and molecules
Colour
Einstein, Albert
Electricity
Electronics
Energy
Faraday, Michael
Forces and pressure
Galilei, Galileo
Gravity
Heat
Light
Magnets
Matter
Newton, Isaac
Radiation
Sound
Waves

◀ Physicists at work inside the European particle physics laboratory near Geneva, Switzerland. Part of the laboratory's complex equipment is housed in this tunnel, which is built in a ring shape 27 km long.

Photography *see* Cameras • **Photosynthesis** *see* Plants • **Planets** *see* Solar System

Plants

Plants range in size from giant trees to tiny mosses. They include the largest and the oldest living things. But unlike animals, plants do not usually move around. Instead, they grow rooted in the soil or attached to the ground or to rocks.

Plants do not feed like animals, although they have to take in chemicals from the soil or from their surroundings to grow. Instead of eating, most make their own food in special 'chemical factories' in their leaves.

Green factories

The most important difference between plants and animals is how they get their food, and this also helps to explain the shape and form of a typical plant. Most plants are green in colour and have leaves. These leaves are spread out in a way that catches most sunshine.

Plants, like animals, are made up of microscopic 'building blocks' called cells. The plants are green because their cells contain a green chemical called *chlorophyll*, and the chlorophyll is bundled into packages called *chloroplasts*. The chloroplasts are the chemical factories that make the plant's food. To do this, the plant also needs two 'raw materials' from its surroundings. These are the gas carbon dioxide, which is common in the air, and water. The carbon dioxide passes into the plant's leaves through special pores in their surface, while the water is taken up by the plant's roots. The

▼ Flowers like the ones on these cacti are designed to attract insects, which then help the plant by carrying pollen to another flower so that fertilization can occur. The shape and colour of different flowers attract particular insects. This helps to ensure the pollen is carried only to the right kind of plant.

chlorophyll in the plant's leaves absorbs energy from sunlight, and this energy is used to turn carbon dioxide and water into various kinds of energy-rich sugars. These sugars are the plant's food. The whole process of making food using sunlight is called *photosynthesis*.

A waste product of photosynthesis is the gas oxygen. This is fortunate for humans and other animals, because we need oxygen to breathe. In the process, we breathe out carbon dioxide, which would eventually poison us, if plants did not turn it into oxygen. Plants therefore have an important role in recycling the air that we breathe.

Food stores

The sugars produced by plants in photosynthesis can be joined together and stored as more complex chemicals called starches. These are often stored in parts of the plant's roots or underground stems, which swell up into bulging growths called tubers. Sometimes we eat these starch stores as food. Carrots, for example, are swollen roots, and potatoes are swollen underground stems.

The plant can break down the starch and the sugars whenever it needs energy, for example at night when there is no sunlight to provide energy, or when it needs extra energy to grow or to produce seeds. Plants also need other chemicals (called *minerals*) to build all the parts that make up their cells. These chemicals are taken in by the plant's roots, dissolved in water. The roots also anchor the plant in the ground. Tube-like cells inside the stem carry water from the roots to the leaves, and other tubes transport sugars to wherever the plant needs them for energy.

Spreading the kind

Because plants do not move about like animals, they cannot find their way to new places where it might be better to live, and they cannot meet and mate with others of their kind, as animals do. Plants therefore need outside help both to breed and to spread themselves. Flowering plants produce male and female sex cells in different parts of their flowers. They rely either on the wind or on animals to carry the male sex cells (called pollen) to the female sex cells of another flower. There, the sex cells can join, in a process called fertilization, to produce seeds.

Seeds allow new plants to grow, and help to spread their kind. They are usually enclosed in a fruit. The fruit is designed to carry the seed away

• The coastal redwood is the tallest living tree and can grow up to 110 m tall. It belongs to the group of conifers, and is found in North America.

• There are some groups of living things that are very like plants, but which scientists do not regard as true plants. Both algae (including seaweeds) and fungi (including mushrooms and toadstools) are usually placed in separate kingdoms.

• The study of plants is called botany, and people who study them are called botanists.

▼ (1) Roots reach down into the soil to gather the water and minerals the plant needs for growth. (2) The roots of some plants swell up and are used to store the plant's food, as in a carrot.

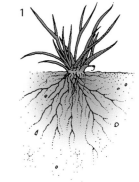

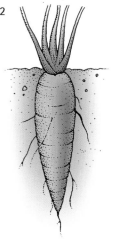

from the parent plant. This helps the plant invade new areas, and ensures that the young plant does not compete with its parent for space and sunlight.

Different life cycles

Other plant groups spread and multiply their kind in slightly different ways. Conifers, for example, also have tiny flowers that spread pollen for fertilization. But their seeds are usually produced on a woody cone that does not completely enclose the seed. Some conifers, such as yew trees, have juicy berries instead of cones, but the seed is still not completely enclosed. The seeds from cones are spread by the wind, while the berries are spread by animals.

Ferns, mosses and liverworts have more complicated lifecycles. Instead of seeds they spread by *spores* – dust-like particles that are spread in the wind. The spores grow into young plants that are quite unlike the adults; they are tiny green flaps that can only survive in damp places. These produce sex cells in tiny pockets on their underside. The male sex cells swim through a film of moisture on the surface of the flap to the pockets containing the female sex cells, which they then fertilize. An adult fern, moss or liverwort then develops from the fertilized cells.

▲ Mistletoe grows as a parasite on other plants.

find out more
Cells
Ecology
Genetics
Living things

▼ Plants are divided into different groups, according to how they reproduce.

SPORE-PRODUCING PLANTS

Mosses and liverworts spread by means of spores, usually produced in box-like capsules held up to the wind on stalks. There are about 16,000 different kinds.

liverwort

The 10,000 or so types of **fern** and their relatives also reproduce by spores, usually produced in 'warts' on the underside of their leaves.

fern

moss

CONE-BEARERS

monkey-puzzle tree

cone

About 500 different kinds of **conifer** (and related plants) are known. They usually have needle-like leaves, and produce their seeds on woody cones.

FLOWERING PLANTS

monocotyledons

The 240,000 known types of **flowering plant** are divided into two groups, depending on the number of leaves that spring directly from their seeds. Monocotyledons produce a single leaf inside each seed.

grass

tulip

dicotyledons

Dicotyledons are flowering plants with two leaves ready-formed inside their seeds.

oak tree

sunflower

Plastics

You can find things made of plastics all around you: telephones, television sets, computers, tapes and disks, toothbrushes, clothes, and countless other things. Plastics are chemically made materials which can easily be moulded into any shape. They can be very hard and strong or they can be soft and stretchy. With such a wide range of properties, plastics have become some of the most useful modern materials.

In some ways, plastics are better than natural materials, such as wood, metal, glass and cotton. They do not rot like wood, or rust like iron and steel. Plastic bottles and cups do not break if you drop them. Electrical appliances are made of plastics because they do not conduct electricity. Plastics can be made with a wide range of different characteristics and shapes. They may be transparent, like glass, or made in any colour; they can be formed into ultra-light solid foams for packaging or into flexible synthetic fibres that are woven into cloth.

Making plastics

Plastics are made from gases and liquids, most of which are extracted from crude oil. The chemicals used to make plastics have small molecules (particles). When heated, often under

pressure, the small molecules join up in chains to form long molecules. Substances with long-chain molecules, such as plastics, are called *polymers*. When the long-chain molecules of a plastic bend, this makes the plastic flexible. When the molecules interlink so that they cannot bend, the plastic is a rigid and tough one.

▲ Helmets and other protective sportswear are made from a very tough plastic called polycarbonate.

▼ Two methods of making plastic objects.

Blow moulding

1 hot plastic inserted into mould

2 mould closed

3 compressed air forced in, shaping plastic to mould

mould   tube of plastic

compressed air   finished bottle

Extrusion

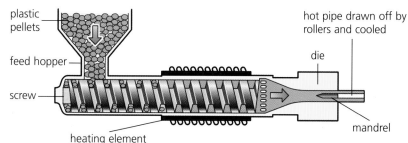

plastic pellets

feed hopper

screw

heating element

hot pipe drawn off by rollers and cooled

die

mandrel

Plastic pellets are fed through a hopper into a barrel. They are heated to turn them into a liquid, which is pushed by a screw through a die and mandrel. The die and mandrel shape the plastic into a pipe.

Some common plastics

Name	Properties	Uses
polythene	strong, flexible, not easily damaged by gases or liquids	bags, sacks, pipes, bottles
nylon	strong, hard-wearing	clothes, carpets, other textiles
PVC (polyvinyl chloride)	flexible, water-resistant, insulates electricity	hoses, boots, rainwear, covering for electrical wires
Kevlar	very strong, bullet-proof	bullet-proof vests, cables, aircraft parts
fibreglass-reinforced plastic	very strong, water- and weather-resistant	boat hulls, storage tanks
acrylic	clear, rigid, weather-resistant	car lights, motorcycle windscreens
polystyrene	lightweight, good insulator against heat and cold	food packaging, disposable cups

find out more
Atoms and molecules
Materials
Oil

Pollution

We cause pollution when we do damage to our surroundings. Leaving litter is one form of pollution. But chemicals and waste from factories, farms, motor cars and even houses cause much more serious pollution, which can affect the air, water and the land.

Pollution is not something new. Six hundred years ago, the air over London was thick with smoke from coal fires. Over the years, laws have been passed to stop some kinds of pollution. Many countries now have government departments whose job is to limit the damage pollution does.

Air pollution

Factories, power stations and motor vehicles make waste gases, soot and dust, which are all released into the air. The polluted air damages people's lungs. Some kinds of air pollution can even cause brain damage. Waste gases in the air can also cause acid rain, which damages trees, lake and river life, and buildings.

Ozone is a gas produced naturally from oxygen in the upper atmosphere. A thin layer of ozone surrounds the world, and protects us from the harmful ultraviolet rays in sunlight. Ozone is destroyed by pollution from burning fuels and by chemicals called CFCs released from some refrigerators and aerosols. If the ozone layer is badly damaged, more people will get skin cancer.

Water pollution

Acid rain can pollute lakes and rivers. But there are many other kinds of water pollution. Some towns and villages pump untreated sewage into rivers or the sea, while factories sometimes release poisonous chemicals and wastes. These pollutants can kill fishes and other water animals and plants. Farmers use fertilizers and chemical pesticides that can also be washed into rivers and streams after heavy rainfall. The sea can also be polluted by spillages of oil from oil tankers and oil rigs.

Pollution on land

People cause pollution when they thoughtlessly dump their rubbish or litter. Some kinds of rubbish rot away quite quickly, but many plastic materials will never decay.

Radioactive waste from nuclear power stations could cause very serious pollution. Nearly all nuclear waste is safely contained for now, but small amounts do sometimes escape into the air or water. Many scientists are worried about the long-term effects of this type of pollution, because nuclear waste can stay radioactive for thousands of years.

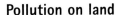

◄ Water pollution in New Zealand. The wastes from a factory pour out from a pipe directly into the sea, close to a beach.

▲ Pollution is causing thinning of the ozone layer, especially over the Poles. This satellite picture taken above the Antarctic shows ozone levels in the upper atmosphere. In the blue, purple and grey area at the centre there is virtually no ozone at all.

▲ In some large cities, the air is so polluted that people wear face masks to filter out dust and soot from the air.

find out more
Aerosols
Atmosphere
Ecology
Energy
Greenhouse effect
Motor cars

Power stations

• Waste materials such as paper or the gas from rubbish tips are burned by some power stations as a useful additional source of power. One power station in the USA even burns drugs captured by the police.

▼ How power stations work.

When you plug a kettle, a television or another electrical appliance into the mains, the electricity comes from a power station that may be hundreds of kilometres away. The most common kind of power station burns coal or oil. Other important kinds burn natural gas or are powered by nuclear fuels.

In a power station, the electricity comes from huge generators. To deliver power, the generators must be turned. Usually, they are driven by huge wheels with fanlike blades or vanes on them.

These wheels are called *turbines*. When a stream of moving liquid or gas strikes them, they spin round. Most turbines are turned by jets of steam from a boiler. However, they can also be turned by running water, wind or gas. The power output of a large power station is 2000 megawatts (2 billion watts) – enough to supply electricity to over a million homes.

Different types of power station

Power stations which use fuels are of three main types: coal- or oil-fired, nuclear-powered, or CCGT (combined-cycle gas turbine). In a *coal- or oil-fired power station*, oil or powdered coal is burned to turn water in the boiler into steam, which drives the turbines. After use, the steam is cooled, condensed (changed back into a liquid) and reused in the boiler. To cool the steam, cooling water passes through huge cooling towers where the heat is removed by an upward draught of air. The cooled water can then be used again in the cooling tower, or it is pumped into a nearby river or lake.

Instead of a furnace for burning fuel to raise steam, a *nuclear power station* has a nuclear reactor to do the same job. The core of the reactor contains a nuclear fuel, such as the radioactive metal uranium-235. In the reactor, heat is released by the fission (splitting) of the atoms of uranium-235. This process releases an enormous amount of heat which is used to boil water. In a pressurized-water reactor (PWR), heat is carried away from the core by water. In an advanced gas-cooled reactor (AGR), carbon dioxide gas is used instead. Control rods are lowered into the reactor's core to slow the rate of fission. Of the 400 or more nuclear power stations in the world, more than half use PWRs.

Combined-cycle gas turbine power stations have a jet engine which uses gas as its fuel. The shaft of the engine turns one generator. The heat from the jet exhaust makes steam to drive another generator. CCGT stations produce less power than other kinds of power station, but they can start up rapidly when demand for power rises. Also, they are more efficient so they can extract more energy from each litre of fuel burned.

Waste heat

Fuel-burning and nuclear power stations use heat energy to drive their generators. Unfortunately, they deliver less than a half of their energy as electricity. The rest is wasted as heat, although this loss is not due to poor design. Once heat has been removed by the cooling

Oil- or coal-burning power station

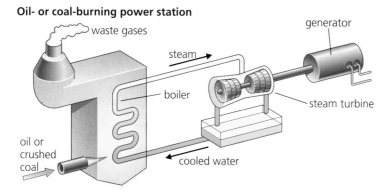

Nuclear power station

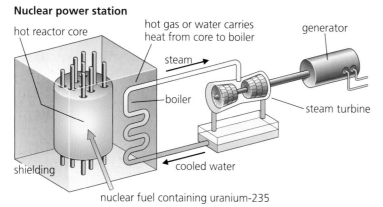

Combined-cycle gas turbine (CCGT) power station

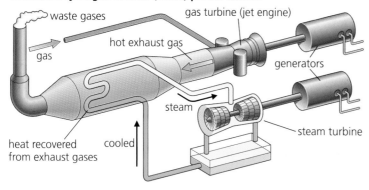

Power stations

◄ Electricity from this coal-fired power station is carried by wires to nearby cities and towns, and to other areas where it is needed.

• In 1986, a major accident at the Chernobyl nuclear power station in the Ukraine released a huge cloud of radioactive material into the atmosphere. Thirty-one people were killed in the accident itself, and thousands are still suffering from its after-effects.

• A typical nuclear power station produces about 60 tonnes of waste every year, of which about 1 tonne is highly radioactive.

• When the nuclei of hydrogen atoms fuse (join) together, large amounts of energy are released in a process called nuclear fusion. (Fusion is the source of the Sun's heat.) In the 21st century, fusion power stations may become an important source of electricity. Unlike today's nuclear power stations, they will produce almost no radioactive waste.

water, it becomes so spread out that it is no longer useful for the generating process. To make steam, concentrated heat is needed at a high temperature. Some power stations use their cooling systems to supply hot water to the houses in their area. This cuts down on energy wastage by using the fuel more efficiently.

Polluting gases

Fuel-burning power stations pollute the atmosphere with unwanted exhaust gases from their chimneys. All give out carbon dioxide, which adds to global warming. Coal-fired stations also give out sulphur dioxide, which causes acid rain. The amount of damage can be reduced either by burning only low-sulphur coal, or by fitting special equipment in the chimneys to control the amount of polluting gases released. However, such equipment is expensive and does not get rid of all the harmful gases.

Nuclear power stations do not burn their fuel, so they do not produce large amounts of polluting gases. However, they produce highly radioactive waste which needs safe storage for thousands of years. Also, very high safety standards are needed to make sure that nuclear power stations do not leak radioactive materials into the atmosphere.

Alternative power schemes

The world's supplies of oil, natural gas and coal are limited, so, where possible, it makes sense to use power stations that do not need these fuels and that produce no polluting gases. Although it may be difficult to provide all the electricity we want without nuclear power, some people say that the risks are too great. We need to find safer and less polluting ways of generating power.

Hydroelectric power uses the flow of water from a lake behind a dam to drive its turbines. Tidal power schemes use the power of the rising tide. Wind farms are collections of aerogenerators: generators turned by giant windmills.

Geothermal power stations use the heat from underground rocks to make steam for their turbines. Cold water is pumped down to the rocks through one borehole and comes up a second borehole as hot steam. In areas where hot water occurs naturally deep in the ground, steam comes out of cracks in the ground.

► FLASHBACK ◄

The world's first power station, with a water-driven generator, was built in Surrey, England, in 1881. It supplied power for a new electric street-lighting system. The first power station in the USA opened in 1882. Its generator was driven by a steam engine. Power stations with steam turbines appeared in about 1900. The first power station to use a nuclear reactor was opened at Obninsk, in Russia, in 1954. The first nuclear power station to provide electricity for public use began working in 1956 in the UK.

find out more
Atoms and molecules
Electricity
Energy
Engines
Greenhouse effect
Pollution
Radiation
Sun

◄ The core of a nuclear reactor. This reactor is being used for research and not to generate power. The nuclear fuel rods at the centre are being heated to very high temperatures. The blue glow is caused by highly charged particles travelling through water faster than light does.

Printing

Printing is a way of making many identical copies from one original. For every page in a magazine, for every stamp, poster, book or cereal packet, there is one original. A printing plate is made from this original, and then hundreds, thousands or even millions of copies are printed.

Nearly all the printed material we see is made up of type (words or numbers), photographs and artists' illustrations. This article has all three. A novel may have only type, while a stamp usually has type and a photograph or illustration.

Type is mostly set on a computer very similar to a word processor, and all the typefaces (different kinds of type) and sizes are stored electronically in its memory. Sometimes artists' illustrations and photographs are also stored in this way. Designers can also use the computer to arrange the type and illustrations on the page.

A finished page can be stored electronically and used to produce film from which the printers can make printing plates. Alternatively, the computer can print out just the type on special paper, and use it together with the illustrations and photographs to make the finished original, which is called camera-ready artwork.

Printing plates

Before any printing can be done, the words and pictures on the camera-ready artwork have to be transferred to the *plate* (printing surface), which is usually metal. The plate is coated with a light-sensitive material, which hardens when exposed to light. The image of the original is transferred by placing a negative film of the original over a printing plate and exposing it to bright light. After exposure, the plate is washed. Those parts of the plate that were masked from the light wash away, but the image of the original remains in those areas where the light shone through the negative.

Type is solid black, but black-and-white photographs and illustrations need a range of different tones from black to very light greys. The tones are produced by breaking the picture up into a pattern of very small dots called a *halftone*. Each dot prints solid black, but little dots with big white spaces between them appear light grey. Big black dots with very little white spaces between them appear almost black.

Printing processes

We use two main printing processes: *lithography* and *gravure*. A third process, *letterpress*, using a printing surface with a raised image, was for many years the main printing technique, but it is now little used.

▲ The main photo shows a print worker checking the quality of a sheet of colour printing (part of the printing press can be seen on the right). The enlarged section above shows how printed colour photos are made up from tiny dots of just four colours: magenta (a bluish red), yellow, cyan (a greenish blue) and black. All other colours can be made by combining these four.

The letter image is greasy and so attracts printing ink.

One roller spreads water over all the plate except for the greasy parts.

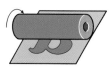

A second roller spreads ink which sticks to the greasy letters. It is repelled by the wet parts of the plate.

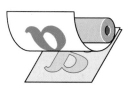

The inked letter is transferred to the paper.

◄ Lithography is the most widely used printing process today.

Lithography ('litho') is the most widely used printing process today. The image on the printing plate is the whole 'picture' of type, illustrations and photographs. Litho plates are usually made of aluminium, which can be easily wrapped around a cylinder. On the printing press, the inked image is offset (transferred) from the plate onto a rubber cylinder and from there onto the paper.

In gravure the printing plate has cells (like tiny wells) sunk into its surface. Making gravure plates is very expensive, so this process is usually used for very large print runs such as for magazines or packaging.

▶ FLASHBACK ◄

The first printed books were made in China by hand-carving characters and designs back-to-front onto a flat block of wood, then inking the block and pressing paper or cloth against it. The earliest surviving book was printed in China in AD 868.

Movable type, which consists of a different piece of type for each character, was invented in China by Pi Sheng between 1041 and 1048.

All printing in Europe was done from wooden blocks until about 1450, when Johann Gutenberg of Germany developed movable metal type which could be used again and again. This is the letterpress form of printing. Around 1800 the process of lithography was introduced.

find out more
Photocopiers
Word processors

▼ To print this colour picture, four printing plates are needed. Each plate makes its impression separately. Black is always printed last.

 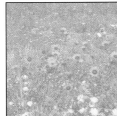 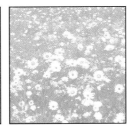  

yellow plate magenta plate cyan plate black plate

Radar

Radar is short for RAdio Detection And Ranging. It can tell us the position of a moving or stationary object, even when it is far away or in dark or foggy conditions. Radar tells air-traffic controllers the height and position of aircraft around busy airports. It has many other important uses, including catching speeding motorists.

Most large aircraft have on-board radar to warn them of nearby planes as well as bad weather ahead. A ship's radar equipment detects other ships or hazards in the area. Weather forecasters use radar to detect approaching storms or hurricanes. Radar helps scientists to study the atmosphere and other planets, and to track spacecraft before they reach their orbits. It can also warn of attacking missiles, aircraft or ships.

Radar was invented by a British scientist, Robert Watson-Watt. In 1935 the British government asked him to find out whether beams of radio waves could destroy enemy aircraft. During his research he realized that radio waves would bounce off a plane. He devised a way of using reflected waves from an aircraft to find out its position and the direction it was moving. Watson-Watt had invented the first radar system for detecting enemy planes.

find out more
Radiation
Radio
Waves

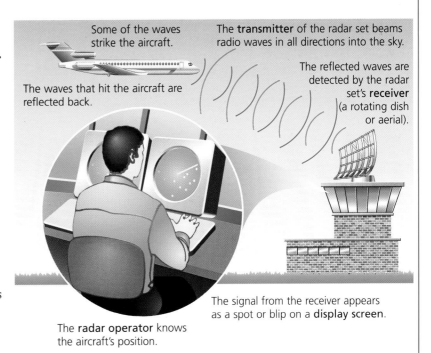

Some of the waves strike the aircraft.

The waves that hit the aircraft are reflected back.

The **transmitter** of the radar set beams radio waves in all directions into the sky.

The reflected waves are detected by the radar set's **receiver** (a rotating dish or aerial).

The signal from the receiver appears as a spot or blip on a **display screen**.

The **radar operator** knows the aircraft's position.

Radiation

Radiation is energy on the move. Some kinds of radiation energy, such as radio signals and light, travel as invisible waves. Other kinds of radiation are tiny particles that shoot out from atoms at enormous speeds. The cosmic rays speeding around out in space are made up of tiny particles.

The materials inside the reactors of nuclear power plants are examples of *radioactive materials*. Radioactive materials can produce a mixture of radiations, some of which are particles and some of which are waves.

Radioactivity

The atoms inside radioactive materials can change into different kinds of atom by throwing out tiny atomic particles. There are two kinds of particle, called alpha and beta. Alpha particles travel more slowly than beta particles, but they are much heavier and generally have more energy. Alpha particles lose their energy easily and can be stopped by a thick sheet of paper. Beta particles lose their energy less easily and can pass through a sheet of aluminium.

Radioactive materials also throw out gamma rays. These travel as waves, and can pass through several centimetres of lead.

Radiation dangers

Small amounts of nuclear radiation come from radioactive materials inside the Earth all the time. This is called *background radiation*, and it

▶ This computer picture shows the spread of radioactivity across the northern hemisphere following an accident at the Chernobyl nuclear power plant, in the former Soviet Union, in April 1986. Many people died or became ill with radiation sickness.

normally does us no harm. However, too much radiation can be dangerous. For example, a natural radioactive gas called radon leaks up through the ground in some places and can collect in people's homes. Special pumps can get rid of the gas.

The radioactive materials in nuclear power plants are surrounded by thick concrete walls to stop the radiation escaping. A serious accident at a nuclear power plant can release radioactive dust and gas into the environment, contaminating water supplies and food. The radiation released in this way may cause cancer, perhaps many years later.

▶ FLASHBACK ◀

In 1873 James Clerk Maxwell predicted the existence of invisible kinds of radiation similar to light. Heinrich Hertz discovered radio waves in 1887, and so confirmed Maxwell's predictions. Then, in 1895, William Röntgen discovered X-rays. In 1896 Henri Becquerel found that uranium gives off an invisible radiation that affects photographic plates. He called this effect radioactivity.

▼ Most types of wave radiation belong to the same family. They are called *electromagnetic waves*. You can see the different types in the chart below.

• Doctors sometimes use nuclear radiation to destroy cancer tumours. Although the doses given are quite small, there are often unpleasant side-effects for the patients.

find out more
Atoms and molecules
Curie, Marie
Energy
Heat
Light
Power stations
Radio
Scanners
Sound
Stars
Waves
X-rays

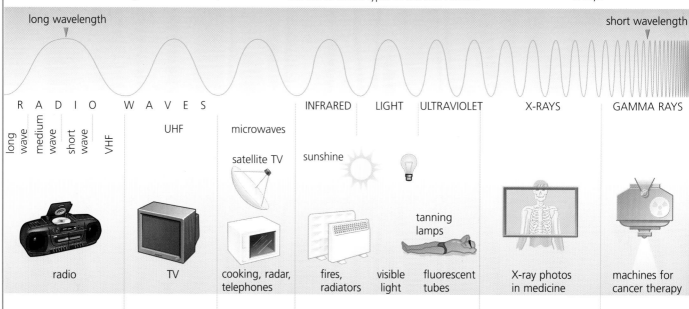

long wavelength | short wavelength

R A D I O   W A V E S | INFRARED | LIGHT | ULTRAVIOLET | X-RAYS | GAMMA RAYS

long wave | medium wave | short wave | VHF | UHF | microwaves

satellite TV | sunshine | tanning lamps

radio | TV | cooking, radar, telephones | fires, radiators | visible light | fluorescent tubes | X-ray photos in medicine | machines for cancer therapy

Radio

Radio lets you listen to someone speaking into a microphone thousands of kilometres away. The sounds themselves do not travel that far. Instead, they are changed into radio waves which travel through the air. When they reach your radio, they are changed back into a copy of the original sounds.

Radio waves are a kind of electromagnetic radiation. Like other kinds of radiation, such as light and X-rays, they can travel long distances at incredible speed – 300,000 km per second (the speed of light).

Sending sounds by radio

When someone speaks, their voice sends sound vibrations through the air. A *microphone* turns the vibrations into tiny changing currents called electrical signals. A *transmitter* is a device for making powerful radio waves, which are sent out in a continuous stream called a *carrier wave*. In simple transmitters, the electrical signals from the microphone control the strength of the radio waves being sent out, making them pulsate to match the sound vibrations. The pulsating waves are sent out from the transmitter through an *aerial* (a metal rod or wire). If the transmitter is powerful enough, the radio waves can travel thousands of kilometres.

The radio waves (called radio signals) are picked up by an aerial in a *receiver* (such as your radio at home). The receiver turns the pulsations into electrical signals, which are then turned back into a copy of the original sound in a *loudspeaker*.

Uses of radio

We use radio waves for many types of communication, apart from sound broadcasting. Police, fire, taxi and ambulance crews use two-way radios. Mobile phones are linked to the main telephone network by radio. Ships and aircraft use radio for communication and for navigation. Television uses radio waves for transmitting pictures and sound.

▶ FLASHBACK ◀

Radio signals were first transmitted over a distance of more than 1.5 kilometres by the Italian inventor Guglielmo Marconi in 1895. In 1901 he sent a radio message across the Atlantic Ocean from Cornwall, England to Newfoundland, Canada. It was later found that the radio waves bounced off an upper layer of the atmosphere, which explained how they could travel so far.

An American station, KDKA, started the first regular public broadcasting in 1920. In the 1950s the first small, portable radios began to appear.

◀ This little boy is listening to a portable radio in a street in Beijing, China. Portable radios are powered by batteries and can be used almost anywhere.

• Different radio stations broadcast on different frequencies, which are measured in hertz (Hz). The frequencies are marked on the radio's tuning scale. A frequency of 200 kilohertz (kHz) means that the transmitter is sending 200,000 radio waves every second.

find out more
Atmosphere
Electronics
Radiation
Recording
Satellites
Television
Waves

◀ How sounds are sent from a broadcaster at a radio station to your radio at home.

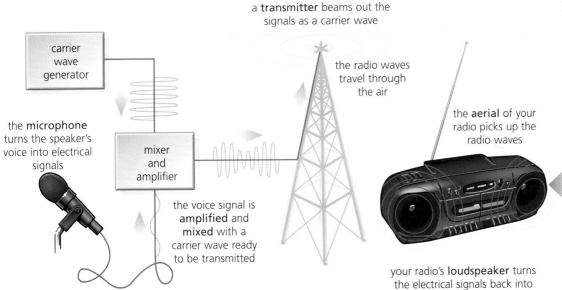

a **transmitter** beams out the signals as a carrier wave

carrier wave generator

the radio waves travel through the air

the **microphone** turns the speaker's voice into electrical signals

mixer and amplifier

the voice signal is **amplified** and **mixed** with a carrier wave ready to be transmitted

the **aerial** of your radio picks up the radio waves

your radio's **loudspeaker** turns the electrical signals back into sounds that you can hear

In the radio, you use a **tuner** to pick up the signals from a particular radio station. An **amplifier** boosts these signals for the **demodulator**, which separates the original voice signals from the carrier wave. Another **amplifier** boosts them for the loudspeaker.

Railways

Railways run on smooth metal tracks that allow heavy loads to be moved more efficiently than on roads. Locomotives (railway engines) are used to pull trains carrying either passengers or freight. A single locomotive may pull a load weighing thousands of tonnes.

Commuter trains carry large numbers of people to and from their work. High-speed passenger trains are widely used in Europe and Japan, the fastest ones travelling at speeds of over 300 kilometres per hour. Freight trains carry cargo. They are often manufactured specially to carry materials or goods such as oil, chemicals and cars. Some freight trains are over 500 metres long, and several locomotives may be needed to pull very heavy loads.

Types of locomotive

Most railway locomotives are powered either by electricity or by diesel engines similar to those in trucks and buses. In big diesel locomotives, the engine turns a generator which supplies electricity to motors between the wheels. Locomotives that use this system are known as diesel-electric locomotives. Electric locomotives can be small but powerful. Electric motors turn the wheels, supplied with electricity either from overhead wires or from an extra rail alongside.

Recent developments in locomotive design have involved lifting trains above the track, either with a cushion of air (the hover-train) or by the use of magnetic levitation (the maglev). Powerful magnets fitted onto the vehicle and onto a guide

▲ On many railways, traffic is controlled from signal centres fitted out with sophisticated computer equipment.

rail below are used to make the maglev trains 'float' above the track, clear of the rails. These trains can travel at high speeds because there is no contact with the track and so no friction to slow them down. In Germany and Japan maglev test vehicles have reached speeds of about 500 kilometres per hour. Not all maglev trains travel at high speeds. The low-speed, driverless trains used to transport people around some large airports are also maglev vehicles.

Constructing railways

The route for a railway needs to be as level as possible. Any slope or gradient has to be very gradual to stop the locomotive wheels from slipping. Curves have to be gentle because a train cannot turn sharply at high speed. Viaducts are built to carry the railway across valleys, and tunnels carry it through hills.

The railway track is made of steel rails laid on concrete or wooden sleepers. These help to take the weight of the passing train and keep the rails level. Short gaps are often left between the lengths of railway track to allow the rails to expand in warm weather. Without the gaps, the rails would bend out of shape. The two rails are laid a fixed distance apart, known as the *gauge*.

Railway signals

To avoid collisions, a railway line is divided into sections with a signal at the beginning of each section. A train can pass a signal only if it shows the right colour or the right position. The signals are operated from a signal box. In modern signal boxes, a computer ensures that only one train is travelling on each section of line. The signal box also controls the route of each train. The train is steered by special moving rails, called *points*, which make it change direction wherever the tracks divide.

Railway firsts

1804 The first steam locomotive is built by Richard Trevithick and runs in an ironworks in Wales.

1825 George Stephenson opens the first passenger railway, between Stockton and Darlington in England.

1863 The first part of the London Underground is built.

1960s Steam locomotives go out of service in many countries.

1981 The French high-speed train, the TGV (*Train à Grande Vitesse*), begins service between Paris and Lyon, travelling at an average speed of 210 km/h.

1990 The TGV reached a top speed of 515 km/h.

find out more
Engines
Magnets
Tunnels

▼ The high-speed Eurostar train carries passengers between Britain and mainland Europe via the Channel Tunnel.

Rain *see* Water • **Rainbows** *see* Colour • **Rayon** *see* Textiles

Recording

Recording is a way of keeping sounds or video pictures so that you can hear or see them later. People record music and sound on cassette tapes or compact discs (CDs), and moving pictures on video. Professional recordings are made in specially designed studios. But you can make recordings at home with a tape recorder or a camcorder.

• Most music recordings are made in *stereo*. This means that there are two versions of the music on the recording, each containing different parts of the original music. When the tape or CD is played, the sounds of the tracks come out of different loudspeakers.

We hear sounds when vibrations in the air enter our ears. We see pictures when light enters our eyes. We cannot save sound vibrations or light rays directly, so they need to be saved in some other way. When we record something, the sounds and pictures are turned into electrical signals. These signals are then used to make the recording. On a tape, sounds and pictures are recorded as patterns in a magnetic coating. On a CD they are recorded as microscopic pits in the surface of the disc. A tape player, CD player, video player or computer turns the recording back into sounds or pictures.

Tape and CD recordings

A microphone can turn sounds into electrical signals; a video camera can do the same with pictures. To record on a tape, the electrical signals are sent to a recording head. A cassette tape is coated with millions of tiny magnetic particles. The recording head magnetizes these particles weakly or strongly, depending on the strength of the signal. In this way, the signal is recorded as a magnetic pattern.

A CD recording is a pattern made by millions of microscopic pits arranged in rings on the surface of the disc. When the disc is played, a laser beam in the CD player reads the pattern in a similar way to a bar-code reader at a supermarket. Most CDs are 'read only': the recording on them cannot be deleted or recorded over. However, it is possible to record on to some kinds of CD, as with cassette tapes.

Analogue and digital

Any recording can be made either in analogue form or in digital form. An analogue recording is a direct copy or image of the electrical signal produced by the microphone or camera, recorded as a magnetic pattern. Until quite recently all recordings were analogue. Analogue recordings suffer from the problem that they can become distorted as they are copied or played back.

To make a digital recording, the signal is coded by turning it into a long list of numbers. This process is called *digitization*. It is carried out by an analogue-to-digital (A-to-D) converter. The converter measures the strength of the analogue signal thousands of times every second, and records each answer as a binary number (a number made up of only 0s and 1s). The long list of numbers is called a *digital signal*. Once a recording has been digitized, it is much less likely to be distorted or altered, and it can be copied exactly time after time.

Tape recordings can be either analogue or digital. On an analogue recording the magnetic pattern varies in just the same way as the original electrical signal. On a digital recording

▶ Analogue recording and playback.

microphone: sound waves make a crystal vibrate. This generates electric signals.

loudspeaker: electric signals make a coil vibrate. The coil's vibrations move the cone, which gives out sound waves.

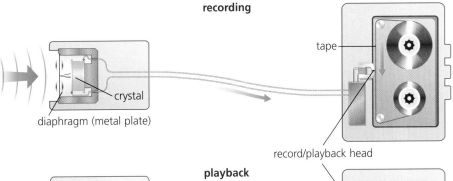

recording

crystal

diaphragm (metal plate)

tape

record/playback head

cassette recorder: electric signals through the recording head put a magnetic pattern on the tape.

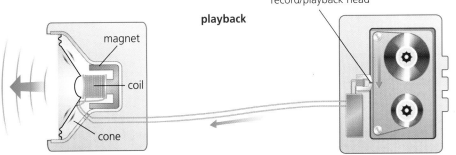

playback

magnet

coil

cone

cassette player: the magnetic pattern on the tape generates electric signals in the playback head. The signals are boosted by an amplifier.

the binary numbers 0 and 1 are stored as on-and-off magnetic patterns on the tape. CD recordings are always digital. The microscopic pits in the surface of the disc represent the 1s of binary numbers, while the areas with no pits represent 0s.

Recording studios

Simple sound recordings can be made with a single microphone and tape recorder, but most music recordings are made in a recording studio. In the studio, different voices and instruments are picked up by different microphones and recorded separately. Each recording is called a *track*. The different tracks are mixed together to make the final recording.

In an analogue recording studio, tracks are recorded on wide magnetic tapes. In a digital studio, the signals are digitized and recorded on a computer. The sound engineer then mixes the tracks on a computer screen.

▶ FLASHBACK ◀

The first successful sound-recording machine was built in 1878 by the American inventor Thomas Edison. The machine, called a

phonograph, recorded sound by making a groove on a cylinder covered in tin-foil or wax. The recording was made mechanically, because there were no electronics at the time. Flat discs (records) were first used for recording in 1888, and vinyl records in 1948. Magnetic tape was developed in the 1930s, and compact discs in the early 1980s.

◀ The sound-mixing desk in a large recording studio. Each of the sets of sliders controls the sound from one track of the recording. This is a 64-track studio – 64 tracks of sound can be recorded separately. It is also an analogue studio; in a digital studio the tracks are displayed on a computer screen and controlled through a keyboard.

find out more
Compact discs
Edison, Thomas
Radio
Sound
Television
Video

Refrigerators

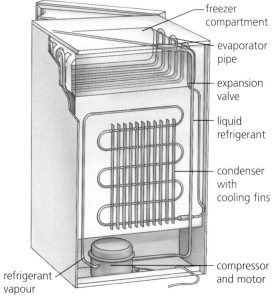

freezer compartment
evaporator pipe
expansion valve
liquid refrigerant
condenser with cooling fins
compressor and motor
refrigerant vapour

▲ In a compression refrigerator, a compressor pumps the refrigerant vapour through the condenser pipes, where it gives out heat and turns to liquid. As the liquid refrigerant passes through the evaporator pipe, it evaporates, taking in heat and producing a cooling effect. The vapour returns to the compressor and the cycle is repeated.

Refrigerators ('fridges' for short) are machines for keeping things cold. Small fridges are used in people's homes to store fresh food, and sometimes small amounts of frozen food as well. Very large fridges may be fitted inside container lorries and in ships. They are used to transport perishable foods over long distances.

Refrigerators keep food at a temperature of about 5 °C (5 degrees above freezing). They work by evaporation. When a liquid changes to a vapour, it takes heat from its surroundings. Refrigerators move heat, taking it away from the inside, which becomes colder, and giving it to the outside, which gets warmer. This cooling process is done by evaporating a special substance called a *refrigerant*. The refrigerant circulates around a sealed system of pipes.

Some fridges use a device called a *compressor* to pump the refrigerant around the circuit of pipes. Others use the heat from a gas flame to circulate the refrigerant. Refrigerators like this have no moving parts and make no noise, but they are much less efficient than compression refrigerators and cost more to operate.

• Freezers work in the same way as refrigerators, but are more powerful and give a greater cooling effect. In a freezer, food stays frozen at about −18 °C.

• Early refrigerators used ammonia as a refrigerant, but this was poisonous, and corrosive if it leaked. Safer, synthetic refrigerants were not developed until the 1920s.

find out more
Heat
Matter
Pollution

Roads

Modern motorways and ring roads help us to travel quickly from one place to another, avoiding busy city centres and residential areas. Yet many people feel that the building of new roads brings more traffic to an area, causing an increase in pollution. Local people often campaign very strongly against plans to build a new road in their area.

▲ These road workers in Nepal are spreading tar by hand onto the surface of a newly built road.

Motorways are fast roads with several lanes in each direction which are separated by a central reservation. They have no sharp bends, steep hills, crossroads or roundabouts. Traffic can travel a long way at high speeds without stopping. Many countries have motorway systems that link up the major cities. Dual carriageways are main roads with a carriageway

▼ This aerial photograph shows a busy intersection on the M62 motorway in northern England. At complex intersections like this one, the various roads are usually built on more than one level.

in each direction. Unlike motorways, they may have roundabouts and crossroads. Urban ring roads provide bypass routes around city centres to avoid traffic jams and residential areas. In country areas narrow, winding roads often follow the routes of ancient tracks.

Road construction

Before a new road can be built, the best route has to be chosen. This may not always be the most direct way between two places. Damage to the countryside, loss of wildlife habitats, inconvenience to local people, and the cost all have to be considered. Sometimes natural obstacles like rivers or hills have to be avoided.

When the route has been chosen, surveyors mark out the area ready for the huge earth-moving vehicles. A machine called a scraper loosens the top layer of soil, which is pushed aside by large bulldozers. The road has to be as level as possible, so cuttings are made through hills and the soil used to fill in small valleys and form embankments. Bridges and tunnels may also be needed.

The engineers then spread foundations of crushed rock to ensure the road can carry the weight of the predicted traffic. Sometimes cement or bitumen is added to the soil to form a solid base. Then a layer of concrete, called the base course, is put on the foundations. A machine called a spreader adds the top layer of asphalt (tar mixed with gravel) or concrete slabs joined by bitumen. The concrete is often strengthened with steel mesh. Road markings, lights and direction signs are added to help control the traffic.

▶ FLASHBACK ◀

The first paved roads were built in Mesopotamia (now Iraq) in about 2200 BC. Two thousand years later the Romans began to build hard, straight roads paved with stones. These roads connected together the various parts of the empire, allowing soldiers to travel quickly across Europe and North Africa. In the 15th and 16th centuries, the Incas of South America created a network of paved roads.

In the early 19th century John McAdam invented a new method of road building. The ground beneath the new road was drained and covered with small stones. Later, a coating of tar or bitumen was added to seal the surface, making it suitable for the rubber tyres of the motor car.

Robots

Most robots are machines that work in factories, doing jobs that would be boring, dangerous or very tiring for people. Androids are walking, talking robots that look like humans, but they are still a thing of the future. A robot would have to be very clever to do all the things you might do in a day!

Robots working in factories are called industrial robots. They work completely automatically, spraying cars with paint, cutting out car parts, stacking up heavy boxes, or welding pieces of metal together. Robot vehicles, including submarines and bomb-disposal robots, work in places which are too dangerous for people or too difficult to reach, and are remote-controlled by an operator. In some car factories, automatic robot vehicles collect and deliver parts by following lines drawn on the factory floor. They have bump sensors which stop them if they run into anything.

How robots work

Robots are moved by electric motors, or they may be hydraulic or pneumatic (powered by water or compressed air). Their movements are controlled by computer. The computer sends instructions to each of the robot's joints, telling it which way to move, and how far. The computer checks that the robot's arm is in the correct position. Even the largest robots can be positioned accurately enough to thread a needle.

Before a robot can do a job, such as spraying a car with paint, it must be taught the correct movements. An engineer does this by holding the spray gun and carrying out the movements. The robot's sensors detect the movements, and the computer remembers them so that it can repeat them exactly over and over again.

• The word 'robot' comes from the Czech word *robota*, which means 'compulsory service'. It was made up by Czech writer Karel Čapek in 1920.

• Robotics researchers are trying to make a robot that can find its way about and identify objects with video eyes. With artificial intelligence, the robot's computer brain gradually learns from its mistakes.

◀ This robot arm has been programmed to perform welding tasks on a car production line. The vast majority of motor cars made in the developed world are now produced by robots.

find out more
Computers

Rockets

The first rockets were made about 1000 years ago in China. They were like the firework rockets of today. The huge rockets that launch spacecraft and satellites into space work in exactly the same way as these firework rockets.

Rockets are full of fuel which burns to make a lot of hot gas. The gas expands rapidly, and when directed downwards through a nozzle, the force of this expansion pushes the rocket upwards.

Space rockets

The first long-distance rocket, the V-2 war rocket, was designed in 1942. Almost all space rockets are built along the same lines as the V-2. They have to be very powerful to escape from the pull of the Earth's gravity.

Space rockets usually have two or more sections called stages. Each stage has an engine and fuel supply. The first stage, at the bottom, lifts the rocket off the ground until the fuel runs out. It then falls away, and the second-stage engines take over, and so on.

Booster rockets attached to the sides of some space rockets often burn solid fuel. The boosters lift the main rocket up through the atmosphere. But most space rockets use liquid fuel. Fuel will not burn without oxygen, and because there is no oxygen in space, rockets carry another tank full of oxygen. Most rockets can only be used once, but the boosters from the Space Shuttle are recovered and used again.

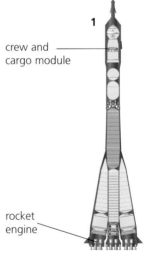

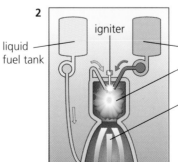

1
crew and cargo module
rocket engine

2
igniter
liquid fuel tank
liquid oxygen tank
combustion chamber
hot gases

◀ (1) A cutaway view of a liquid-fuel space rocket. It is carrying both the fuel and the oxygen (for burning) which it needs to work in space. (2) A diagram of a single rocket engine. The liquid fuel and liquid oxygen mix in the combustion chamber, then the igniter explodes the mixture.

• A speed of at least 40,000 km per hour, about 20 times as fast as Concorde, is needed to escape completely from the Earth's gravity.

find out more
Engines
Space exploration

Rocks and minerals

Rocks are the hard, solid parts that make up the Earth. You can find them all around you: in hillsides and mountains, in cliffs along the seashore, in the walls of large buildings, in the broken pieces of stone in the surface of the road. Rocks also lie beneath the oceans and seas, and under the ice in polar regions. Minerals are solid crystal shapes that are the building materials of rocks. Every kind of rock is made up of one or more minerals.

There are three main types of rock. *Igneous* rocks are formed at high temperatures from molten rocky material, either deep within the Earth or at the surface. *Sedimentary* rocks are formed from sand or mud (*sediment*) that has been laid down on land or in ancient rivers, lakes or seas. *Metamorphic* rocks are formed from sedimentary or igneous rocks that have been buried and heated up or put under great pressure.

Igneous rocks

Igneous rocks form from a hot molten mass of rocky material, called *magma*. Magma forces its way up through the Earth's crust from deep below the surface. Sometimes it reaches the surface as the lava (molten rock) which flows from an erupting volcano. When the magma cools, it hardens and forms rock. The kind of igneous rock that forms depends on what the magma is made of, where it cools, and how long it takes to cool. On cooling, the minerals in the magma form crystals. These crystals, like grains of sugar, have particular shapes depending on their chemical composition. The longer it takes the crystals to cool, the larger they become.

Igneous rocks formed deep in the Earth's crust are called *plutonic* rocks. A common type is granite, which consists of the minerals quartz, mica, feldspar and hornblende. Igneous rocks formed nearer the surface have finer grains and contain minerals such as olivine and magnetite but much less quartz. *Volcanic* rocks, which are formed at the surface, include basalt and pumice.

Sedimentary rocks

Soft and moving sands and muds at the bottom of rivers, lakes and seas form sedimentary rocks such as sandstone, mudstone and limestone. These rocks form part of the great cycle of erosion and deposition that takes place all the time. Rocks on land are broken down by the

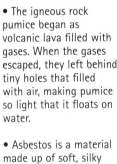

• The igneous rock pumice began as volcanic lava filled with gases. When the gases escaped, they left behind tiny holes that filled with air, making pumice so light that it floats on water.

• Asbestos is a material made up of soft, silky fibres obtained by crushing asbestos rock. It helps to insulate things from intense heat or fire, and is woven into protective clothing for fire-fighters. Asbestos can be very harmful to health, so strict safety rules must be followed wherever it is used.

▶ How different kinds of rock are formed, and, above, an example of each of the three main types.

Granite is an **igneous** rock. It is rich in the mineral quartz. Granite is the most common type of rock in the Earth's crust.

Shale is a soft **sedimentary** rock formed from fine clay. The fossil of an animal has been preserved in the stone.

Schist is a **metamorphic** rock formed from mudstone and limestone. It consists of fine bands of different-coloured minerals.

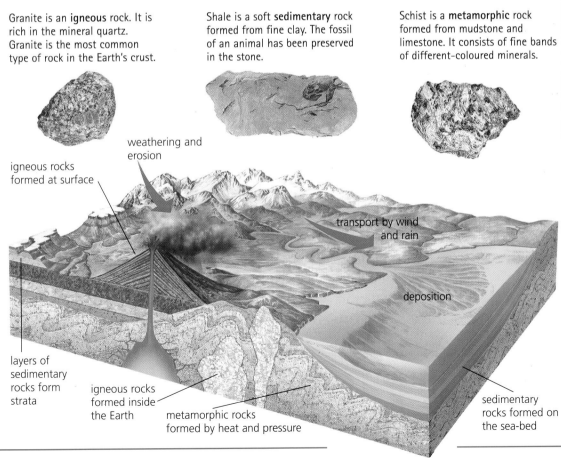

weathering and erosion

igneous rocks formed at surface

transport by wind and rain

deposition

layers of sedimentary rocks form strata

igneous rocks formed inside the Earth

metamorphic rocks formed by heat and pressure

sedimentary rocks formed on the sea-bed

95

find out more
Crystals
Earth
Metals
Mining

◀ The rocks that form these cliffs at Eleonore Bay, Greenland, have been built up in layers. These rocky layers are known as *strata*.

Large-scale metamorphism can take place when mountains are forming. For example, when major plates of the Earth's crust collide, great pressures are created. Both pressure and heat may alter ocean-floor sediments like mudstone and sandstone to form metamorphic rocks such as slate and schist.

action of wind, water, ice and plant roots. Small fragments of sand, silt or clay are then blown away or washed down into rivers or lakes. Over the years, millions of grains may be deposited (laid down) in a single place, building up into thick layers on land or underwater. The largest areas of sediment deposition are in the sea, where sediment is also eroded from the coastline by the action of the sea itself.

Sedimentary rocks also form when material from plants and animals that lived long ago is deposited, usually on the ocean floor. This kind of material is known as 'organic sediment'. On land, the plant material hardened to form beds of peat and coal. In the sea, the skeletons and shells of tiny animals hardened to form rocks such as chalky limestone. A famous example of this rock is the white cliffs of Dover, in southern England.

Two main changes have to take place in order for these sediments to form rock. First, the deeper layers of sediment are pressed down by the weight of sand or mud above, and the water is squeezed out of them. During the second stage, a kind of cement forms. The water that remains around the sediments contains dissolved minerals. As more water is lost, these minerals form crystals that fill the spaces between the rocky grains.

Metamorphic rocks

The word 'metamorphic' means 'later (or changed) form'. Metamorphic rocks have been altered by heat, or by heat and pressure. When magma forces its way up inside the Earth's crust, it heats the surrounding rock. If it passes through sandstone, this may be baked into hard quartzite. Limestone may be baked into marble. This process, which is called *metamorphism*, only affects small amounts of rock that are close to the rising magma.

Minerals

When you look in detail at a piece of rock such as granite, you can make out smaller pieces of individual minerals, often in a variety of colours and shapes. Minerals include such everyday substances as rock salt, asbestos, the graphite used as pencil lead, the talc used to make talcum powder, and the china clay used to make crockery. They also include gold and silver, and the ores of metals such as copper, tin and iron. Minerals that are prized for their beauty and rarity, like diamonds, are known as gems.

Some rocks are made up of only one mineral, while others contain many. Scientists have identified more than 2500 different minerals, but some of these are quite rare. You can identify a mineral by the shape of its crystals as well as by its colour or lustre (the way it reflects light). You can also do a 'streak' test. When minerals are scratched against a rough white surface, many of them leave a distinctive streak of colour. Haematite, the commonest form of iron ore, always produces a red streak.

• During metamorphism, the tremendous heat can melt the rock into a liquid. When the liquid cools, impurities come together to form new minerals. A very unusual example of this is the formation of diamonds in coal layers that have been heated by igneous rocks.

▼ Erosion by the wind has created these unusual sandstone rock shapes in the Arches National Park, Utah, USA.

Rubber

Rubber is a material used to make products as different as car tyres and surgeon's gloves. Its most important property is that it is elastic: it can be stretched or squeezed out of shape, but returns to its original form.

Natural rubber is made from a liquid called latex, obtained from the trunk of the rubber tree. The rubber tree originally grew in Central and South America. Today it is grown on plantations in hot parts of the world, particularly in South-east Asia. Since World War II synthetic rubber, made from chemicals obtained from oil, has become important. Over two-thirds of all rubber produced is now synthetic.

From tree to factory

Rubber is obtained from trees by a process called 'tapping'. The rubber tapper makes a shallow, diagonal cut in the bark of the tree. The milky latex slowly runs down from the cut into a cup fastened to the tree trunk. The latex is thickened and solidified into doughy sheets, then dried to make raw rubber.

Raw rubber is hard when cold and sticky when hot. It has to be processed before it is useful. The most important process is *vulcanization*. This involves mixing the rubber with sulphur. The resulting material is stronger and more elastic than raw rubber. Woven fabric or wires are often added to the material to strengthen it.

Over half of all rubber is used for vehicle tyres. Other uses include rubber gloves, hoses, tubing, elastic, tennis balls, and rubber seals to prevent leakage of water or oil in engines and pipelines.

◀ A rubber tapper in Indonesia. Once started, the latex will flow for a few hours, giving about 150 grams of rubber. A tapper can visit about 400 trees each day. Trees can be tapped only every two days, so each tapper looks after about 800 trees.

• Rubber balls were made by the Maya people in South America over 900 years ago.

• The vulcanization process was invented in 1839 by Charles Goodyear, when he accidentally spilled some rubber and sulphur on a hot stove.

find out more
Plastics
Springs

Satellites

A satellite is an object that travels around a larger object. The natural satellites of planets are often called moons. Many artificial satellites are launched into space by rockets or the Space Shuttle. Some send out radio, television and telephone signals, others take photographs of the Earth's surface or look into the depths of space.

A satellite travels in space along a path called an orbit. The orbit can be a circle or an oval shape. A satellite keeps going round and does not fly off into space because the planet's gravity holds onto it.

A satellite 300 kilometres from the Earth goes round in about 90 minutes, while one that orbits at a height of 36,000 kilometres goes round in 24 hours. A satellite in *geostationary orbit* is one which is in orbit above the Equator and moves round the Earth in the same time that the Earth takes to spin around its axis once. It always stays directly above the same point on the Earth's surface. The International Telecommunications Satellite Organization (Intelsat) has a network of communication satellites in geostationary orbit above the Earth. Other satellites travel round the Earth in a north–south direction. This is called a *polar orbit*. Each time the satellites come round, they pass over a different part of the Earth's surface.

Most artificial satellites get their power from panels of solar cells that turn sunlight into electricity. Some satellites are space stations where the crew can do experiments.

▼ The European Remote-Sensing Satellite (ERS-1) above the coast of the Netherlands. The satellite monitors shorelines and ocean currents. It can also be used to study crop growth and to detect oil spills.

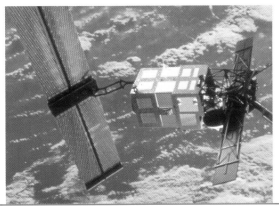

Types of satellite
♦ *Communications* satellites send telephone, television and radio signals between the continents.
♦ *Navigation* satellites send out radio signals that help aircraft and ships to find their way.
♦ *'Spy'* satellites take photographs of the land for military use.
♦ *Weather* satellites photograph cloud patterns and movements to help forecast the weather.
♦ *Scientific* satellites carry special measuring instruments.

find out more
Gravity
Moon
Navigation
Rockets
Solar System
Space exploration

Scanners

Scanners are machines used in hospitals to take pictures of the inside of a person's body. Scanners produce pictures with more detail than an ordinary X-ray photograph. They 'scan' the body, one thin strip at a time.

• The beam from a CAT scanner is made as weak as possible because X-rays are harmful.

CAT scanners (short for computerized axial tomography) X-ray a thin 'slice' of the body from many different angles. A computer processes the information to produce a picture of the slice. Doctors use CAT scanners to help them diagnose infections and broken bones as well as to detect certain diseases.

MRI scanners (short for magnetic resonance imaging) also take pictures of slices of the body, but without using X-rays.

• Ultrasound scanners are used to look at an unborn baby inside its mother's womb. They provide a safer method than using X-rays, which might harm the growing baby.

The scanner sends out powerful radio signals that make certain atoms within the patient's body wobble. The atoms then give out their own radio signals, which are detected by the scanner. It converts the body's signals into an image on a monitor. MRI scanners are mostly used to take pictures of the head and spine.

Ultrasound scanners give less detailed pictures, but are much cheaper, and more convenient for some jobs. They work by beaming sound waves into the body. A probe picks up the waves reflected from different layers inside the body, and the computer builds up its picture.

▼ Another method of taking scans is called positron emission tomography (PET). These scanners work by picking up the radiation from a radioactive material that is put into the patient's body. Here, the scanner's screen shows colour-coded images of 'slices' through the patient's brain.

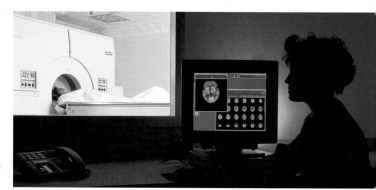

Scientists

Scientists ask questions about the world around us and how it works. To find answers to their questions, they make observations and try out experiments. They investigate everything from the tiniest sub-atomic particles to volcanoes, stars and the human brain.

There are several different branches of science. *Chemists* investigate all the different substances in the Universe and also make new ones. *Physicists* are interested in the particles that make up the Universe, and in different forms of energy such as heat, light and electricity. *Biologists* study living things. They look at their structure, how they behave, how they evolve, and how they interact with each other and their environment. *Geologists* examine what our planet Earth is made of and how it has developed since it formed. *Astronomers* are interested in stars, planets and galaxies, and how the Universe itself began.

All scientific investigations begin with a question. What is water made of? How far away are the stars? The next step is to think up an experiment that might help to answer the question, and make measurements to try to find answers. From the results of their experiments scientists develop a theory about what is happening. Often the theory uses mathematics to describe how things behave. They then make predictions from the theory to test whether it is useful or not. They set up new experiments to check whether or not the predictions are correct.

▶ Not all scientific experiments are done in laboratories. This scientist with the British Antarctic Survey is taking snow samples in the Rutford Ice Stream, using his sledge as a makeshift ladder.

Scavengers *see Ecology*

Seasons

As each season arrives, the length of daylight and the daily weather alter. Summer days are longer and warmer, while winter ones are shorter and cooler. Throughout the year, the different seasons bring changes to the world around us.

• In the night sky, the constellations you can see change day by day. The stars you see in the summer are quite different from the ones you can see in winter.

▲ This time-lapse photograph of the Midnight Sun was taken over northern Norway in midsummer. It shows the position of the Sun in the sky at one-hour intervals. Although the Sun is low in the sky at midnight, it never drops below the horizon.

Midnight Sun
Close to the North and South Poles, there are places where the Sun never sets for days or weeks in midsummer. These places experience the Midnight Sun. In midwinter, the opposite happens and the Sun never rises. This effect happens because the Earth's axis is tilted. The places that get the Midnight Sun lie inside the Arctic and Antarctic circles. The Antarctic has no permanent inhabitants, but people living near and inside the Arctic Circle have to adapt to long periods of continuous daylight or night-time.

In spring, after the short days of winter, the amount of daily sunshine increases as the Sun climbs higher in the sky. Summer is the warmest time of the year. The higher the Sun is, the stronger the warming effect of its rays. In autumn, the days shorten again, many trees drop their leaves, and the weather gets cooler as winter approaches.

Near the Equator, the number of hours of daylight does not change much through the year and it stays hot all year round. But the amount of rain that falls varies, so some tropical places have just two seasons: a wet one and a dry one. The seasonal changes are more extreme the further you are from the Equator. Near the Poles, there are enormous differences between the length of winter and summer days, but it never gets really warm because the Sun is not very high in the sky, even in midsummer.

The changing seasons

The Earth takes one year to travel around the Sun. We have seasons because the Earth's axis (an imaginary line going through the North and South Poles) is tilted to its path round the Sun at an angle of $23\frac{1}{2}°$. From about 21 March to 21 September, the North Pole is tilted towards the Sun and places in the northern hemisphere have spring followed by summer. At the same time, the South Pole faces away from the Sun. From September to March, the North Pole is tilted away from the Sun. Places in the northern hemisphere have autumn and winter while the southern hemisphere has spring and summer.

Each year, on or near 21 March and 23 September, the hours of daylight and darkness everywhere in the world are equal. These days are known as *equinoxes* (equinox means 'equal night'). At midday on the equinoxes, the Sun is directly overhead at places on the Equator. The days when the number of hours of daylight is greatest and smallest also have a special name. They are called the *solstices* and fall on or about 21 June and 21 December.

▼ Places on Earth receive different amounts of sunlight during the year as the Earth travels around the Sun.

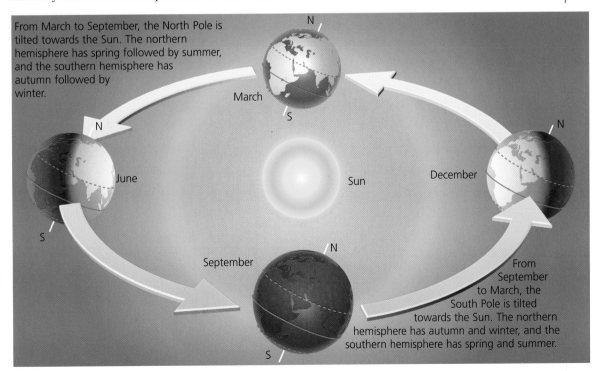

From March to September, the North Pole is tilted towards the Sun. The northern hemisphere has spring followed by summer, and the southern hemisphere has autumn followed by winter.

March

June

September

Sun

December

From September to March, the South Pole is tilted towards the Sun. The northern hemisphere has autumn and winter, and the southern hemisphere has spring and summer.

Ships and boats

Ships are large, sea-going vessels, usually with engines that drive an underwater propeller. Ships used to carry sails and to rely on the wind, but there are very few large sailing ships in use today. Boats are much smaller craft and can be propelled by people using oars or paddles, by small sails or by an engine. Boats are used worldwide on rivers and along coasts.

- Clippers got their name from the way they could 'clip' time off their sailing schedules. In the 1850s, a clipper could carry a cargo of wool from Australia to Britain in just over two months.

- The first steamships carried sails to assist their engines. Modern ship designers have looked at this idea again as they search for ways of saving fuel and cutting pollution from engines.

Boats, which in the past were built of wood or reeds, are generally now made of materials such as aluminium, plastic, rubber and fibreglass. Modern ships are built of steel and other metals. Most have one propeller (also called a screw), but some ships have two or even three. Usually, the propeller is driven by a diesel engine, but a gas turbine or a steam turbine may be used instead. For a steam turbine, the steam comes from a boiler using the heat from burning oil or from a nuclear reactor.

Boats

Boats are small craft, often with little or no deck. They are not generally large enough to be used safely in the open sea. Coracles and canoes are small boats, with no keel, which are moved through water by a paddle or a sail. *Coracles* are made from a frame of woven wooden strips covered with canvas or flannel. A covering of tar or pitch makes the boat waterproof. *Dugout canoes* are hollowed out from tree trunks. Craft such as these are found in many parts of Africa and Asia. In West Africa, for example, they are used for fishing near the shore. The Inuit people of North America build *kayaks*, which are wooden-framed canoes covered with sealskin.

▲ A Tirio Indian uses an outboard motor to help his dugout canoe through some rapids on the Tapanahoni River in Suriname, South America.

Sailing ships

The earliest sailing ships had just one mast and sail. As ships grew larger, more and taller masts were added, and several sails were carried on each mast. Most large sailing ships were *square-rigged*, which means the sails were set at right-angles to the length of the ship. The square-rigged clippers were the fastest sailing ships of all. Small sailing ships are still used for trading in many parts of the world. For example, *dhows* are used in the Middle East and *junks* in the Far East.

Cargo and passenger ships

Most modern cargo ships are specially designed to carry one type of goods only. The cargo might be several hundred cars, containers packed with washing machines, or grain pumped aboard through a pipe. Passenger ships are either ferries or luxury liners taking people on holiday cruises. In the past, before air travel became popular, huge passenger liners provided regular services between all the major ports of the world.

▼ Different types of ship and boat. (These drawings are not to scale.)

coracle

rowing boat

sailing yacht

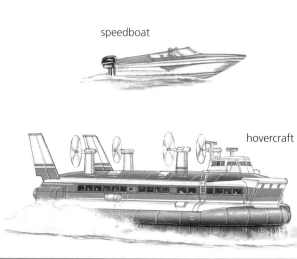

speedboat

hovercraft

Ships and boats

Lifeboats

A lifeboat is a boat specially built for saving people who are in difficulty at sea. Lifeboats are self-righting, so that if they capsize, they will turn the right way again by themselves. A lifeboat needs to have powerful engines and must be strong enough to withstand the force of the waves. Many big lifeboats have now been replaced by small inflatable rubber boats. These are better suited to rescue work close to the shore, helping people in trouble on yachts and small fishing boats.

Hovercraft

Hovercraft carry people and goods over land and sea. Some are used as passenger and car ferries. They are sometimes called 'air-cushion vehicles' because they float on a cushion of air, which is made by pumping air downwards underneath the hovercraft. The vehicle is pushed forwards by propellers on top, usually driven by ordinary aircraft engines. Hovercraft are able to travel over any fairly flat surface and move easily from water to land without stopping. In Canada, for example, they work across land, water and ice.

▶ FLASHBACK ◀

The ancient Egyptians built long reed boats as far back as 4000 BC. The Greeks and Romans used long narrow galleys powered by lines of rowers. Between about 700 and 1000 AD, the Vikings

invaded much of northern Europe in their famous long ships. In the 16th century sailing ships called galleons were used to carry cargoes and as fighting ships.

Ships driven by steam engines started to replace sailing ships in the early 1800s. The first steamships were propelled by large paddle wheels. The engineer Isambard Kingdom Brunel had a major influence on modern ship design. His ship the *Great Britain* was a revolution in design. Launched in 1843, it had a screw-propeller and was built of iron. Steamships needed huge supplies of coal as fuel, so they became much bigger.

▲ A crowded ferry crosses the Mekong River in Cambodia, South-east Asia.

find out more
Canals
Engines
Matter
Navigation
Radar
Submarines

container ship

cruise liner

Silver

Silver is a brilliant-white shining metal. Along with gold and platinum, it is one of the so-called precious metals. Silver is widely used to make jewellery, tableware and ornaments. It is also used to coat other cheaper metals in a process called silver-plating.

Some silver is found in the ground in its pure state, but it is mostly found combined with other substances. Silver can easily be beaten into shape or be given a highly polished surface. It is used to coat mirrors because it reflects light well. Silver is also a very good conductor of electricity. It is used in the electrical switches inside computers and other electronic equipment.

Silver has a special use in photography. When silver is combined with certain other substances, such as chlorine and iodine, it forms salts which are very sensitive to light. If a light shines on them, they turn black. For this reason, large quantities of silver are used to make photographic films and special, light-sensitive papers.

Many nations have at various times used silver coins. Nowadays, though, alloys (mixtures) of other metals are often used instead, except for coins to celebrate special events.

▶ A silver vesta box for keeping matches in. The four marks that make up the hallmark can be seen along the rim.

• In many countries, objects made of silver, gold or platinum must be tested and hallmarked before sale. The hallmark guarantees that the object contains a high enough proportion of the precious metal. It may also give information on the manufacture and on the year and place in which the object was tested.

find out more
Metals
Mining

Soaps and detergents

Soap is a natural detergent – a chemical that we add to water when we want to clean things. Soap helps the water to get right into the fabric of the things being washed, and to remove any dirt or grease. Synthetic detergents work in a similar way, by helping water to spread out and clean things.

Washing soap is made by adding plant oil or animal fat to a strong alkali. Soap and a substance known as glycerol or glycerine are produced. The glycerine is washed out, and perfumes, preservatives and colourings are added. Finally, the soap is cooled and cut or shaped.

Soaps do not work well in hard water, which contains lots of calcium and magnesium salts. The soap reacts with these salts to form a 'scum'. This scum leaves rings on baths and a whitish film on glassware. Because they do not form a scum, synthetic detergents are now used instead of soaps for many cleaning purposes. They are made from chemicals obtained from oil. Other substances are added to detergents to make them clean better and to make the water look soapy.

• Soap was made from animal fats and wood ashes until the end of the 18th century. Then caustic soda was used in place of wood ashes, and plant oils such as olive oil and palm oil began to replace animal fats.

• The first synthetic detergents were developed during World War I (1914–1918). Household detergents became common in Europe and North America in the 1950s.

find out more
Acids and alkalis
Water

How detergents work

This is a magnified view of the structure of a detergent molecule. The head of the molecule is attracted to water, and the tail is attracted to grease.

When dirty clothes are washed in detergent, the tails of the detergent molecules bury themselves in any greasy dirt, leaving the molecule heads in contact with the water.

As the clothes move about, the greasy dirt breaks free from the fabric. Detergent molecules surround the greasy particles, which are rinsed away in the water.

Solar System

The Sun and all the things in orbit around it make up the Solar System. It includes a family of nine planets, most of which have one or more moons. Lots of other smaller objects, such as asteroids (minor planets) and comets, are also travelling around the Sun.

- The word 'solar' means 'to do with the Sun'. It comes from *sol*, the Latin word for Sun.

- Venus comes nearer to Earth than any other planet in the sky. You can easily find it by looking for a really brilliant object in the western sky in the evening or in the eastern sky in the morning.

▼ The major planets in the Solar System, in order from the Sun, and a plan of their orbits around the Sun. The planets are drawn to scale, so their sizes can be compared with the Sun. (The distances between the planets are not drawn to scale.)

1 Sun
2 Mercury
3 Venus
4 Earth
5 Mars
6 Jupiter
7 Saturn
8 Uranus
9 Neptune
10 Pluto

The Sun, which is a star, is by far the largest body in the Solar System. Planets are different from stars because they do not give out any light of their own. They shine because they reflect light from the Sun.

The nine planets

Mercury, Venus, Earth and Mars are small rocky planets that together make up the inner Solar System. Jupiter and Saturn are giant balls of gas. Uranus and Neptune are giant planets made of gas and ice. Pluto, the smallest planet, is composed of rock and ice. The diameter of Jupiter, the largest planet, is about one-tenth of the Sun's diameter. The Sun could contain a thousand bodies the size of Jupiter.

Some of the planets are surrounded by a system of rings. Saturn is circled by beautiful coloured rings made up of pieces of ice and rock and particles of dust. Uranus has a set of 10 very narrow rings, which were only discovered in 1977 when the planet crossed in front of a star and the rings cut out the starlight for a few moments.

All of the planets, except Pluto, have been visited or passed by spacecraft carrying cameras and scientific equipment.

The paths of the planets

The orbits of the planets round the Sun are not circles but have a squashed oval shape called an ellipse. A planet's distance from the Sun changes as it moves along its elliptical orbit. Most of the planets vary only slightly in their distance from the Sun, but Pluto varies from about 30 to about 50 times the Earth's distance. Although Pluto is further away than Neptune most of the time, a small part of its orbit crosses just inside Neptune's.

Apart from Pluto's, none of the planetary orbits is tilted by much, so the Solar System is like a flat disc. Pluto's orbit is tilted by 17°, so when it crosses Neptune's orbit it passes above Neptune and there is no danger of a collision. The way gravity acts means that the further a planet is from the Sun, the longer the period of time it takes to complete an orbit. The Earth takes one year to travel round the Sun, Mercury 88 days and Pluto nearly 248 years.

The spaces between the planets are huge compared to their sizes. For example, if the Sun were the size of a football, the Earth would be the size of this spot • and would be 30 metres away! ▶

Average distance of each planet from Sun, and time taken to orbit Sun

planet	million km	days
Mercury	58	88
Venus	108	224.7
Earth	150	365.3
Mars	228	687.0

planet	million km	years
Jupiter	778	11.86
Saturn	1427	29.46
Uranus	2870	84.01
Neptune	4497	164.8
Pluto	5900	247.7

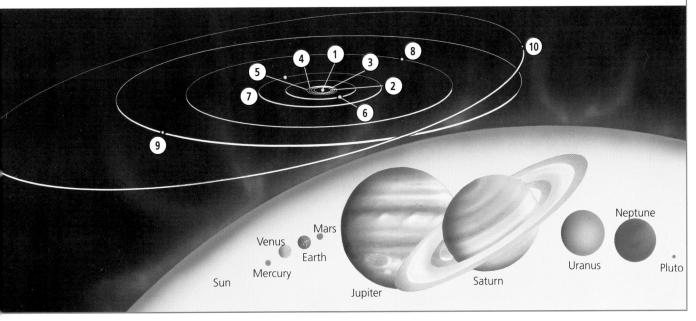

◄ This picture of Mars clearly shows the polar ice-cap that covers the planet's northern tip. The dark area around the polar region is a huge plain measuring about 10,000 km across. The plains in the northern hemisphere of Mars are lightly cratered, while those in the southern hemisphere have many more craters.

▼ In July 1997 the spacecraft *Pathfinder* landed on the surface of Mars. On board was this robot vehicle called *Sojourner*. It was powered by a solar panel, allowing it to move for a few hours each day. The 63-cm-long *Sojourner* carried equipment to study the planet's rocks.

• Jupiter, the giant of the Solar System, is wrapped in bands of swirling clouds. It has no solid surface but consists mostly of liquid hydrogen. Its largest cloud feature, called the Great Red Spot, has existed for at least 140 years.

Discoveries

1543 Copernicus publishes his theory that the planets circle the Sun.

1609 The German astronomer Johannes Kepler shows that the planets move in oval (elliptical) orbits round the Sun, not in circles.

1609–1610 Galileo finds four of Jupiter's moons and the rings of Saturn.

1686–1687 Newton publishes his laws of gravity and motion, which explain the movements of the planets.

1781 The British astronomer William Herschel discovers the planet Uranus.

1846 Neptune discovered by Johann Galle in Germany, following the predictions of two mathematicians, John Couch Adams and Urbain Leverrier.

1930 Pluto discovered by the American astronomer Clyde W. Tombaugh, again following predictions.

Moons

Seven of the planets have moons that orbit around them. These moons are natural satellites, and altogether more than 60 of them are known in the Solar System. The biggest moons are the four major moons of Jupiter, Titan (one of Saturn's moons), and the Earth's Moon.

Asteroids and comets

In the gap between the orbits of Mars and Jupiter, thousands of pieces of rock circle the Sun. These are the minor planets, or asteroids. The largest asteroid is Ceres, which measures about 940 kilometres across. However, most asteroids are much smaller than this, and there are only about 200 asteroids with a diameter of more than 100 kilometres. Ceres is a round globe, but asteroids usually have an uneven shape.

Astronomers have recently discovered a number of icy asteroids beyond the orbits of Neptune and Pluto. These objects are probably part of a huge ring of icy bodies called the Kuiper Belt.

A comet is a lump of ice, dust and rock that travels through the Solar System. Comets usually travel in a very stretched-out orbit around the Sun. Some of the comets come from the Kuiper Belt.

Astronomers think that others come from a huge cloud of icy bodies, called the Oort Cloud, which surrounds the Solar System and stretches out to a distance of about one light-year (about 10 million million kilometres).

Birth of the Solar System

Most astronomers believe that the Solar System was formed when a huge cloud of gas and dust fell together, pulled by its own gravity, just under 5 billion years ago. The cloud was spinning very slowly at first, but as it fell inwards, it began to spin faster and faster until it formed a central ball surrounded by a flattened sheet of gas and dust. As it continued to fall together, the central ball became hotter. Eventually it became hot enough to shine like a star and became our Sun.

In the surrounding sheet of gas and dust, tiny particles of dust collided and stuck together to form small rocky or icy bodies. These then collided with each other to form complete planets like the Earth, and the cores (central parts) of the four giant planets (Jupiter, Saturn, Uranus and Neptune). Huge amounts of gas fell in to surround the core of each of the giant planets. Many of the remaining lumps of material collided with the newly formed planets and moons and blasted out craters on their surfaces. The lumps that were left over are the asteroids and comets that we see today.

find out more

Astronomy
Comets
Copernicus, Nicolas
Earth
Galilei, Galileo
Gravity
Meteors and meteorites
Moon
Space exploration
Sun

Sound

Sounds are caused by vibrations. They travel to our ears in the form of waves. Sounds can be high or low, loud or quiet. If they are too high, we cannot hear them. If they are too loud, they can damage our hearing.

If you pluck a guitar string, it vibrates, and the air next to it is squashed and stretched over and over again. As a result, lots of 'squashes' and 'stretches' travel through the air, rather as ripples spread across water. These are *sound waves*. You cannot see them, but when they enter your ears, they make your eardrums vibrate and you hear a sound. Sound waves can travel through solids, liquids and gases. But they cannot travel through a vacuum (empty space).

Speed of sound

Sound waves travel through air at a speed of about 330 metres per second, although this varies with temperature. Sound travels nearly a million times more slowly than light, which is why you see a distant flash of lightning before you hear it.

Supersonic aircraft travel faster than sound. When they do so, they create shock waves, rather like the bow wave at the front of a fast boat. You hear a 'sonic boom' as each shock wave passes you.

Echoes

Sound is reflected from hard surfaces. If you stand well back from a cliff and shout, you hear a reflected sound a few moments later. This is called an echo. Ships use underwater echoes to measure their distance from the sea-bed (or other objects). The system is called *sonar*. It involves sending out sound pulses and measuring the time taken for them to be reflected back. The longer the time taken, the greater the distance.

Frequency and pitch

When something vibrates, for example a guitar string, the number of vibrations per second is called the *frequency*. It is measured in hertz (Hz). A string that vibrates 1000 times per second has a frequency of 1000 Hz. The higher the frequency, the higher the *pitch* of the note – the higher it sounds to your ear.

The human ear can hear sounds between about 20 Hz and 20,000 Hz, although the upper limit becomes lower as you grow older. Sounds above the range of human hearing are called *ultrasonic* sounds. Some of these can be heard by dogs, cats and bats.

Loudness and noise

Big vibrations produce louder sounds than small ones. They make the air vibrate more. If a sound is too loud or unpleasant, we call it noise. Noise levels need to be checked because very loud sounds can permanently damage the ears.

▶ Scientists measure noise levels using the decibel (dB) scale. Here are some typical values on the scale.

• The speed of sound is called Mach 1. The aircraft Concorde cruises at Mach 2.2, which is more than twice the speed of sound.

▼ In factories, noise levels are checked to make sure that they do not go above the legal limit. Continuous loud noise damages hearing and may lead to deafness later in life.

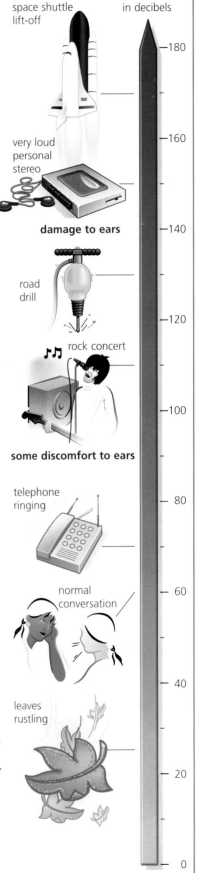

noise level in decibels

space shuttle lift-off — 180

— 160

very loud personal stereo

damage to ears — 140

road drill — 120

rock concert

— 100

some discomfort to ears

telephone ringing — 80

normal conversation — 60

— 40

leaves rustling — 20

— 0

Space exploration

Since the beginning of the Space Age in October 1957, human beings have continuously looked for new ways of exploring space. Astronauts have walked on the Moon's surface, and can now live and work for months in space stations. Robot spacecraft have already explored much of our Solar System. Despite these achievements, it would take any spacecraft thousands of years to reach the nearest star after the Sun.

The Space Age began in October 1957, when the former Soviet Union launched the artificial satellite *Sputnik 1* into orbit around the Earth. One month later, *Sputnik 2* carried the dog Laika into space. By the 1960s rockets from both the Soviet Union and the USA were carrying men and women into orbit around the Earth.

Astronauts

Astronauts, or cosmonauts as they are called in Russia, are people who leave the Earth and travel into space. They may spend many months in space on board a spacecraft or space station. Once they are in orbit, away from the pull of the Earth's gravity, astronauts become weightless and float around inside the spacecraft.

In space, astronauts study the Earth below, the distant stars and galaxies, and the space around them. They launch and repair satellites. They measure the effects of weightlessness on themselves and other creatures, and they make things, such as certain kinds of medicine, that would be difficult to make on Earth.

Going to the Moon

The exploration of the Moon began when the unmanned Soviet spacecraft *Luna 1* flew past the Moon in January 1959. In 1966 the probe *Luna 9* made the first soft landing on its surface. In July 1969 three US astronauts flew to the Moon in the *Apollo 11* spacecraft. The main spacecraft, piloted by astronaut Michael Collins, orbited the Moon, while Neil Armstrong and Edwin Aldrin landed in the tiny Lunar Module. During five more Moon missions, the last in 1972, astronauts explored the Moon's surface, collecting rock samples and setting up scientific equipment.

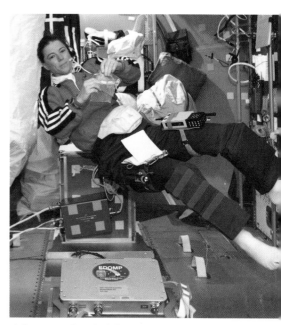

▲ Astronaut Bonnie J. Dunbar floats weightlessly in the Space Shuttle's *Spacelab* science module. To stay in one place, astronauts must fix themselves to something, and they sleep strapped into sleeping bags.

The Space Shuttle

In April 1981 the first US Space Shuttle was launched. Unlike earlier spacecraft, the Shuttle can fly into space many times. Only the huge main fuel tank is new for each flight. The Shuttle takes off upwards like a rocket, but lands back on Earth like a glider on a runway. On board, astronauts conduct scientific experiments and launch satellites from the cargo bay. In 1990 the Shuttle *Discovery* launched the space probe *Ulysses*, which flew over the north and south poles of the Sun. In the same year the Shuttle placed the Hubble Space Telescope into orbit.

Space stations

A space station is a home in space where astronauts can live and work. It contains everything that they need, including water, food and air, which must all be brought up from Earth. The first space station was *Salyut 1*, launched by the Soviet Union in 1971. The most

• The USA is currently building a replacement for the Space Shuttle, the X-33 *VentureStar*. It will be fully reusable, with no expensive throw-away fuel tanks.

▼ These astronauts are servicing the Hubble Space Telescope, which is docked onto the Shuttle *Endeavour*. Outside the spacecraft astronauts must wear a protective spacesuit. Its outer layers protect against radiation, and visors provide protection from the Sun. The backpack contains the air and power supplies.

◀ The first human in space was Yuri Gagarin from the Soviet Union. On 12 April 1961 he orbited the Earth once in Vostok 1, in a trip lasting 108 minutes.

Missions to the planets

Since the Moon missions, most space exploration has been carried out by unmanned spacecraft travelling to other planets. They take photographs and use radar and other instruments to collect information, which they send back to Earth by radio. Some spacecraft fly past planets, but others orbit or land on the surface.

The first successful planetary spacecraft was *Mariner 2*, which flew past Venus in 1962. The *Viking 1* and *2* spacecraft (1976) landed on Mars and dug up samples of soil. The two *Voyager* spacecraft sent back detailed pictures of Jupiter (1979), Saturn (1980–1981), Uranus (1986) and Neptune (1989) before passing out of the Solar System altogether. The probe *Galileo* was launched in 1989. It flew past Venus (1990), then back past Earth, and in 1995 it launched a probe into Jupiter's atmosphere, before beginning an exploration of Jupiter's moons. In 1997 the *Pathfinder* spacecraft landed on Mars. It released a tiny robot vehicle called *Sojourner*, which sent back high-quality photographs of the planet's rocky surface.

More space missions are planned for the future. *Cassini* is on a long mission to Saturn and its moons, and other spacecraft are intended to meet up with asteroids and comets.

recent space station is the Russian *Mir*, launched in 1986. Work is now under way on a new space station, the ISS (International Space Station), which should be completed in 2004. But astronauts should be able to stay in it full time before then.

• The longest stay in space was by Russian cosmonaut Dr Valery Polyakov, who returned to Earth on 22 March 1995 after spending 438 days on board the space station *Mir*.

find out more
Moon
Rockets
Satellites
Solar System

Springs

Springs are usually made of metal and come in many different shapes – thin flat strips, wires or rods. Springs store energy that can be allowed to escape quickly or slowly. As energy escapes, the spring can move something or drive a piece of machinery around. Coiled-up springs are used in the 'clockwork' motors inside some toys.

• A material has passed its elastic limit when it stays out of shape, or breaks, when dented. Brittle materials such as china and chalk are hardly elastic at all. They break very easily because they cannot bend or stretch.

• Even your body has elastic fibres in it. For example, try pinching the skin on the back of your hand. As soon as you let go, the skin returns to its original shape.

find out more
Clocks and watches
Materials
Motor cars

A spring is usually made of a special type of steel so that it will return to its original shape, however much it has been squeezed, bent or stretched. The steel in the spring must also not crack or break after it has been bent a large number of times.

Springs are made of stretchy or springy materials that we call elastic. A rubber band is elastic. Wood, steel and plastic are much less stretchy than rubber bands but they are still elastic. For example, a plank of wood sags when you walk on it but straightens when you step off. Rubber and rubber-like plastics called *elastomers* can act as springs too. They are often used to cut down vibration. Engines are usually mounted on rubber or elastomer, and some bicycles have suspension systems with elastomer springs. In some springs air is used as the elastic material. If you put your finger over the hole in a bicycle pump and push in the handle, you find that trapped air is springy. This idea is used in gas springs and in some vehicles.

▼ Some different kinds of spring.

Helical (coil) springs are used in some bed mattresses to make them soft to lie on.

In a clockwork motor, a coiled-up strip of steel unwinds slowly to turn the wheels.

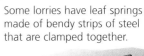

Some lorries have leaf springs made of bendy strips of steel that are clamped together.

The spring in a door bell is a strip of bendy metal.

Stars

On a clear, dark night you can see hundreds of twinkling stars in the sky. These stars are huge glowing balls of gas like our Sun, but they are fainter because they are so much further away. Light from even the nearest stars takes years to reach us. We look up at the stars through air that is constantly blowing about, so their light is unsteady and they seem to twinkle.

Our Sun is one ordinary star among millions of other stars. In the centre of all stars, particles of hydrogen gas crash into each other and give off large amounts of nuclear energy. This process, called nuclear fusion, is what makes stars shine. The stars are all speeding through space but they look still to us because they are so far away. The patterns they make in the sky stay the same. Groups of stars that make patterns in certain parts of the sky are called *constellations*.

Some bright stars look quite red, while others are brilliant white or bluish; the Sun is a yellow star. The stars shine with different colours because some are hotter than others. The Sun's surface is about 6000 °C. The red stars are cooler and the blue-white ones hotter, at about 10,000 °C or more.

The birth of a star

Stars are being created all the time. They begin as clumps of gas and dust in space. Once this material begins to collect, the force of gravity makes it pull together even more strongly. In the middle it gets warmer and denser until the gas is so hot and squashed up that nuclear fusion can start. When this happens, a new star is born. Often, lots of stars form near to each other in a giant cloud to make a family of stars, which we call a *cluster*.

Giants and dwarfs

Astronomers have worked out that stars cover a huge range of sizes. They often call the large ones 'giants' and the small ones 'dwarfs'. The Sun is a smallish star, though some are even smaller. The kind of star called a *white dwarf* has a diameter

- About 5780 stars can be seen by the naked eye without a telescope. On a clear dark night around 2500 are visible from one place on Earth at any one time.

- In 1997 scientists discovered a new star in our galaxy, which is bigger than any other star yet discovered. It is over 100 thousand times as big as our Sun. If it were at the centre of our Solar System, it would engulf all the planets as far out as Mars. It is invisible from Earth because it is obscured by gas and dust.

▶ The birth and death of two stars. The top star, a star more massive than our Sun, will become a red supergiant. This will eventually explode as a supernova and end up as either a neutron star or a black hole. The bottom star, which is more like our Sun, will first become a red giant and then end up as a white dwarf. The blue arrows show how the material blown off the stars is recycled into nebulas, which become future stars. (This illustration is not to scale.)

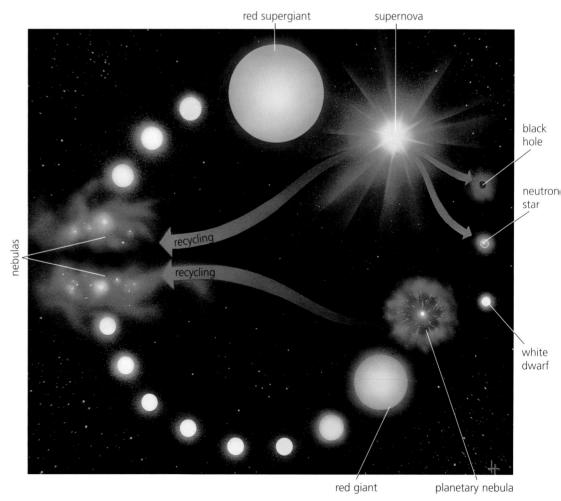

red supergiant · supernova · black hole · neutron star · white dwarf · planetary nebula · red giant · nebulas · recycling · recycling

The Horsehead Nebula in the constellation Orion. Astronomers use the word 'nebula' to describe misty patches of light in the sky that are not stars. These glowing clouds of gas and dust either give out their own light or reflect light from nearby stars.

• In 1987 a supernova exploded in a galaxy very near to our own called the Large Magellanic Cloud, which can be seen from countries in the southern hemisphere.

less than one-hundredth that of our Sun. In contrast, there are some truly immense stars, called *red giants*, which are several hundred times the Sun's size. The bright red star called Betelgeuse, in the constellation Orion, is about 500 times bigger than the Sun.

Double stars

The Sun is a single star on its own, but most stars are in pairs. The force of gravity keeps them together and they orbit round each other like the planets going round the Sun. Sometimes the two stars in a pair pass in front of one another. This blocks out some of the starlight and makes the pair look fainter for a short time. The brightest star in the sky, Sirius, is a double.

The death of a star

Stars do not live for ever. Eventually the hydrogen gas fuel in their core is used up. When this happens, the star changes and eventually it dies. Old stars swell up into red giants. They can blow off some of their gas into space, like a big smoke ring. Astronomers can see stars like this at the centres of shells of glowing gas.

The Sun is already about 5000 million years old and is reckoned to be about half-way through its life. In the far future, the Sun will become a red giant and swallow up the planets near to it. After that, it will shrink until all its material is squashed into a ball about the size of the Earth. It will then be a white dwarf and fade away.

Stars rather more massive than the Sun finish up with a tremendous explosion, called a *supernova*. When a supernova goes off, it shines as brightly as millions of Suns put together for a few days. Only three supernovas have definitely been recorded in our own Galaxy during the past 1000 years.

Following a supernova, the remains may shrink into a *neutron star*. A neutron star is only about 20 kilometres across, but it is so dense that it has the same mass as several Suns. Often a neutron star is a *pulsar*, which sends out beams of radio waves as it spins very rapidly. On Earth we detect its signals as a series of rapid pulses. After a very big star explodes in a supernova, the remains may collapse inward to form a black hole. A *black hole* has such a strong gravitational pull that no matter or energy – not even light – can escape from it.

Star names

Many of the bright stars have their own names. Most of them were named by early Arab astronomers of centuries ago. Arabic names often start with the two letters Al, such as Altair, Aldebaran and Algol. Others come from Greek or Latin, such as Castor and Pollux, the 'heavenly twins' in the constellation Gemini. Stars are also called after the constellation they are in, with a Greek letter in front. Alpha Centauri, the nearest bright star after the Sun, is one example. Fainter stars do not have names and are known just as numbers in catalogues.

• Stars are not scattered evenly through space. They form into large groups of stars called *galaxies*. Our own Galaxy (also called the Milky Way) contains around 100,000 million stars. It would take light 100,000 years to cross it (light travels at a speed of 300,000 km per second). There are billions of galaxies in the Universe.

find out more
Astronomy
Atoms and molecules
Black holes
Galaxies
Gravity
Solar system
Sun

The Pleiades, or Seven Sisters, is one of the easiest star clusters to see in the night sky. It has six bright stars, and many more are visible through a telescope. The blue area of the picture is a cloud of cold gas and dust between the stars.

Submarines

Submarines are sea-going vessels that can travel underwater as well as on the surface. Most submarines are naval ones that patrol the oceans and can fire torpedoes or missiles. Special submarines called submersibles are used for engineering and exploration.

Submarines have long hollow ballast tanks, which can be filled with air or water. To dive and stay underwater, the tanks are filled with water so that the submarine can sink to a particular depth and then remain there. To return to the surface and float there, the water is blown out of the ballast tanks by compressed air. This makes the submarine lighter and so it rises again.

A submarine is driven forward by propellers, and fins called hydroplanes tilt to force it downwards or upwards. Submarines cannot use diesel or petrol engines when submerged, because these kinds of engine cannot work without oxygen. Instead, small submarines use electric motors and batteries. Larger ones are nuclear-powered. Their nuclear reactor boils water, producing steam that turns turbines to drive the propellers. Nuclear submarines can stay submerged for many weeks.

Submersibles

Submersibles can reach much greater depths in the ocean than a diver. They are used to collect scientific information as well as to carry out maintenance work on oil rigs and undersea pipelines. Most submersibles carry a small crew of people, although some carry only equipment, such as television cameras. The crew on board a manned submersible use movable arms to hold tools or to pick up objects and samples from the sea-bed.

▶ FLASHBACK ◀

The first vessel to travel underwater was built by the Dutch inventor Cornelius Drebbel. It was propelled by oars from Westminster to Greenwich on the River Thames in 1620. The first proper submarine was the *Turtle*, a wooden vessel built by the American engineer David Bushnell in 1776. In 1875 the Irish engineer John Holland built the first of a series of submarines in the USA. The modern naval submarine is descended from them. In 1958 the world's first nuclear submarine, the USS *Nautilus*, travelled under the Arctic ice and surfaced at the North Pole.

▲ This research submersible, the Johnson Sea-Link, is being launched for use in underwater exploration.

● When a submarine cruises just below the surface of the sea, the crew use a special telescope called a *periscope* to see where the submarine is going and to identify other vessels on the surface. The periscope is raised up like a hollow mast, and it has a sloping mirror at each end and lenses inside.

◀ How a submarine dives underwater and surfaces.

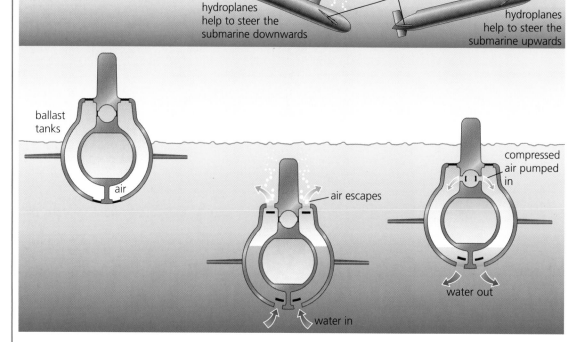

DIVING   SURFACING

hydroplanes

hydroplanes help to steer the submarine downwards

hydroplanes help to steer the submarine upwards

ballast tanks

air

air escapes

compressed air pumped in

water out

water in

● The world's biggest submarines are the Russian Typhoon Class. They weigh over 26,000 tonnes.

find out more
Matter
Ships and boats

Sugars *see* Carbon

Sun

The Sun is a giant ball of hot gas, 150 million kilometres from the Earth. Although it is an ordinary star, like the thousands of others you see in the night sky, without it there would be no life on Earth. Human beings and all other livings things on the Earth need the heat and light energy from the Sun to stay alive. People have always recognized how important the Sun is and have often worshipped it as a god.

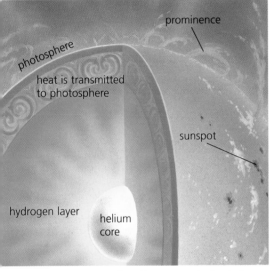

▲ A cross-section of the Sun. Energy travels slowly from the core through the thick hydrogen layer and heats the photosphere (surface).

The temperature near the outside of the Sun is about 6000 °C, but in the centre it is more like 16 million °C. Inside the core, enormous amounts of energy in the form of heat and light are produced by a process called nuclear fusion. This energy makes the Sun shine.

The Sun also gives out harmful X-rays and ultraviolet rays. Most are soaked up in our atmosphere and do not affect us. Sunlight is very strong and no one should ever stare at the Sun or look at it through any kind of magnifier, binoculars or telescope. Even with dark sunglasses it is still dangerous to look at the Sun. Astronomers study the Sun safely by looking at it with special instruments.

Activity on the Sun

Close-up pictures of the Sun show that it looks like a bubbling cauldron as hot gases gush out and then fall back. Some of the gas is streaming away from the Sun all the time into the space between the planets.

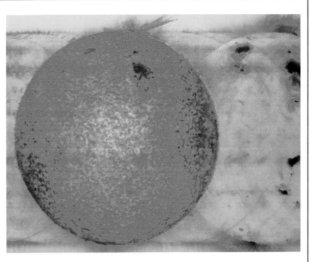

▶ Giant tongues of hot gas called *prominences* leap out violently from the Sun to heights of 1 million km or more. The prominence in this ultraviolet photograph of the Sun consists of glowing gases moving violently outwards from the Sun's surface.

Sometimes dark blotches called *sunspots* appear on the Sun's yellow disc. The average number of spots on the Sun goes up and down over a cycle of about 11 years. Near to sunspots, flares like enormous lightning flashes can burst out. When particles that shoot out from the Sun reach the Earth, they cause the lights in the night sky that we call an aurora.

▼ Solar panels on the roofs of buildings can trap the Sun's heat to provide hot water. When we use energy from the Sun as heat, or turn it into electricity, we call it *solar power*.

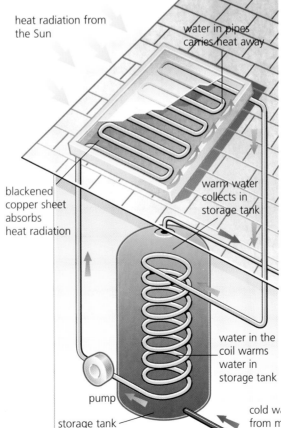

find out more
Atmosphere
Atoms and molecules
Eclipses
Ecology
Electricity
Energy
Heat
Light
Plants
Power stations
Seasons
Solar System
Stars

● Light from the Sun, travelling at 300,000 km per second, takes 8.3 minutes to reach the Earth.

● Solar cells can turn sunlight directly into electricity. Satellites in space have huge panels of solar cells to supply their electricity. In remote areas of some hot countries, solar cells provide electricity to pump water and to power appliances.

Telephones

A telephone lets you talk to other people almost anywhere on Earth, simply by pressing a few buttons. There are hundreds of millions of telephones in the world. They are all linked by a complicated telecommunications network which carries telephone calls, fax messages, television and radio signals, and computer data.

When you speak into a telephone receiver, sound waves of your voice go into the mouthpiece. A microphone there changes the sounds into patterns on a tiny electric current, which are called signals. These signals travel from the receiver into the telephone network. When people telephone you, signals come from the network to the earpiece of your receiver. A thin metal diaphragm inside the earpiece vibrates to produce sound waves that enter your ear.

When you press the number buttons on your telephone, the receiver sends signals to your local telephone exchange. The exchange uses the numbers to route your call through the telephone network – to another local telephone, to another telephone exchange, or to the telephone network of another country.

Electrical and digital signals

Signals go from your telephone to the local exchange along copper cables. Most exchanges are linked by optical-fibre cables through which the signals travel as pulses of laser light. Microwave beams, sent between dishes on tall towers, link some signals. International calls go along undersea optical-fibre cables or via satellites high above the Earth.

Before they go through the telephone network, most signals are changed into digital signals (the changing electric current is changed into patterns of the digits 0 and 1). It is easy to send these as pulses of electricity, light or microwaves. The digital signals turn back to normal signals before reaching your telephone. Signals from mobile telephones go by radio to a radio mast and then into the telephone network. Mobile phones only work when close to a radio mast.

▶ FLASHBACK ◀

The first device to send messages by electricity was the telegraph. The messages were sent by tapping out a special code, known as the Morse code. Invented by Samuel Morse in 1838, the code uses different combinations of short and

long bursts of electric current to represent different letters of the alphabet. The Scottish-American inventor Alexander Graham Bell was experimenting with a telegraph machine in 1875 when he realized it was transmitting sounds. In this way he invented the telephone almost by accident. The first telephone exchange, which connected 21 people, was opened in 1878. Although the first automatic exchange was built in the 1890s, operators still worked most exchanges until the 1920s. A transatlantic telephone cable was laid in 1956, and the first communications satellite, Telstar, was launched in 1962. Optical fibres carrying digital signals have been widely used since the 1980s.

◀ Light beams emerge from the end of a cable of optical fibres. The fibres are made from flexible glass. Telephone conversations travel along optical-fibre cables as pulses of laser light. A thin optical-fibre cable can carry 40,000 digitized telephone calls at the same time.

find out more

Fax machines
Information technology
Radiation
Radio
Satellites
Waves

• There is a photograph of Alexander Graham Bell in the article on Inventors.

▼ This illustration from a 1904 edition of *Le Petit Journal* shows the telephone exchange for the Paris Opera in France. Patrons used to call the Opera and listen to the evening's performance over the telephone.

Telescopes

When you look through a telescope, distant things seem nearer and bigger. A telescope collects light and funnels it into your eye, allowing you to see things that are too faint to be seen by the eye alone. A telescope also lets you see more detail than you would otherwise see. Telescopes range in size from simple tube-shaped ones that you hold in your hands to the huge telescopes used by astronomers to study the stars.

Telescopes that collect light are known as optical telescopes. The simplest kind, called a *refracting telescope*, has a tube with a lens at each end. The front lens collects light and brings light rays together to form an image of a distant object. The image is then magnified by the *eyepiece*, the lens that you look through. A *reflecting telescope*, or reflector, uses a concave (dish-shaped) mirror to collect light. The main mirror concentrates the light onto a smaller mirror which then reflects it into an eyepiece.

The bigger the main mirror or lens, the more light it collects, and the fainter the things it can see. Larger telescopes also show more details than small ones. The blurring effects of the atmosphere often prevent telescopes from showing as much as they should, so they are often built on high mountains or put into space.

Radio telescopes collect radio waves from distant stars and galaxies. These telescopes consist of big dishes to collect the radio signals. Radio telescopes can be used in daylight as well as at night.

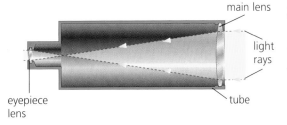

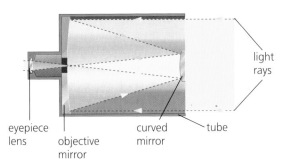

eyepiece lens

objective mirror

curved mirror

tube

◀ A refracting telescope. The main lens focuses light from a distant object to form an image in front of the eyepiece. The eyepiece lens magnifies this image.

◀ A reflecting telescope. Light is focused by a large curved mirror. The eyepiece lens magnifies the image of the distant object.

• Orbiting clear of the atmosphere, the Hubble Space Telescope (HST) can see far more clearly than telescopes on the ground. Shuttle astronauts had to correct the main mirror in December 1993, and carried out further repairs to the telescope in 1997.

▶ FLASHBACK ◀

Hans Lippershey, a Dutch spectacle-maker, is usually said to have invented the first telescope in 1608. The next year, the Italian astronomer Galileo Galilei built a telescope and turned it on the sky. In 1671 Isaac Newton announced that he had made the first reflecting telescope.

Observatories

Observatories are buildings from which astronomers look at the sky. The two most important types of ground-based observatory are optical observatories and radio observatories. In space, unmanned observatories orbit the Earth on satellites.

Optical observatories have ordinary telescopes housed in big domes. At night, the dome opens and can turn to point the telescope at different parts of the sky. Many telescopes are now operated by computers. Optical observatories need to be built away from city lights and in cloud-free places. The best sites are on mountain-tops in warm places. The telescopes in radio observatories do not need to be inside buildings. Also, radio waves from space can pass through clouds, so it is not important where the observatory is built.

Thousands of years ago, astronomers watched the movements of the Sun, Moon and stars from observatories, long before the invention of telescopes. Over 4500 years ago Stonehenge was constructed in Britain, possibly for use as an observatory. At this time Babylonians watched the night sky from stepped towers called ziggurats.

Telescope records

Largest radio telescope
Puerto Rico, Caribbean: 300 m across

Most powerful radio telescope
Very Long Baseline Array (VLBA), USA: consists of 10 dishes spread along a line 8000 km long

Largest optical telescope
Keck telescope, Hawaii: 10 m across and weighs 270 tonnes

find out more
Astronomy
Galilei, Galileo
Lenses
Mirrors
Newton, Isaac
Space exploration

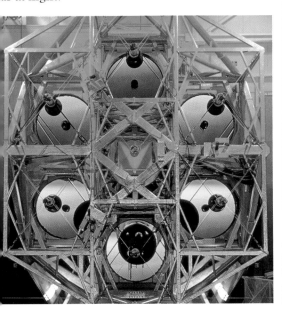

◀ A close-up view of the Multiple Mirror Telescope (MMT) on Mount Hopkins in Arizona, USA. One of the world's largest reflecting telescopes, it has six separate mirrors (each measuring 1.8 m across), which work together to form a single large mirror.

Television

Television is a way of sending moving pictures from one place to another. It lets us watch events from around the world as they happen, whether they are sporting competitions, wars or natural disasters. Television has a huge effect on the lives of many people. For most of us, it is our main way of getting news and entertainment. In developed countries, almost every home has a television set.

A television (TV) camera turns moving pictures into electrical signals. The signals are sent to your television set by radio waves, via satellites, or through cables under the ground. The television set uses the signals it receives to make a moving picture on its screen and to make sound through its speaker.

In Western countries most people watch a few hours of television each day. If they have the right receiving equipment, they can choose from dozens of channels broadcasting a wide range of programmes, from soap operas to wildlife films and current affairs discussions. Advertisers pay huge sums of money to have their products shown during the commercial breaks in television programmes, especially the programmes they know millions of people will be watching.

What is a TV picture?

Moving pictures are made by showing still pictures one after another very quickly. Each still picture, called a frame, is slightly different from the one before. Our eyes cannot react quickly enough to see one picture change to the next, and our brains are fooled into seeing a moving picture. Each frame is made up of hundreds of thin horizontal lines, and each line is made up of hundreds of coloured strips. You do not see the lines or strips because they all merge together to make up the complete picture.

In most of Europe, television pictures are made up of 625 lines, and 25 frames are shown every second. In the USA and Japan, pictures have 525 lines and 30 frames are shown every second. In a new kind of system, called high-definition television (HDTV), pictures are made up of thousands of lines instead of hundreds. This makes the pictures far more detailed.

From camera to TV set

The lens of a television camera collects light from a moving scene, just like an ordinary camera.

• All TV pictures were in black and white until 1953, when the first successful colour pictures were broadcast in the USA.

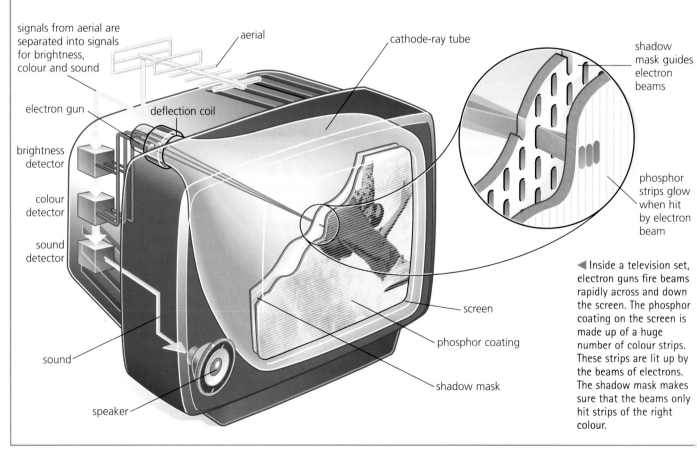

signals from aerial are separated into signals for brightness, colour and sound

aerial

cathode-ray tube

shadow mask guides electron beams

electron gun

deflection coil

brightness detector

colour detector

sound detector

phosphor strips glow when hit by electron beam

sound

screen

phosphor coating

shadow mask

speaker

◄ Inside a television set, electron guns fire beams rapidly across and down the screen. The phosphor coating on the screen is made up of a huge number of colour strips. These strips are lit up by the beams of electrons. The shadow mask makes sure that the beams only hit strips of the right colour.

- The largest TV screen in the world was built by Sony for an international exhibition in Tokyo. It measured 45 m by 24 m.

- The smallest TV screen is on a Seiko TV-wrist watch. It is black and white, and measures just 30 mm across.

TV pioneers

In 1926 a Scottish engineer John Logie Baird (1888–1946) gave the first public demonstration of television in England. He used a cumbersome mechanical camera, and the pictures produced were shaky and blurred.

Earlier, in 1923, a Russian inventor and engineer, Vladimir Zworykin (1889–1982), invented an electronic image-scanning device. In the 1930s a receiving device was developed using a cathode-ray tube. This all-electric system quickly replaced Baird's relatively crude device.

▲ John Logie Baird was one of the pioneers of television. In 1929 his equipment was used to make the first television broadcast (without sound). He was also responsible for the first outside TV broadcast (of the Derby horse race in 1931).

Inside the camera is a light-sensitive device which scans the pattern of light, line by line, strip by strip. It works out how much green, red and blue light there is in each strip, and codes this information in an electrical signal. When it has scanned one frame, it starts on the next. In this way, the moving scene is turned into an electrical signal. Sound is added to the signal later.

There are several ways of getting the signals from a television camera to your television set. In *terrestrial* (Earth-based) television, the signals are sent from a transmitter as radio waves and are picked up by a normal television aerial. In *satellite* television, the signals are sent by microwaves to a satellite orbiting the Earth. The

satellite sends them down again, scattered over a wide area. To collect them, you need a small satellite dish. In *cable* television, the signals travel through electrical cables under the ground, straight to your television.

In *digital* television, television signals are made up of a list of numbers. This gives clearer pictures. In the future, all television will be digital. It will also be in widescreen format, just like movie pictures.

How a TV set works

Signals from many different television stations arrive at your television set. The first thing it does is pick out the signal from the station you want. This is called *tuning*. Next, it takes the signal apart to make signals for red, green and blue, for brightness, and for sound. It uses these signals to re-create the picture on its screen and to make sound. Behind a television screen there are three 'guns' which shoot streams of tiny particles called electrons at the back of the screen. The red, green and blue signals control the output of one electron gun each. The beams of electrons are not themselves coloured, but they make red, green and blue light when they hit the screen. The sound signal is sent to an amplifier and a speaker.

▶ In September 1997, thousands of people watched the funeral of Diana, Princess of Wales on giant TV screens in London's Hyde Park. Millions of people around the world saw pictures of the funeral on their television sets.

Textiles

Textiles are all around you. They form the clothes you wear during the day, and the bedding that you sleep in at night. Towels, carpets, curtains and furniture covers are made of textiles. Cars contain textiles on the seats and inside tyres. And textiles are used for many other useful things, such as belts, parachutes, tents, sails, and bandages.

A textile is a cloth or fabric made from fibres. These might be natural fibres that come from plants or animals, such as cotton, silk, flax and wool. Or they could be synthetic fibres made in factories, such as nylon, polyester and acrylics. Many textiles contain a mixture of natural and synthetic fibres.

Other kinds of textile

Denim: a strong woven cotton cloth used for jeans and other tough garments.
Linen: a fabric made from the flax plant.
Satin: a fabric woven with a smooth surface, so that it appears shiny.
Tweed: a heavy woollen cloth with a rough surface.
Lycra®: shiny fabric made with stretchy synthetic fibres, used to make sportswear.
Gore-Tex®: a 'breathable' waterproof fabric used for outdoor clothing and tents.

Making textiles

The first step in producing most textiles is to twist the fibres together to form a yarn or thread, like the cotton on a reel or the wool in a ball of wool. Yarn is made by *spinning* the fibres to twist them together, either by hand or using a machine. Most synthetic fibres are made from chemicals extracted from oil. The fibres are produced by forcing the chemicals through tiny holes in a nozzle called a *spinneret*. As the fibres emerge, they are spun to make yarn.

The yarn may then be dyed before being made into cloth or fabric. This is mainly done by *weaving*, in which lengths of yarn are criss-crossed on a loom, or by *knitting*, in which the yarn is linked in loops. A pattern can be formed by weaving or knitting different-coloured yarns together. *Felting* is a third way of making textiles, in which the fibres are matted together.

Once made, a textile may next need some kind of treatment – washing or cleaning to remove dirt and impurities, bleaching to whiten it, or waterproofing or fireproofing. Many textiles have patterns printed on their surface. This is done using large rollers which carry a pattern of coloured dyes.

Textile properties

The properties of a finished textile depend partly on the fibres from which it is made. Textiles made from natural fibres are generally softer, absorb moisture better and are more heat-resistant than synthetic fabrics. Synthetic textiles are stronger, harder-

▼ A Guatemalan woman using a simple loom. It is called a backstrap loom, because the warp threads are kept tight by a strap that runs around the weaver's back. With her left hand, the woman is lifting up one set of warp yarns to create a gap (the *shed*). With her right, she is pushing the weft tight, using a tool called a *reed*.

▶ Weaving involves passing a yarn, called the *weft*, over and under many parallel yarns, called *warp* threads.

1 Each warp thread is attached to a wire loop called a *heddle*.

2 Using the heddles, one set of warp threads is raised and another lowered. The weft is passed through the gap (the *shed*), using a *shuttle*.

3 The warp threads are reversed, so that the lower one is above, and the higher one is below. The weft passes through the shed again.

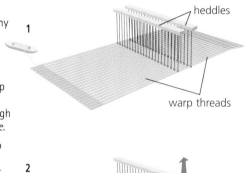

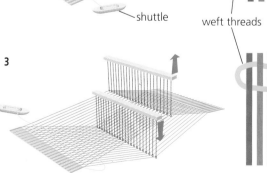

1 — heddles — warp threads

2 — shed — shuttle — weft threads

3

wearing and more crease-resistant than natural fabrics. Modern textiles may be made from a mixture of natural and synthetic fibres to give the best combination of properties for a particular product. Cotton–polyester shirts, for example, are soft and comfortable, but they are also hard-wearing and easy to iron.

► FLASHBACK ◄

Weaving was one of the first crafts. Remains of cotton seeds and clothes have been found that date back to 3000 BC. Cotton was grown in places as far apart as Mexico, northern India and China, and silk fabrics were woven 4000 years ago in China. In medieval Europe most textiles were made from wool, although the richest people wore silks. The Arabs introduced cotton fabric to Europe, but at first it was not very popular. Indian cotton became fashionable in Europe during the 17th century, and in the early 18th century cheaper cotton fabrics began to be made in England, using cotton grown in the USA.

During the Industrial Revolution, two important machines for making textiles were invented in the UK. These were the spinning jenny, which spun yarn, and the power loom, which wove cloth. These machines could spin and weave much faster than people. American cotton was shipped to Britain, where it was made into cloth using the new inventions.

The first synthetic fabric, rayon, was invented at the end of the 19th century. It was made from cellulose, a plant fibre that is extracted from wood pulp. Nylon was introduced in the 1930s, and in the 1940s many other synthetic fabrics were produced.

▼ The quality of these synthetic yarns is being tested, using a machine that measures how strong a pull is needed to break the yarn.

find out more
Materials
Plastics

● Silk is made from fine threads unwound from the cocoon of the silkworm, which is the caterpillar of a kind of moth.

Time

We see time passing in the natural world around us: the seasons and the weather change, plants grow, the stars shine at night and the Sun shines during the day. All over the world people need to keep to the same standard time and to measure it in the same way. International time is kept by atomic clocks in laboratories around the world.

● If we use a 12-hour clock, we have to add a.m. or p.m. to show whether a time is before or after the middle of the day. By using the 24-hour clock we can avoid confusion, so 1.00 p.m. is called 13.00 hours, 2.00 p.m. is 14.00, and so on.

● The basic unit of time used by scientists is the second. There are 60 seconds in a minute, 60 minutes in 1 hour, and 24 hours in 1 day. A day is the time it takes the Earth to turn once on its axis.

find out more
Calendars
Clocks and watches
Einstein, Albert
Seasons

◄ In this view of the Earth taken from space, you can see the outline of California, on the west coast of the USA. The USA, which includes Alaska, spans a total of six time zones. When the time is 12 noon in New York on the east coast, for example, it is only 9 a.m. in Los Angeles, California.

The day is our most important period of time. Day begins when the Sun rises in the east, and night comes when the Sun sets in the west. Noon (midday) at a particular place occurs when the Sun reaches its highest point in the sky. As the Earth spins round, places across the world, from east to west, have noon one after the other. Places further east are already having their afternoon or evening while places further west still have not reached midday.

Measuring time

People used to measure time from when it was noon, but this meant that at every longitude in the world the time was different. In 1880, the whole of Britain adopted the average local time at Greenwich in London as its standard time. It was called Greenwich Mean Time (GMT). At an international conference in 1884, the world was divided up into 'time zones', each about 15 degrees of longitude wide. The standard time in each zone differs from the zones on either side by one hour. If you travel to another country, you usually have to alter your watch. The further you go, east or west, the bigger the time change.

Tidal power *see* Power stations • **Tin** *see* Metals • **Toadstools** *see* Living things

Tools

We use tools around the home to prepare food, to work in the garden or to mend the car. A tool is any device which helps you do a job. In factories, much larger machine tools are used for cutting and shaping metals, plastics and other materials.

Hand tools use the force of your muscles. Power tools are driven by another energy source, such as electricity or compressed (squashed) air. Specialized electric power tools include screwdrivers, hammer drills, chainsaws and hedge-trimmers. They are powered either from the mains or by rechargeable batteries. Extra parts can be attached to hand-held electric drills to convert them into jigsaws, circular saws, or sanders.

Machine tools are generally faster, more powerful and more accurate than hand-held tools. Many machine tools are now controlled by computers. Machine tools can make lots of identical parts one after another. Specific machine tools include lathes, grinders, shapers, planers, and drilling and milling machines.

For gripping
A high gripping force can be produced by lever action or by turning a screw thread.

G-clamp to hold parts together for glueing

▲ ▶ A selection of commonly used hand tools and power tools.

For making holes
Hand drills have gearwheels to make the bit turn faster. Electric motors turn very fast anyway, so electric drills have gearwheels to slow the bit down.

bit

electric drill for boring holes

For shaping and smoothing
Some shaping and smoothing tools cut into the material with a sharp edge. Others have hundreds of tiny points to rub the material away.

plane for smoothing wood

For hammering
A heavy metal head gives most force when hammering, but a wooden or plastic head is less likely to damage the material being struck.

claw hammer for driving in nails and pulling them out

For measuring and checking
Before materials are cut, drilled or fixed, it is important to check that all sizes and positions are correct.

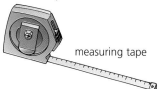

measuring tape

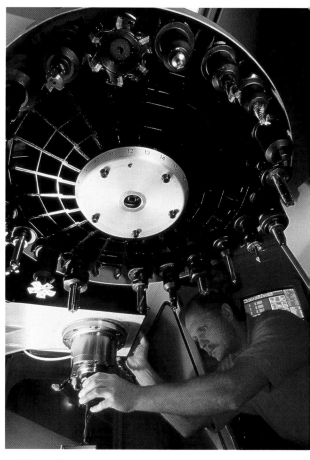

▲ This machine tool is controlled by computer. In the 1980s the computerized control of machine tools brought about a 'second revolution' in mass production.

For cutting
Some cutting tools have a sharp, smooth blade. Others have a jagged blade with small teeth along the edge.

axe for chopping wood

electric jigsaw for cutting curves

For screwing and bolting
Nuts, bolts and screws have special tools to turn them. Tools like this must fit properly to give a firm grip, so they are made in a range of sizes.

straight-headed screwdriver for slotted screws

open-ended spanner

find out more
Forces and pressure
Machines
Motors
Robots

Towers

Towers are buildings that are much higher than they are wide. They can stand alone or form part of a building.

Greater understanding of how structures work has been the key to constructing taller and taller towers. Some medieval builders built church towers that collapsed. The tallest medieval church tower still standing belongs to Lincoln Cathedral in England. It is 160 metres tall.

Buildings of over 10 storeys were made possible by the invention of lifts in the late 19th century.

Now, skyscrapers can be built that have over 100 storeys.

Some of the world's highest towers are radio and TV masts. The tallest free-standing tower is the CN Tower in Toronto, Canada, at 553 metres. The tallest building in the world is the Petronas Twin Towers, in Kuala Lumpur, Malaysia. It stands 452 metres high.

• One of the most famous towers in the world is the Leaning Tower of Pisa, in Italy. It leans because its foundations, laid in 1174, are not secure and are 'settling' unevenly. Despite recent attempts to strengthen the foundations, the structure is still in danger of collapse.

find out more
Building

height in metres

500

400

300

200

100

0

Petronas Twin Towers, Malaysia 1996

Eiffel Tower, France 1889

Pharos of Alexandria, Egypt about 280 BC

Great Pyramid of Khufu, Egypt about 2580 BC

Lincoln Cathedral, England 1307

Empire State Building, New York 1931

CN Tower, Canada 1976

Tunnels

Tunnels are underground passages that are built for different purposes. Tunnels in cities carry road and rail traffic beneath the streets and buildings. In the countryside, road and rail vehicles use tunnels to pass under rivers or through hills and mountains. Deep below the waters of the English Channel, the Channel Tunnel links Britain with the rest of Europe.

In cities, people use subways (short tunnels) to cross under busy roads. Tunnels also bring water supplies to the city and take away waste water or sewage. Narrow tunnels may contain telephone and other cables. Underground mines consist of tunnels dug into deposits of coal or minerals. Mines are by far the deepest tunnels of all.

Building a tunnel

Tunnels that are to lie just below the surface may be built by the cut-and-cover method.

A large long ditch is dug, and then covered over to form a tunnel.

Most tunnels have to go deeper and are dug down into the ground. Cutting machines are used to gouge out soft rock or soil, or the rock is blown out with explosives. Supports or a lining made of steel or concrete prevent the tunnel collapsing. A tunnelling machine is often used to build a tunnel. Powerful motors push the machine forwards, and its cutting teeth or tools excavate the rock or soil.

• The longest tunnel in the world is in the USA. It carries water 169 km from a reservoir to New York City, and was completed in 1944.

find out more
Building
Explosives
Mining
Railways
Roads

▶ The Channel Tunnel consists of two main train tunnels, with a third service tunnel between them. Cross-tunnels link the main tunnels to each other and to the service tunnel.

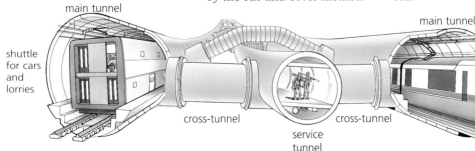

main tunnel

shuttle for cars and lorries

cross-tunnel

service tunnel

cross-tunnel

main tunnel

passenger train

Universe

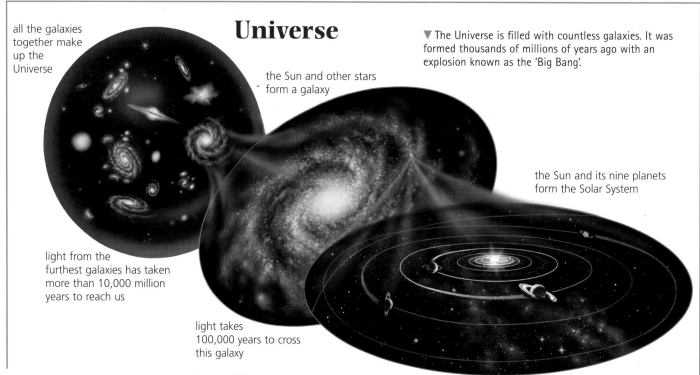

all the galaxies together make up the Universe

the Sun and other stars form a galaxy

▼ The Universe is filled with countless galaxies. It was formed thousands of millions of years ago with an explosion known as the 'Big Bang'.

the Sun and its nine planets form the Solar System

light from the furthest galaxies has taken more than 10,000 million years to reach us

light takes 100,000 years to cross this galaxy

light takes about one day to cross the Solar System

▲ This image is made up from over 200 separate pictures taken by the Hubble Space Telescope. It shows masses of very faint and distant galaxies.

find out more
Astronomy
Atoms and molecules
Galaxies
Solar System
Space exploration
Stars

We use the word 'Universe' to mean everything that exists, from the Earth to the most distant parts of space. The Universe contains countless galaxies of stars. The furthest ones we can see are so distant that their light takes billions of years to reach us.

People used to think that the Earth was the centre of the Universe. Although the Earth is important to us, we know now that it is a little planet going round the Sun, which is just one of millions of ordinary stars in our Galaxy. Because the light from the stars takes so long to reach us, we are seeing them now as they actually were long ago. When we look deep into space, we are looking a long way back in time as well.

The Big Bang

Scientists believe that the Universe started about 15 billion years ago with an event that they call the 'Big Bang'. This was an explosion in which all the matter and energy in the Universe were created. It was the beginning of time and space.

At first the Universe was incredibly dense and hot, but as it expanded, it began to cool down. Initially, it contained vast numbers of fast-moving particles called quarks and electrons. These joined together to form new particles called protons and neutrons, some of which combined into bunches. At this stage, matter in the Universe consisted almost entirely of the nuclei (central parts) of hydrogen and helium atoms.

Three hundred thousand years later, when the Universe was much cooler, the electrons had slowed down and the nuclei captured them to form atoms, the building blocks of everyday matter. Matter, light and other kinds of radiation spread out ever more thinly as space continued to expand. Huge clouds of gas began to collapse on themselves about a billion years later. Each of these clouds became a galaxy.

The Universe is still expanding, and the galaxies are moving further and further away from each other. If there is enough matter in the Universe, the pull of gravity will eventually halt the expansion and cause the galaxies to fall together until everything collides in a 'big crunch'. If the Universe does expand forever, millions of millions of years in the future all the stars will have run out of fuel and died. Much further in the future all that will be left will be a few widely separated particles in cold, empty, but still expanding space.

▶ FLASHBACK ◀

In 1929 the American astronomer Edwin Hubble showed that the galaxies are moving away from each other and the Universe is expanding. This forms the basis of the 'Big Bang' theory. The British physicist Stephen Hawking argues that our Universe, and an infinite number of universes like it, are all part of one great 'super-universe'.

Video

We use video recorders at home for recording and watching programmes and feature films. Camcorders record family events and holidays. Video is also used for television news reporting, for pop videos and for making adverts.

A video recorder plays video tapes on a television, and records television programmes so that you can watch them later. Video recorders record pictures on video tape as a magnetic pattern. The signals which are recorded are the signals that a television needs to create pictures on its screen. The signals are recorded on the tape in diagonal stripes.

A video camera records moving pictures that can be shown on television later. It uses a light-sensitive microchip to change the picture into electrical signals. The signals can be recorded on video tape to be played later. A camcorder records pictures on a mini video tape. Some camcorders are small enough to fit on the palm of your hand.

Video pictures can also be recorded digitally. Digital recordings code signals as numbers (digits). These signals can then be moved to a different medium, for example a computer, where they are converted back into signals for pictures or sounds, and called up onto the screen.

▶ When you load a cassette into a video recorder, levers wrap the magnetic tape around a metal drum. This has recording and playback heads. As the tape moves slowly past, the drum spins, making the heads move across the tape in diagonal lines.

find out more
Electronics
Recording
Television

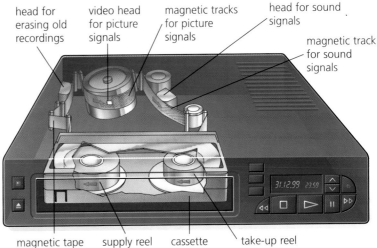

head for erasing old recordings

video head for picture signals

magnetic tracks for picture signals

head for sound signals

magnetic track for sound signals

magnetic tape   supply reel   cassette   take-up reel

Virtual reality

Virtual reality (VR) is a way of simulating (re-creating) a world using pictures and sounds generated by a computer. You can enter this 'virtual world' by wearing a special headset that shows three-dimensional pictures in tiny television screens, and creates sounds through headphones.

Virtual reality makes you feel as if you are really part of the environment that the computer creates. In training and education, VR can simulate almost any situation in the real world. For example, a virtual aircraft can be used for pilot training and a virtual car for driver training. Virtual training is cheaper and safer than the real thing.

Objects in a virtual world do not have to be the same size as in the real world. Scientists have designed chemicals by joining huge virtual atoms which seem to float in mid-air. Manufacturers can construct virtual objects, such as cars, to test them before they make them for real. Amazing virtual worlds can be invented for computer games and for the rides found in some theme parks.

Creating a virtual world

Every VR system has a powerful computer. It needs to be quick at drawing the three-dimensional pictures. Plugged into the computer are a headset, containing television screens and headphones, and a hand-held controller. Data held in the memory of the computer describe the shape, size, colour and position of every object in the virtual world. The computer looks at this database so that it can draw the world. Finally, a computer program decides exactly what happens in that world.

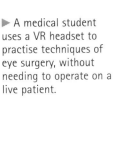

▶ A medical student uses a VR headset to practise techniques of eye surgery, without needing to operate on a live patient.

find out more
Computers
Information technology

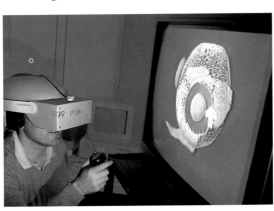

Water

• In Europe, an average family of four people uses about 500 litres of water every day. You use 10 litres of water every time you flush a lavatory, and more than seven times that amount to have a bath.

Water covers almost three-quarters of the Earth's surface. The oceans hold about 97 per cent of the world's water. Frozen water forms the ice-caps at the North and South Poles. In the sky, clouds of water vapour bring rain, and where the rain falls and the rivers flow, plants and animals thrive. We use water in our homes for drinking, cooking, washing, cleaning, and flushing the lavatory. Factories need huge amounts of water for manufacturing things. Without water there would be no life on Earth.

Like many other substances, water is made up of molecules. Every molecule of water consists of two atoms of hydrogen joined to a single atom of oxygen.

Two-thirds of your body is water. Most of your blood is water. Your brain, heart, muscles and liver all contain water. Every day your body loses lots of water. About a litre goes down the toilet, and half a litre is lost as sweat and when you breathe out. You need about a litre and a half of water each day to stay alive.

Plants need water to grow. They usually take it in through their roots. They use water and other chemicals to make the substances needed for growth. They also use water to carry substances between their roots and leaves. The pressure of water in their cells helps plants to stay firm.

The water cycle

Water goes round and round in a process called the water cycle. In some parts of the cycle the water is a liquid (rain); in other parts it is a gas (water vapour) or a solid (ice). The warmth of the Sun evaporates water from seas, rivers and lakes, and also from the soil and plants on the land. The water turns into an invisible gas called water vapour. This process is called *evaporation*. The water vapour cools as it rises into the atmosphere. Cool air cannot hold as much water vapour as warm air, so some of the vapour turns into water droplets. This process is called *condensation*.

In the sky, the tiny water droplets form clouds. If these droplets combine to form larger droplets,

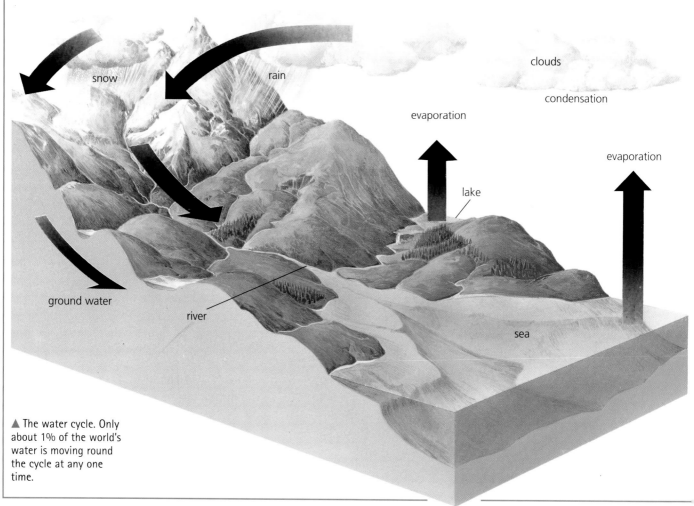

snow   rain   clouds

condensation

evaporation

evaporation

lake

ground water

river

sea

▲ The water cycle. Only about 1% of the world's water is moving round the cycle at any one time.

hey will fall to Earth as rain, hail or snow. Much of the water that falls on the land flows to the sea in streams and rivers. Some soaks into the ground and some stays as ice. The water eventually finds its way into rivers and seas, where the water cycle begins again.

Water supplies

The water we use in our homes is rainwater from reservoirs, wells or rivers. Before this water can be pumped to your home, it must be cleaned at the waterworks. The water is then pumped through pipes to storage tanks, and finally to your home.

Plumbing is the name given to all the pipes which carry clean and dirty water around a house. Water flows through copper pipes to cold taps, toilet cisterns and tanks in the roof.

Plastic pipes carry away the waste water to drains and sewers, and then on to the sewage works.

Hard and soft water

On its long journey to your home, rainwater washes over rocks and flows along rivers, dissolving gases from the air and many different substances from the rocks. Where there are chalk and limestone rocks, these dissolve in the rain and join with the dissolved gas, carbon dioxide, to form a substance called calcium bicarbonate. This and other similar chemicals produce 'hard' water. It is difficult to make a good lather with soap in hard water. Water that does not have these particular substances is called 'soft', but it still contains lots of different chemicals.

▼ Water from this village well in India is drawn up in buckets attached to a moving chain. The chain is driven round by a wheel moved by the oxen.

Waves

The word 'waves' probably makes you think of waves on the sea. Yet there are many other kinds of waves. Sounds reach our ears in waves, and radio and TV programmes travel to our homes in waves, although you cannot see them.

Some waves are started by something that is wobbling in a regular way, for example a tuning fork or a guitar string. This wobbling or shaking is called *vibration*. When something that is wobbling makes the air near it vibrate, we may hear a sound. As the tuning fork vibrates, the air is alternately squashed and expanded, and the squashes travel out as waves.

An electric current is surrounded by invisible electric and magnetic fields. If the electric current wobbles, these fields vibrate too, and the wobbles travel as waves. These are called *electromagnetic waves*.

Waves in the sea

The wind makes waves at sea by pushing against ripples and making them bigger. The water in a wave does not move from place to place. It travels in a circle, upwards and forwards on the wave crest, then down and back as the wave passes.

• A radio wave (a kind of electromagnetic wave) might have a frequency of 1 million vibrations a second: 1 million hertz (Hz), or 1 megahertz (MHz).

find out more

Light
Radiation
Radio
Sound
X-rays

▶ We can measure the speed, the frequency and the wavelength of a wave. Its *frequency* is the number of wave crests that pass a particular point every second. Its *wavelength* is the distance between any two crests.

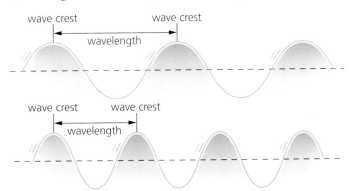

wave crest · wave crest
wavelength

wave crest · wave crest
wavelength

Longer waves
Longer wavelength: longer distance between crests
Lower frequency: fewer wave crests passing each second

Shorter waves
Shorter wavelength: shorter distance between crests
Higher frequency: more wave crests passing each second

Watt, James *see* Steam engines • **Weight** *see* Gravity • **Wheels** *see* Machines

Word processors

A word processor is a computer which can be used as a typewriter. You type at the keyboard and the words and numbers (the text) appear on a screen. Some word processors can handle pictures (graphics) too. In offices across the world, reports, letters, magazines and newspapers are prepared using word processors. The articles in this encyclopedia were prepared in this way.

Word processors have now mostly replaced typewriters. Like a typewriter, most word processors have a 'qwerty' keyboard. It gets this name from the first six keys on the top row of letters on the keyboard. By using special keys, you can change the text and move it about. You can store or save the text on computer disk until you need it again. Some word processors have special spelling and grammar checkers. An electronic printer prints out the text on paper.

Most word processors plug into the mains electricity. Some run on batteries and are small enough to be used on trains and planes. These

are usually small portable computers called *laptops*. Many word processors are just ordinary desktop computers with a special program in them for word processing. Some even 'learn' words you use a lot and complete them as soon as you have begun to type them.

Journalists use word processors to design and prepare whole pages for magazines and newspapers. This is sometimes called *desktop publishing*. At the printer's, signals from a word processor can be sent straight to the machine which makes the printing plates.

find out more
Computers
Information technology
Printing

• Many organizations use word processors to send out 'personal' letters. Everyone receives the same basic letter, but the word processor changes the name and address each time.

◄ This scientist is using a word processor to update scientific information on screen. The information appears on the World Wide Web, a computer network that connects millions of computers across the world.

X-rays

X-rays are a kind of energy which can be both useful and dangerous. The Sun and other stars produce some X-rays, but our atmosphere protects us from these. We use X-rays in hospitals, factories and laboratories.

X-rays are waves like radio waves and light, but they have much more energy. They travel at the same speed as light, but can go right through some solid things which light cannot penetrate.

Doctors and dentists use X-rays to take pictures of broken bones and growing teeth. X-rays make shadow pictures because they go through soft parts of your body, like skin, but are stopped by the hard bones or teeth. Computers can build up

very detailed X-ray pictures of the inside of a patient's body. Doctors sometimes use carefully measured amounts of much stronger X-rays to kill cancer cells in the body.

X-rays can check inside machines for cracks or faults. Airport staff use them to check luggage for weapons and bombs. Scientists use X-rays to study how atoms are arranged in solid materials such as crystals.

► **FLASHBACK** ◄

Wilhelm Röntgen, a German physicist, discovered X-rays in 1895. He was experimenting with electric current flow inside a glass tube when he realized that rays were escaping from the tube. He found that these mysterious rays, which he called X-rays, passed through some solid materials.

• Astronomers study the X-rays that come from the stars. These rays can show where black holes might be.

• X-rays have to be used carefully by people who work with them regularly. A screen, often made of lead, protects the X-ray machine operator while an X-ray picture is taken. You wear a lead shield to protect your body when your teeth are X-rayed.

find out more
Black holes
Radiation
Scanners
Waves

▼ A radiologist (a doctor who specializes in using X-rays) takes accurate measurements of a human knee joint from a life-size X-ray picture. The measurements will be used to make an artificial knee joint to replace the patient's diseased one.

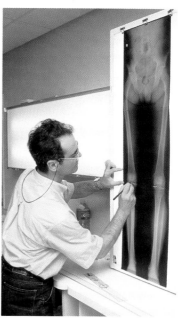

Index

If an index entry is printed in **bold**, it means that there is an article under that name in the A–Z section of the encyclopedia. When an entry has more than one page number, the most important one may be printed in **bold**. Page numbers in *italic* mean that there is an illustration relating to the entry on that page.